HOLY DREAD

James Lees-Milne and John Martin Robinson photographed by
Gavin Stamp on the doorstep of 19, Lansdown Crescent, Bath
(see entry for 7 March 1982)

Holy Dread

DIARIES, 1982–1984

James Lees-Milne

Edited by Michael Bloch

JOHN MURRAY
Albemarle Street, London

Frontispiece: Photograph by Gavin Stamp

© Michael Bloch 2001

First published in 2001
by John Murray (Publishers) Ltd,
50 Albemarle Street, London W1S 4BD

A catalogue record for this book is available from the British Library

ISBN 0-7195-6205 8

Typeset in 11.5/13pt Bembo by Servis Filmsetting Ltd, Manchester
Printed and bound in Great Britain by
Butler & Tanner Ltd, Frome and London

*To Charles Orwin
(publisher, born 1951)
who first introduced the editor
to the diaries of James Lees-Milne*

Contents

Preface

James Lees-Milne was seventy-three when this volume of his diaries (the ninth) opens in 1982, and had been living with his wife Alvilde at Essex House, Badminton for six years. The had gone there, after an unsatisfactory year of residence in Lansdown Crescent, Bath, thanks to Alvilde's friendship with Caroline Somerset, whose husband David was cousin and heir of the tenth Duke of Beaufort, owner of the Badminton estate. The Duke, known as 'Master' owing to his eminence in the hunting world, was still active in his eighties, living in the decaying Palladian grandeur of Badminton House and ruling over his extensive land and many villages in something of the manner of an eighteenth-century continental princeling. Jim found him splendidly patrician, rather intimidating, and somewhat absurd: their relations, always uneasy, had reached a low point in 1979 when the Duke threatened to have the Lees-Milnes' whippets shot after they had chased a fox. The Duchess was a sweet-natured woman who, being Queen Mary's niece, gave Badminton a royal connection; but she had long been eccentric and was now deranged. Since arriving at Essex House, Alvilde had created a celebrated garden in the French style; and within the past year or so she (who had never worked before) had embarked on a successful career as a garden designer and compiler of books on gardens.

Jim himself remained a hard-working author in his mid seventies. In these pages he rarely shows himself at his desk. Yet it was there that he spent most of his daylight hours: on a normal weekday, he would drive after breakfast from Badminton to Lansdown Crescent, where in his beloved library, originally created for William Beckford, he would work furiously from ten until five. His industry was extraordinary. When these diaries begin, only a few weeks had passed since the publication of the second volume of his biography of Harold Nicolson; yet he had recently produced no fewer than four other

works which were due to appear in 1982–3: a country house anthology for Oxford University Press; a book on Bath for Bamber
Gascoigne; a third volume of diaries, covering 1946–7; and a history
of the Stuarts in exile, which he had drafted some years previously and
was now revising. He had also worked out the plot of a new novel
(somewhat 'gothick', like his previous excursions into fiction); and he
continued to pour out articles, obituaries and book reviews on
demand. But he took no great pride in these works, and felt unfulfilled. He longed to find another challenging biographical subject in
which he could immerse himself, as he had done with Nicolson. At
first he thought of William John Bankes, the friend of Byron whose
house in Dorset, Kingston Lacy, had recently been donated with its
contents (including family papers) to the National Trust. By the end
of 1982, however, he had decided to devote himself to writing the life
of another, more recent personality, no less enigmatic and unconven-
tional than Bankes.

Jim's desire to plunge into an arduous literary project likely to
occupy him for years was remarkable in view of his age and his health.
Though essentially stoical by nature, he was all his life a dedicated
hypochondriac, constantly fussing about ailments real or imagined
and predicting his own imminent demise. By the time this volume
begins, however, failing eyesight, deafness, arthritis and heart mur-
murings have become very present realities; and before it ends, the
spectre of cancer has raised its head. He was also increasingly preoc-
cupied by the health of his wife; and almost every week brought news
of the deaths (faithfully recorded with appropriate reminiscence) of
old friends. These intimidations of mortality, far from resulting in less-
ened activity, seem to have induced in him an almost frantic determination to carry on vigorously. As he writes on New Year's Day, 1984:
'It is … relaxation which is the killer.' He was anxious to fulfil himself
as a writer before his powers faded: on learning that he would have to
undergo a major operation, his first thought was that it would keep
him from his book. Fortunately, the process of physical decline,
although accompanied by bouts of exhaustion and depression, did not
unduly affect his acuteness as an observer, his literary talent, or his wit,
all of which continued to flourish almost until his death in his ninetieth year.

During these years I enjoyed a happy friendship with Jim – largely
carried on by letter and telephone, as we were usually only able to meet
on those occasions when he visited London and I was not (as was often

then the case) abroad. He was a wonderful mentor who encouraged my own early writing career; and he showed me his manuscripts, paying too much attention to my immature suggestions. The disagreements with his wife which had been a feature of the previous three years (and of which I appear to have been the unwitting cause) now cease: they were growing close to each other in old age, though continuing to lead rather separate lives. To a large extent he had his own friends, and she hers; and when they went to London together, they stayed in separate places – he with bachelor friends or at Brooks's, she at the Lennox Berkeleys'.

Jim kept the bulk of his diaries in the form of a typescript which he updated at irregular intervals. The fact that less than twenty years now separate writing and publication imposes a greater duty of discretion, and I have cut the original by about one-quarter, rather more than the previous volume. When Jim travelled abroad he kept another, more detailed sort of diary, handwritten in notebooks; but of five such notebooks referred to in the typescript, only one has been found – the rest having presumably been mislaid when he vacated his library in Bath the year before his death. I have included the survivor (an account of an Italian visit in the spring of 1982) as an appendix, and have tried to make good the absence of the others by quoting, where appropriate, from letters he wrote to me at the time. The fact that Jim ended nearly fifty years of association with the National Trust when he retired from its Properties Committee in 1983 seemed to call for another appendix. While taking full responsibility for the final text and annotations, I am grateful to all who read it at various stages of editing and made useful suggestions, or who provided material for footnotes, including Desmond Briggs, Bruce Hunter, R. B. McDowell, Grant McIntyre, Diana Mosley, Gail Pirkis, Stuart Preston, Liz Robinson, Nick Robinson, John Saumarez Smith and Tony Scotland.

This volume comments on the appearance of Jim's first peacetime diaries, *Caves of Ice*, in 1983. Although they dealt with a period almost forty years in the past, he was at moments dismayed by the mild scandal they created. On 8 June, he declares himself 'overcome with embarrassment at my foolish and impertinent anecdotes and criticisms. Wish I had never published these bloody diaries. Can't think what came over me.' By the end of 1984, he has the next volume ready for publication. One hopes this instalment will not offend the living – but Jim's diaries would not be Jim's diaries if they caused no eyebrows to rise.

Weave a circle round him thrice,
And close your eyes with holy dread,
For he on honey-dew hath fed,
And drunk the milk of Paradise.

Samuel Taylor Coleridge, *Kubla Khan*

1982

J.L.-M. was inspired to thoughts of mortality by the deaths, in the last days of 1981, of his wife Alvilde's former husband, Lord Chaplin, and the last surviving retainer from his childhood home at Wickhamford Manor, Worcestershire, Mrs Haines.

Wednesday, 6th January

On the way to Mrs Haines's funeral, I kept thinking incongruously of Anthony Chaplin.[*] He has been dead three weeks and is already forgotten. One short succinct account of his life in *The Times*. No follow-up, no appreciation of his musical talents by Lennox Berkeley or William Glock. And Anthony was a thinker, not a doer. What did he think about? He pondered as Shakespeare must have done the awful destinies of life and death, without conviction, without faith. His love and understanding of animals, his discoveries of their means of living and dying, are unrecorded. It is as if he had never been.

Then I reached the Cheltenham Crematorium, that ghastly place where I attended services of my father, my mother, and old Haines himself. I had been thinking so deeply about Anthony that I failed to leave the motorway at Gloucester, went on to Tewkesbury and had to return to Prestbury. Anyway I was in time, and joined Simon[†] who came over. We entered that empty, hospital-like waiting room, boiling hot from radiators hidden, no furniture or pictures, only seats and a central table with copies of *The Casket*, such jolly reading under the circs. I rootled out an undertaker to whom I gave my sorry wreath made in Wotton, some mimosa and chrysanthemum tied with yellow ribbon. Then we were called as though to enter Concorde at Heathrow. The previous funeral was over, its cortège driving to the

---

[*] Anthony, 3rd Viscount Chaplin (1906–81); composer and zoologist, Secretary of Zoological Society of London, 1952–5; m. 1st 1933 Alvilde Bridges, 2nd 1951 Hon. Rosemary Lyttelton.

[†] J.L-M's nephew Simon Lees-Milne (b. 1939), o. c. of his brother Richard ('Dick') (1909–84) and Elaine *née* Brigstocke (1911–96); m. 1st 1962 Jane Alford (m. diss. 1974), 2nd 1976 Patricia Derrick.

far end of the cemetery for burial. No burial for Mrs Haines. Simon
and I followed a handful of mourners of this ninety-two-year-old
woman and sat in a back pew, or rather bench, of yellow pitch pine.
All clinically clean. On the bench in front of mine was a small,
screwed-up handkerchief of floral pattern, left by a mourner at the
previous ceremony. A whirring noise was of scented disinfectant from
the roof, probably needed since poor Mrs H. died a fortnight ago.
Service sheets much thumbed and soiled, protruding from hideous
plastic covers. 'The Lord is my Shepherd', of course, intoned by
parson and congregation alternately. Only I raised my voice and
answered responses. Then the clergyman, a nice man, gave a short
address, or rather read out basic facts about Mrs Haines – born
ninety-two years ago, daughter of a Badsey market gardener, lived all
her life at Wickhamford, her husband chauffeur of L.-M. family. He
praised her sense of duty, her knitting garments for troops in both
wars, her public spirit, her friendliness, her charity. When I remember how uncharitable the dear old thing was to her neighbours, refusing to speak to the nice Leathers family who for twenty years lived
in the other part of her semi-detached cottage at Wickhamford. We
filed out. Jackie Haines has developed a nice, rather good face, but
his sister Peggy, whom I remember as the prettiest, most blooming
girl, is now tiny and wizened with bad false teeth. Shook hands with
them all, murmured words of sympathy, received murmured words
of thanks, and that will be all. Shall I ever see them again? Mrs H. has
left me Barraclough's portrait of my mother, which I shall have to
fetch one day.

Tuesday, 12th January

A[lvilde] and I motored to London on the 7th to dine with the Beits.*
Pompous party, agreeable enough, men in dinner jackets. A very
charming Princess d'Arenberg on my left, Lady Wilton† on my right.
Princess told me how at age of twenty-three she had been made
mayor of her local town, whence all but she had fled from invading
Nazis. Said her mother, Spanish, aged eighty-eight and in full possession, disliked the present King, regarding him as a traitor to General

---

* Sir Alfred Beit, 2nd Bt (1903–94), art collector and sometime Conservative MP; m.
1939 Clementine Mitford (cousin of the Mitford sisters).
† Diana Galway; m. (2nd) 1962 John Egerton, 7th Earl of Wilton (1921–99).

Franco.* Stayed the night with Eardley [Knollys].† Next morning woke up to deep snow, and was obliged to spend the ensuing five nights in London without change of clothing. E. sweet about having me. I saw M[ichael Bloch]‡ every day and read part of his book on the Duke of Windsor in wartime. Good it is too. And J[ohn Kenworthy-Browne]§ read my third volume of edited diaries¶ and has written notes for my consideration.

Such a severe winter not known since 1962–3. If anything, worse. Roads blocked. I was obliged to buy a shirt at Harvie & Hudson's sale, reduced from £30 to £20 and nothing special about it. Charming middle-aged assistant, when he saw my cheque, asked what book I was now writing. And whether I had sold a silver porringer six years ago at Christie's (A. had done so), he collecting old silver as an investment. 'Have a good day' he said as we parted, this now being the common expression, vying in fatuity with the air hostess hoping one has enjoyed one's flight.

Went with A. and the Berkeleys‖ to a party given by Charlotte Bonham-Carter,** who must be ninety. She moved briskly about the room, carrying sandwiches and bottles of South African sherry, introducing as though her life depended on it. How can the dear old thing be bothered? While I sat talking to Freda she nodded towards Lennox and said, 'The old man is composing.' Lennox was sitting on a hard chair, totally oblivious of the company, looking straight ahead, his lips

---

* Though groomed by Franco for the succession, King Juan Carlos (b. 1938) had dismantled the General's authoritarian system after coming to the throne in 1975. An attempted military *coup* in 1981 to restore the *ancien régime* had ended in farce.

† Painter (1902–91); formerly on staff of N.T.; friend of J.L.-M. since 1941.

‡ Author and barrister (b. 1953); friend of J.L.-M. since 1979, at which time he was a Cambridge postgraduate student; had since lived in Paris, writing books on the Duke of Windsor at behest of the Duchess's French lawyer, Suzanne Blum; also commissioned to write biography of J.L.-M's late friend, the hostess Sibyl Colefax.

§ Expert on neo-classical sculpture (b. 1931); formerly on staff of N.T. and Christie's; friend of J.L.-M. since 1958.

¶ Covering the years 1946–7, and due to be published by Chatto & Windus as *Caves of Ice*.

‖ Sir Lennox Berkeley (1903–90), composer; nephew of 9th and last Earl Berkeley (d. 1942) but unable to inherit title and estates owing to father's illegitimacy; m. 1946 Freda Bernstein (b. 1923).

** Charlotte Ogilvy (1893–1989); idiosyncratic social figure; m. 1927 Sir Edgar Bonham Carter, colonial civil servant (d. 1956).

moving. Sir Charles Johnston* present, who has translated Pushkin's *Onegin* into excellent English verse. A. and I had a difficult drive home of five hours today.

Wednesday, 13th January

Unable to motor to Bath, the road still absolutely blocked. I resent not being able to work. Yet am paralysed with cold. We have experienced one of the coldest spells ever known. One night the temperature dropped to minus forty. Twice the pipes in my bathroom burst. One evening in London I walked to the Berkeleys' in Warwick Avenue and arrived suffering, I believe, from hypothermia. I could not speak, and did not know where I was; felt almost in a state of coma. I have learnt since that this happens to the old, who ought always to keep extremities warm.

Sunday, 24th January

A. has read my diaries with interest but advised me to omit certain passages relating to my ancient love life. M. has been too busy to read them but has asked me to let him have them on Tuesday when I see him in London. I have begun revising my Stuart book in the light of the recommendations of Professor J. P. Kenyon.†

Have read *Middlemarch* for the third time. I used to think of it as the greatest English novel. Now I am not so sure. There are some splendid characters – Mr Casaubon, Mr Bulstrode, Rosalind Lydgate. But there are touches which I can only describe as provincial. Dorothea's love for Will Ladislaw is not full-blooded or convincing. Am now reading a life of Sonya, wife of that horrid old man Tolstoy. Not well written, by an American woman, but fascinating. How that couple revelled in misunderstanding and hurt feelings. Oh the idiocy of love!

---

* Diplomatist (1912–86); Governor of Aden, 1960–3; High Commissioner to Australia, 1965–71; m. 1944 Princess Natasha Bagration.
† John Philipps Kenyon (b. 1927); Professor of Modern History, University of St Andrew's, 1981–7; expert on Stuart dynasty, on whose qualified recommendation Chatto & Windus had recently agreed to publish J. L.-M's *The Last Stuarts*, the first draft of which had failed to find a publisher in the early 1970s (see *Deep Romantic Chasm*, 1 May 1980 and 26 September 1981).

I seem to have unconsciously told myself that I cannot live much longer and therefore should not bother to try cures for my arthritis and deafness. I will just manage to last out. Whereas twenty years ago I would bother lest I became totally crippled before old age set in. Similarly, I cannot be bothered to learn things which twenty years ago I would have considered worth the effort. For instance, the typewriter shop where I have my machines serviced pressed me to use an electric machine and even gave me one to take away on trial. But I could not manage it. Am too accustomed to banging away. The touch required for the electric is so light that the keys depress themselves almost before one fingers them. This machine is of course easier and more satisfactory and less tiring if one can learn to master it, but I cannot be bothered.

Tony Powell,* who with Violet lunched here yesterday, has a prodigious memory. Told me he and I first met at the Glenconners'† in Regent's Park in 1947. He will not write another book. All the writing he does is a fortnightly review for the *Daily Telegraph*. He can only work in the mornings, no longer after tea as was his wont. Yet with age the urge to work and be busy is more pronounced than ever before. He spends his time reading. He is an observant man. Went upstairs to wash before luncheon and remarked on everything in my bathroom. Like the old silver mug in which I keep my toothbrushes. No one else has ever remarked on this. Yet I do not think he is an imaginative man, and he lacks sparkle in his conversation and, I find, in his writings. Yet I like him very much and enjoy talking with him. We spoke of Henry Yorke,‡ whose biography is being written by Paul Bailey.§ Would he understand, I asked, the upper-class humour of the period? Tony wondered too. He was an exact contemporary of Henry, yet could never endure his novels, which embarrasses him since as a fellow novelist he does not like to appear to deprecate his writings.

---

* Anthony Powell (1905–2000), novelist; m. 1934 Lady Violet Pakenham.

† Christopher Tennant (1899–1983); s. father as 2nd Baron Glenconner, 1920; m. (2nd) 1935 Elizabeth Powell.

‡ Novelist (1905–73) under pseudonym Henry Green, of whom J.L.-M. later wrote a memoir in *Fourteen Friends* (John Murray, 1996).

§ The novelist Paul Bailey (b. 1937) abandoned his life of Henry Yorke in face of obstruction from the family. A much-acclaimed biography by Jeremy Treglown appeared in 2000.

Thursday, 28th January

Last night I had two dreams which I remembered, a rare thing. One was that I had broken my wrist watch. The whole of the works had fallen out. Only a fragment of glass still stuck to the rim. This distressed me very much until I remembered that I had a spare watch. The other was that I was abroad and realised with horror that I had another fortnight before I could return home, and hated being away. Both dreams are concerned with M., I think. For yesterday I went to London to see him and hand him my diaries to read. I booked a table at a Jermyn Street restaurant and waited. A message came that he would be twenty minutes late. By the time he arrived the restaurant had become extremely noisy and hot. I felt uncomfortable and could not hear. He ate little and drank nothing and left after an hour, saying he had to see his publishers. I paid the bill and walked to the London Library, feeling very unhappy. This meeting is the first unsatisfactory one we have had. Through his sensitive politeness I detected boredom. He said he would telephone today. He hasn't, which is unlike him. I ask myself what this relationship is bringing either of us. If we are only to have infrequent meetings in uncomfortable and noisy restaurants, it may be better not to meet at all but only write and telephone. What I think upset me most yesterday was the information that he is going to Paris again next week. I rebuked him for waltzing off at this moment when his publishers are clamouring for his manuscript, but my rebukes do not irk him.

Sunday, 31st January

Of course the dear reliable creature telephoned two days running. On the second occasion he said he had read one-third of my new diary and liked it. This has cheered me. Strange how much I depend on him, how much I love him with a love which is totally unphysical and wholly platonic.

I motored Audrey* yesterday to Wickhamford to tea with Jack Haines and wife, both charming. In spite of Jackie's success in life as a centre-forward for England, he still addresses me as Sir or Mr Jim, and Audrey as Miss Audrey or Madam. Audrey and I later agreed we

---

* J.L.-M's sister (1905–90); m. 1st Matthew Arthur, later 3rd Baron Glenarthur, 2nd Anthony Stevens.

were embarrassed by such address today, but in this particular case thought it best not to invite them to address us by our christian names, which might embarrass them. Anyway, Audrey and Jack embraced warmly on parting. I asked Audrey how well she knew her son-in-law James Sutton,* who stays four nights a week with her. She said she didn't think she really knew anyone. 'And I don't suppose I know you, really,' she added rather sadly.

I collected my mother's portrait which Mrs Haines left me. To my distress it has badly flaked since being removed from Mrs H's damp cottage to the young Haines's overheated bungalow. Now that I examine the portrait I realise how bad it is. Is it worth repairing? And what do I do with it? I cannot bring myself to destroy it.

Wednesday, 10th February

June and Jeremy Hutchinson† told us they had dined at 10 Downing Street, Mrs Thatcher‡ having expressed a wish to meet the heads of the various national museums and galleries, Jeremy being Chairman of the Tate. Jeremy went with an open mind, prepared to like Mrs T. although disapproving of her policy. But it was difficult to do so. She was like a steamroller. He wished to ask some questions, but she never drew breath or gave him an opportunity of putting them. After dinner she conducted them round the house and showed them her private apartments. Even there she interrupted relentlessly the moment he tried to speak. Jeremy says she totally lacks charm, though Mr T. does have some – he stood with his right hand behind his back motioning to a waiter to put a fresh glass of whisky into it. And Alex Moulton,§ who likewise has recently been to 10 Downing Street and is a fervent supporter of Mrs T., admitted she was charmless. But he admired her grasp of the matter – in this case, design in industry – for in taking the

---

* Audrey's daughter Dale Stevens (b. 1944); m. 1964 James Sutton (b. 1940), mechanical engineer, yr s. of Sir Robert Sutton, 8th Bt.
† Jeremy Hutchinson,QC (b. 1915); m. 1st 1940 Dame Peggy Ashcroft, 2nd 1966 June, *née* Capel (daughter of J.L.-M's friend Diana, Countess of Westmorland, and formerly wife of Franz Osborn); cr. Lord Hutchinson of Lullington, 1978; Chairman of Tate Gallery Trustees, 1980–4.
‡ Margaret Roberts (b. 1925); m. 1951 (as his 2nd wife) Denis Thatcher (later 1st Bt); MP (C) Finchley, 1959–92; Prime Minister 1979–90; cr. life peer, 1992.
§ Dr Alexander Moulton (b. 1920) of The Hall, Bradford-on-Avon, Wiltshire; innovating engineer and inventor of the Moulton bicycle and motor-car suspension.

chair she knew her stuff exactly and what she wanted to get from the meeting. Above all he was impressed by her patriotism.

Gervase Jackson-Stops* lunched with me at Brooks's yesterday. He thinks it an admirable idea that I should write a biography of W. J. Bankes.† From the latter's letters to his father which he has seen in the library of Kingston Lacy he believes him to have had a fascinating mind. Gervase also asked me to write an introduction to a book about how writers have been influenced by their houses, and vice versa. Must be N.T. properties of course. He is getting John Lehmann to write on the Woolfs and Monk's House, Tony Powell on Kipling and Batemans, Lord Blake on Disraeli and Hughenden, David Cecil on Coleridge's house, etc.

Saturday, 20th February

M. sent me a telegram on St Valentine's Day and I sent him one back.

On Tuesday last A. and I motored to London for the day. I had my [N.T.] Properties Committee in the afternoon, and Johnnie Churchill‡ to lunch with me beforehand at Brooks's. He was very sweet and affectionate, much calmer, drinking less, and a little pitiable in that he does not make much money from his painting and has not received much acclaim. But is resigned and philosophical. Talked of old days, his father and mother. Says his father was always supposed to be the son of some Edwardian called Jocelyn. So, said J., I ought really to be the tenth Earl of Roden. After the Committee I slipped away in order to see a German film at the ICA§ called *Taxi zum Klo*, strongly recommended by Alex [Moulton]. John Cornforth¶ left the meeting at the same time, and *would* stick to me like a leech. I had to pretend I was going to the Travellers'. Finally shook him off and descended Duke of York's steps to ICA premises. The film was appalling – about a queer Berlin schoolmaster and his doings off-duty. Nothing left to the imagination. When it came to the anti-hero being examined for

---

* Architectural historian and adviser to N.T. (1947–95).

† William John Bankes (d. 1855); friend of Byron, MP, and traveller in the East; owner of Kingston Lacy, Dorset, bequeathed by his successor to the N.T. in 1981 with its contents and estate; obliged to live abroad for much of his life owing to homosexual scandal.

‡ J. G. Spencer-Churchill (1909–94), nephew of Sir Winston; artist; friend of J.L.-M. since they had crammed together for Oxford in 1927–8.

§ The Institute of Contemporary Arts in the Mall, showing *avant-garde* films.

¶ Architectural historian on staff of *Country Life* (b. 1937).

syphilis by a hospital doctor I thought I would be sick. Left and fled
to Brooks's. There met Giles Eyre* and told him of my experience.
He had also been to see it and reacted exactly as I had done. Gave me
a stiff whisky-and-soda to recover. Am I being oversensitive, hypo-
critical, prudish? I felt degraded, debased and embarrassed. I am, all
things considered, a romantic. When I told M. over the telephone of
my disgust at the film he said, 'I told you not to go to it. Why do you
never do what I tell you?'

At the Properties meeting, somebody referred to the likes and dislikes of 'the British people'. John Smith† interpolated, 'It is mislead-
ing to refer to "the British people" nowadays. At most one can talk of
"a group of human beings who happen to live in this island".'

Wednesday, 24th February

A. and I dined with the Hutchinsons in their new little house in
Blenheim Road. The John Griggs‡ present and Celia Goodman,§ one
of the Paget twins I knew years ago. She reminded me that we first
met on a train journey to Salzburg, when she was not yet 'out': I sat
up and she slept in the rack above me. John Grigg criticised the Queen
Mother for having been responsible for the Duke of Windsor's suffer-
ings. She was the force behind George VI's irreconcilable attitude to
his brother. What I did not know (but M. of course knew when I
mentioned it to him later) was that in 1939 the Duke was offered the
Deputy Commissionership of Wales, a humiliating offer but such was
his desire to serve his country that he accepted it, whereupon it was
immediately withdrawn. After dinner, Jeremy and June took us to the
Tate where we had the Landseer exhibition to ourselves. There is a
streak of cruelty in Landseer, a love of violence and blood, allied to
that Victorian sentimentality over animals, dogs particularly. Yet a
splendid artist on occasion, who must have been in great demand by
ducal houses.

---

* Dealer in water-colours and art critic (b. 1922).
† J. L. E. Smith (b. 1923); banker; MP (C) Cities of London and Westminster, 1965–70;
Deputy Chairman of N.T., 1980–5; founder of the Landmark Trust; kt, 1988.
‡ Author (b. 1924), official biographer of Lloyd George; succeeded father as 2nd Baron
Altrincham 1955, but disclaimed peerage 1963; m. 1958 Patricia Campbell.
§ Celia Paget (b. 1916), one of the celebrated Paget twins (the other was briefly married
to the novelist Arthur Koestler and died young); m. (2nd) 1954 Arthur Goodman.

Thursday, 25th February

Went with the [N.T.] Arts Panel in a bus from London to Kingston Lacy, three and a half hours each way. Tiring. Talked on way down with Nancy Lancaster* who strongly disapproves of the film about her aunt Lady Astor,† which gets her grandfather quite wrong. She is a very splendid octogenarian. I still fancy tackling the biography of W. J. Bankes. Got back in time to give a dinner at Brooks's, party of five which cost me £60. M. arrived back from Paris in a tweed suit looking tired and dishevelled. He lent me the typescript of an unpublished book of the Duke of Windsor entitled *My Hanoverian Ancestors*. Not badly written, though I can't make out if the Duke wrote it himself or a ghost did.‡ Not clear why it was never published, unless to spare the Queen embarrassment, for it does deprecate, to put it mildly, the majority of her Hanoverian forebears. Parts of it are very good. A bit too discursive, and too long.

Sunday, 7th March

Have suffered from a cold for a fortnight and felt rotten.

On Friday two young men came to see me about the early days of the Georgian Group – John Martin Robinson§ and Gavin Stamp.¶ Apparently I am the last living person to have attended the first committee meeting in 1937.‖ They are devoting a whole issue of the

---

* Nancy Perkins of Virginia, USA; m. 1st Henry Field, 2nd Ronald Tree, MP, 3rd Colonel Claude Lancaster of Kelmarsh Hall, Northamptonshire; proprietor from 1945 of the London decorating firm of Colefax & Fowler; horticulturist; she d. 1995.

† Nancy Langhorne of Virginia, USA (1879–1964); m. (2nd) 2nd Viscount Astor (d. 1952); MP (U) Plymouth Sutton, 1919–45 (the first woman MP); châtelaine of Cliveden Court, Berkshire.

‡ It was in fact mostly written by the British historian Kenneth Young, who discussed the sources with the Duke and was supplied with a certain amount of family anecdote by him. As J.L.-M. surmised, in view of the unflattering picture presented of his eighteenth-century predecessors the former King decided not to proceed with publication.

§ Librarian to Duke of Norfolk, and writer and consultant on architectural and genealogical subjects (b. 1948); later Maltravers Herald Extraordinary, and Vice-Chairman of Georgian Group.

¶ Architectural historian (b. 1948).

‖ The Group (which still flourishes) had been founded in 1937 under the aegis of the Society for the Protection of Ancient Buildings. J.L.-M. was not in fact the last survivor of the original committee: two others, John Betjeman and John Summerson, were then still alive.

Architects' Journal to the Group and asked me dozens of questions about my colleagues. Both tremendous admirers of Robert Byron* and regard me as a phenomenon for having known him so well. They would take photographs of me. I hate it, and put on a self-conscious face, try as I may not to.

Norah Smallwood† telephoned last week that she finds my new diaries fascinating 'and so funny'. Chatto's will publish early next year.

Tuesday, 9th March

M. telephoned to tell me Geoffrey Gilmour‡ had died. Poor old Geoffrey, he suffered much from cancer at the end. M. sees him as a panda-like figure, the end of a species. He was rich and civilised and had exquisite taste. His flat in Paris was dark and opulent, crammed with beautiful works of art. He was so fastidious that it was pain and grief having guests to stay, lest they leave a dirty handkerchief on a Louis Quinze tabouret. I have known him since Oxford days. He was not interesting, and when he telephoned to announce his arrival in London one groaned a little inwardly. Yet when he did come to stay he was sweet and no trouble. Had a very quiet, dry sense of humour. Diana Mosley§ saw him at least once a week and will be bereft.

Also today *The Times* carried a long obituary of John Blakenham.¶ He was absent from last month's Properties Committee, and inexplicably tried to suicide himself five years ago. His life was the very opposite of Geoffrey's, for he held office in every Conservative government and his activities were legion. A. became fond of him for he was Chairman of her [N.T.] Gardens Panel. A very polite man, but inarticulate since his accident. He wore a patch over the eye which he shot out. Also last week Ursula Rayleigh‖ died. Before she married I had a slight flirtation with her. She was as a girl – and indeed whenever I

---

* Travel writer, Byzantinist and aesthete (1905–41); early Secretary of Georgian Group.
† The dragon-like chairman of Chatto & Windus (1909–84).
‡ Anglo-Argentine art collector resident in Paris (1907–81).
§ Hon. Diana Mitford (b. 1910), m. 1st 1928 Hon. Bryan Guinness (1905–92), 2nd 1936 Sir Oswald Mosley, 6th Bt (1896–80); resident in Paris.
¶ John Hare, 1st Viscount Blakenham (1911–82); cabinet minister, 1956–64; raised to peerage, 1963; Chairman of Conservative Party, 1963–5.
‖ Only dau. of Lieut.-Col. R.H.R. Brocklebank, DSO and Charlotte Carissima, o. dau. of General Sir Bindon Blood, GCB, GCVO; m. 1934 John Arthur Strutt, later 5th Baron Rayleigh (1908–88).

ran into her, which was about once a decade – very correct, laced-in, pursed-up. Her mother was an arrant snob determined she should marry a lord. Well, she did, and was miserable ever after. Had no children. John Rayleigh is besides a maniac who writes indecent letters to the Queen and rises in church to forbid the banns of marriage of young girls he has never known. Ursula's failing was over-politeness.

Thursday, 11th March

To London for the day. M. lunched with me at Brooks's and talked till three, assuring me that he will soon deliver his completed typescript. I went to two exhibitions. One Harold Gilman, Camden Town school, at Burlington House. Sickert-like, very good too. The other Meredith Frampton at the Tate. Extraordinary that he is alive today, aged eighty-eight, and has not painted a single picture since 1945, because at the time his painting was considered so representational and photographic as hardly to qualify as art. Now he is acclaimed. A lot of good it will do the poor man. Just shows one should never be influenced by or pay any heed to fashion. I have lived long enough to see several wheels come round full circle.

On leaving Paddington Station and descending escalator to the tube, I heard my name called with peals of laughter. It was Freda [Berkeley] clutching a bag, she having returned from staying away for the night. I said, 'Had I been up to wickedness you would have told Alvilde you met me and I would have got into trouble. As it is . . .' We parted for different platforms. I still hear Freda's laugh ringing in my ears. It is one of the most attractive things about her.

Saturday, 13th March

A. has returned from seeing Clarissa* in France. I miss her when she is away. The house feels dead.

Rory Cameron† told her this story. Friends of his in New York went out to dinner, leaving their son, aged twelve, behind in their

---

* J.L.-M's stepdaughter, only child of A.L.-M. by her 1st marriage to 3rd Viscount Chaplin; b. 1934; m. 1958 Michael Luke.
† Roderick Cameron (1914–85), garden designer and travel writer, living in South of France; son of Enid, Countess of Kenmare, Australian-born society figure, by her American 1st husband; old friend of A.L.-M.

apartment. They said to him, 'If anyone rings the bell, do not open the door.' Within an hour the doorbell rang. The twelve-year-old opened it. An eighteen-year-old entered and said, 'Hand me the keys to the safe.' 'All right,' said the twelve-year-old, who opened a drawer, drew out his father's revolver and shot the eighteen-year-old dead. Then telephoned his parents, who had left their number with him. He said, 'Mummy, I have shot a man.' She replied, 'What nonsense, go back to bed.' The parents' hosts said, 'Perhaps you had better return to see what has happened.' On their return they found that the eighteen-year-old was the son of their hosts.

Today a fine, sunny day for a change, though a cold west wind. I took Folly* to the Berkeley–Gloucester canal. Covered six miles with no fatigue. At every forty paces there is a cast-iron, white-painted bollard, and at every mile a mile-stone, also of metal. A feel of spring in the air. Saw primroses, white violets and many yellow celandines through the wire fencing. Was inspired to write my novel and worked out the theme in my mind. Must now get from the London Library some book which describes conditions of German prisoners in England during 1914–18 war.†

Wednesday, 17th March

To London for the night at Eardley's. Martin Drury‡ motored me in the afternoon to Osterley [Park] for me to see for myself the surrounding land which the N.T. wants me to get from Grandy Jersey.§ I was horrified by the condition of Osterley outside and in. The garden has become like a public park, grass all worn, south lake margin given a stone curb. All Grandy's land seemed derelict. As for the inside, the rooms empty and drear. No ornaments. Drawing-room carpet faded. The worst things are the Library and Breakfast Room ceilings

---

* One of the L.-Ms' two whippets; the other was Honey.
† For more than two years J.L.-M. had been planning a novel about a German count, a prisoner in England during the First World War, who seduces first an English schoolboy and then the boy's mother (see *Deep Romantic Chasm*, 29 December 1979 and 1 May 1980). It was eventually published as *The Fool of Love* (Robinson, 1990).
‡ Historic Buildings Secretary (1981–95), subsequently Director-General, of N.T. (b. 1938).
§ George Villiers, 9th Earl of Jersey (1910–1998); m. (3rd) 1947 Bianca Mottironi. After complex negotiations conducted with J.L.-M. soon after the war (described in *Caves of Ice*), he had donated his house and estate at Osterley, Middlesex, to the N.T.

lately painted by the V. & A. in garish colours like a merry-go-round. How can these scholars and experts have such appalling taste?

At six went to New Zealand House in Haymarket for Hatchard's Authors-of-the-Year Party, which the Queen and Prince Philip attended. Lovely view over London at dusk from topmost floor, walls of which are of glass. But too hot, so I dared not drink. Knew few people there, but Mark Bonham Carter* most friendly. For Collins apparently own Hatchard's. I stood next to a man who greeted me and said, 'I saw quite a lot of you at Rainbird's when we produced your St Peter's book. My name is . . .', which I didn't hear. I said brightly, 'Of course I remember you well', and we talked. Then I said, 'Do tell me, does John Hadfield still have anything to do with Rainbird's? Is he even alive?' 'But I am John Hadfield,' he answered. I tried to pass it off by explaining that I was extremely deaf.

We stood in a circle, the Queen brought round. She spoke to little groups. When my turn came Mark Bonham Carter mentioned my name, which meant nothing to her. She said, 'Are you an author? I thought I was to meet authors and most of those I have talked to don't seem to be.' I said, 'Yes, I suppose I can call myself one, Ma'am.' 'And what books, what are you . . .?' she began. So, seeing she needed help, I explained that I had recently written a biography of Sir Harold Nicolson. 'Such an interesting man,' she said, 'but it must have been an uphill struggle?' 'It wasn't so much a struggle as rather onerous,' I replied, 'because of the quantity of letters the Nicolsons wrote to each other, all of which I had to read through.' Then we talked about letters. She asked if I kept them. I said I kept a great many, and couldn't bear to throw away ones I thought might be interesting or amusing. Then Mark B.C. joined in, 'And do you keep letters, Ma'am?' 'Oh yes, a lot,' she said; and to me, 'But do you re-read them?' I said I seldom did because I found it sad work. 'Oh, I don't find it sad,' she said. And I, rather cheekily, 'Well, Ma'am, you are so much younger than I am. But most of the letters I have kept are from dead friends.' Then a few more *politesses* and she passed on. But what I found was that, far from being stuffy or awkward, she was bright, extremely natural, and rather funny. I would far prefer to sit next to her than the Q. Mother. There is none

---

* Mark Raymond Bonham Carter (1920–94); elder son of Lady Violet Bonham Carter (d. 1969), daughter of 1st Earl of Oxford, and Liberal stateswoman; Director, William Collins & Co.; MP (Lib) Torrington, 1958–9; Chairman of Race Relations Board, 1966–70; cr. life peer, 1986.

of that sugary insincerity in the Queen. She is absolutely direct. V. dignified notwithstanding. Face to face she is good-looking, with that wonderful complexion. Was wearing a purple two-piece with high collar of black velvet, pearls and diamond brooch. I have a great 'up' on her.

Did not enjoy party otherwise, and hastened away as soon as the royal couple left.

Thursday, 18th March

Norah has handed me back *Caves of Ice*, from which I have to deduct 7,000 words. In return I handed her *The Last Stuarts*, to which I have added about 7,000 words, which will horrify her.

Monday, 29th March

To London for the night to dine with Elizabeth [Cavendish]* and John Betj[eman].† Lately I have had a hunch that John will not last long. Indeed, tonight I was shocked by his condition. When I arrived, he was sitting in his usual chair under the window, his belly swollen and prominent. Not his usual self, but quieter than usual. No guffaws of laughter, and when amused he gave a funny little half-snigger, half-grunt as though it were painful for him to laugh outright. But I tried to cheer him. He began by reciting a new poem he was writing: 'Sir Christopher Wren/ Was dining with some men/He said "If anyone calls/ Say I'm building St Paul's." '‡ 'No, you have not got it right, love,' said Elizabeth. Moving him to table for dinner was a great effort. She walked backwards, holding his outstretched hands. He groaned, as though with pain, and moved to the table in a kind of dancing movement like an old bear. It was rather piteous. Talked of Gavin Stamp. I said how nice he was and clever. J. said he was a very good writer and had a column in *Private Eye* on architecture, under assumed name. J. said he (John) was only interested in young men. Wanted to go to bed with them. This did make him laugh outright. I said, 'We

---

* Lady Elizabeth ('Feeble') Cavendish (b. 1926), dau. of 10th Duke of Devonshire; Lady-in-Waiting to Princess Margaret; long-standing friend of Sir John Betjeman.
† Sir John Betjeman (1906–84); poet, broadcaster and writer on architecture; m. 1933 Hon. Penelope Chetwode (b. 1910); succeeded Cecil Day-Lewis as Poet Laureate, 1972.
‡ Garbled version of well-known lines by E. Clerihew Bentley.

must get used to the fact that this is impossible now.' Talked of David
Linley,* Feeble's godson. A true Messel, he is a craftsman who designs
and makes furniture with his own hands. Thinks of nothing else. This
is good. Talked of the Parsons family. I told them that Lady de Vesci†
was to be a hundred this year and she ought to be recorded on telly
or radio. They thought this an excellent idea. Discussed who should
interview her. Feeble instantly telephoned John Julius [Norwich],‡
who said I should do it because I had known all of them; but I said I
would not be good. Had no experience of such a thing. Someone
needed who could egg on. Agreed it must be a gent who understood
the world Lady de V. came from. At ten John became silent. I realised
I should go but stayed on. So much to say to them both. At 10.15 John
said he must go to bed. So I sprang up and left. They are off to
Cornwall for six weeks on Wednesday. I would not be surprised if he
did not return. Osbert [Lancaster]§ had been talking to them on telephone before I arrived. Asked them to tell me to go and see him too.
He is in a bad way. Can no longer go to club to gossip with cronies,
which he loves doing.

Tuesday, 30th March

In London Library saw Sachie [Sitwell]¶ sitting in reading room
browsing through periodicals. I told him he looked well, which did
not please. 'I am very depressed,' he said, 'and sit here until luncheon
time. It is as good as anywhere else.' Told me he had a volume of
poems to be published by Macmillan's next month. 'It will be my
eightieth book,' he said, 'and my last.' I said I would come and see
him in the summer if he liked. He asked me to stay. But I felt he was
indifferent to everyone and everything. Before catching train home

---

* David Armstrong-Jones, Viscount Linley (b. 1961); o. s. of Princess Margaret and 1st
Earl of Snowdon; m. 1993 Hon. Serena Stanhope; furniture designer.
† Lois Lister-Kaye (1882–1984); m. 1st 1905 5th Earl of Rosse (d. 1918), 2nd 1920 5th
Viscount de Vesci (d. 1958); mother of J.L.-M's friends Hon. Desmond Parsons (d. 1937)
and Michael, 6th Earl of Rosse (d. 1979). See entry for 11 March 1984.
‡ John Julius Cooper, 2nd Viscount Norwich (b. 1929), son of Alfred Duff Cooper, 1st
Viscount, and Lady Diana, *née* Manners; diplomatist, author, broadcaster and Chairman
of Venice in Peril Fund; m. 1st Anne Clifford, 2nd Mollie Philipps.
§ Cartoonist, humourist and dandy (1908–86), of whom J. L.-M., his Oxford contem-
porary, wrote a memoir in *Fourteen Friends*.
¶ Sir Sacheverell Sitwell, 6th Bt (1897–1988); m. 1925 Georgia Doble (d. 1980).

had assignation with M. at our usual café at Paddington. He very talk-
ative and sweet, and said his book really was nearly finished. But
looked scruffy, unshaven. In the train a man got in at Slough and sat
in seat in front of mine. With him came a stink of such potency I was
nearly gassed. Wondered if it meant drugs. This dusky, good-looking
man slept throughout journey.

When I asked Sachie about Roy Campbell* whose biography I have
just reviewed for the *Evening Standard*, and who consorted with the
Sitwells in the Twenties, he said he could not remember him. I said,
'But he was a swashbuckling, violent sort of man, wasn't he?' 'Perhaps
he was,' S. said.

Monday, 5th April

At the shop in Acton Turville, where I had gone to buy some milk, a
very old local stopped to talk about what he called 'the war'.† Said he
knew it was coming. 'My father never would vote because he said if
you had a Tory government there will be war, if a Labour government
there will be starvation. I don't know which be worst.' It is strange
how one cannot take our armada seriously, somehow. Yet the situation
might provoke a world war – if Argentina succeeds in recruiting all the
South American countries; if Russia joins the fray; if (low be it spoken)
our assault were to fail. Yet I think the crisis is uniting the people.

Tuesday, 6th April

Grandy Jersey and his delightful, sprightly Italian wife Bianca lunched,
ostensibly to talk about Osterley Park, the N.T. wishing to acquire
more parkland. Grandy unable to give away anything, all the land he
owns there being tied up in complicated trusts. But he seemed pleased
to see us again after more than thirty years. No longer the delicate,
beautiful, pale, willowy Jersey lily, he now resembles Hugh Grafton,‡

---

* Poet (1902–57).
† Argentina had invaded and occupied the Falkland Islands on 2 April, and a Royal Navy
'Task Force' was preparing to sail to recapture them. The Argentinians surrendered to
British forces on 14 June.
‡ Hugh FitzRoy, 11th Duke of Grafton (b. 1919); m. 1946 Fortune Smith (Mistress of
the Robes to HM The Queen from 1967); Chairman of Society for Protection of
Ancient Buildings. In 1950s, as Earl of Euston, he had been N.T. Historic Buildings
Representative for East of England.

replete, podgy and much aged. Wears Dundrearies cut square on a line with the prim little mouth. These grisly grey appendages make him look older than he need. He pressed us to stay in Jersey, though I would sooner die than go now.

Wednesday, 7th–Thursday, 8th April

The much-deferred two-day tour of Cornwall with Alex [Moulton] in his lovely smooth Rolls-Royce. Agreeable and involved staying the night in a small hotel in Looe. But terribly cold and grey. We visited Lanhydrock, Cothele and Antony. I was impressed by the splendid way these three N.T. houses are kept. An improvement on how they used to be under my jurisdiction. Michael Trinick* has worked marvels. Even the restaurants have good food, and the china and table-cloths are pretty. Alex intends to write an autobiographical book on his career, stressing his impulse to advance from one scientific invention to another. He feels his life has been more than moderately successful and that young engineers must always have an eye on the task ahead.

Easter Sunday, 11th April

We had Billa Harrod† and the Moores‡ to stay. Billa tells me she no longer wants to stay away anywhere. She says this will be her last visit to us. She is happy at home working for the Norfolk churches and local interests. Is only interested in her grandchildren, somewhat indifferent to her contemporaries and when they die hardly laments them.

Tuesday, 13th April

To London for N.T. Properties Committee. In the morning I delivered my diaries to Chatto's, reduced by 7,000 words. I now have four

---

* G. E. M. Trinick (1924–94); from 1953 to 1984 served N.T. as land agent, later Historic Buildings Representative, for Cornwall (of which county he later became Deputy-Lieutenant and High Sheriff).
† Wilhelmina Cresswell (b. 1911); Norfolk conservationist; widow of Sir Roy Harrod (1900–79), Oxford economist and biographer of J. M. Keynes.
‡ Derry, Viscount Moore (b. 1937); son and heir of 11th Earl of Drogheda; m. (2nd) Alexandra, dau. of Sir Nicholas Henderson; photographer.

books in the press,* so to speak, but no book on hand, which makes
me sad. I wonder if I have the impulse to write another, that spring
to which Alex attaches so much importance? Met M. before dinner.
He has handed in the final chapter of his Duke of Windsor book, and
I accordingly handed him the letter I have been threatening to write
him these months past. When it came to writing it I had forgotten
some of the reprimands I had intended to put across. M. very sweet
and apologetic for neglecting his friends lately. It is true he has written
me less, but he is as affectionate as ever. We were joined for dinner in
Paddington by his Cambridge friend Peter Bloxham,† a delicate-
looking chap with quiet good manners.

Wednesday, 14th April

I saw a Bath specialist, nice man, who took tests. Says my prostate
gland is slightly swollen, which accounts for my 'secret sorrow'. But
advises against operation. Says my blood pressure is that of a twenty-
year-old but my pulse is low, which accounts for my languor. This
sounds odd. I am to have a cardiac test.

The Royal Society of Literature has written offering me the
Heinemann Award for *Harold* [*Nicolson*], and asking whether I want
the £1,000 prize. Is this query in view of my declining to lecture to
them? Of course I have written accepting. Am pleased, but not
thrilled as I would have been ten years ago. I pointed out to them what
they might not be aware of, that they gave me this award for *Roman
Mornings* twenty-five years ago.

*J. L.-M's diary of his visit to Vicenza and Asolo with Eardley Knollys,
April–May 1982, is reproduced as Appendix I.*

Saturday, 8th May

Spent ten days in Italy with Eardley. A great success. Eardley is the
ideal traveller. He notices everything, and we invent fantasies about
the people we see in restaurants and bars.

---

* Apart from *Caves of Ice*, these were *The Country House: an Anthology*, *Images of Bath*, and
The Last Stuarts.
† Partner of Freshfield & Co., solicitors (b. 1952).

Since my return I have within two days written Part I of my novel.
I think it rather good, but then it was easy. The feelings of Rupert,
and his seduction, come easily to me. I got so worked up during the
writing that the characters became real to me. It was like writing autobiography, although totally fictitious. Of course, all novels must be
wish-fantasies.

Went for my cardiac test yesterday. When it was over the print-
out was passed to the doctor, who read it like a musical score. A long
roll of zig-zags, showing the pulse beat. He explained that the down-
ward fall never quite reached the level mark on the roll. He said, 'You
have had a small coronary attack during the past three months. Do
you remember it?' Now, I am not sure whether I do or not. I
remember having a pain in my chest once, and there was the occasion when I walked to the Berkeleys' house during the intense cold
in London and felt extremely affected by it.[*] A. thinks that may have
been the occasion. Anyway, doctor suggests no precautionary meas-
ures but stresses the importance of my taking exercise. Says coronar-
ies are usually caused either by excessive smoking and drinking, or
lack of exercise. Tests have proved beyond argument that bus drivers
are more subject to them than bus conductors, postmasters sitting in
their offices than postmen on their rounds. This is encouraging. It
means that I have no excuse not to accompany Derek [Hill][†] to
Mount Athos.

Chatto's write ecstatically about my Heinemann Award and *Caves
of Ice*, and say that Rainbird's are interested in *The Last Stuarts*.

I wrote to Master[‡] yesterday asking if I might illustrate [in *The Last
Stuarts*] his portrait of the Countess of Albany.[§] He telephoned this
morning asking us to dine tonight, which we can't. Said he can't iden-
tify any such portrait in the catalogue. Will I point it out to him? So
I went round there and then. Slowly and painfully he and Mary

---

[*] See entry for 13 January 1982.
[†] Landscape and portrait artist (1916–2000).
[‡] Henry Somerset, 10th Duke of Beaufort (1900–84); m. 1923 Lady Mary Cambridge
(1897–1987), dau. of 1st Marquess of Cambridge (brother of Queen Mary, consort of
King George V); leading figure of the hunting world, known as 'Master' from the age of
nine, when he was presented with a pack of harriers; owner of the Badminton estate.
[§] The name by which Princess Louise of Stolberg (1752–1824) was generally known after
her disastrous marriage in 1772 to Prince Charles Edward Stuart, 'the Young Pretender'
(d. 1788): she later became mistress of the poet Alfieri, and was received at the English
court.

walked up the stairs. We had to go to the top floor. There the portrait was, but it was not labelled Countess of Albany but Princess Stolberg. 'I can't think of any relation of ours called Lady Albany,' he said.* Mary hadn't a clue as to who I was, and begged me to come back and see the pictures another time. They have a red carpet up one side of the staircase. She explained that the Queen Mother had said the last time she stayed that, unless they provided a carpet, never again, too slippery. 'We could not afford more than a small strip,' Mary said. They were very friendly, and rather pathetic. He much more bent than formerly, his head jutting forward.

I notice that Eardley who will be eighty this autumn is inclined to jut his jaw forward in that enquiring, anxious way the old have. Must avoid doing it myself, if possible.

Sunday, 9th May

We lunched with Charlie and Jessica Douglas-Home† at their mill house, out of doors on the lawn. Delicious hot mutton but cold session. Charlie explained much about the workings of *The Times* that I had always wanted to know. He is an autocrat in that he decides policy entirely. He tells the writer of every leader what he wishes him to say. He has two meetings with his staff each day, at 11.30 a.m. and about 5 p.m., at which they discuss the news of the past twenty-four hours and how it should be reported. He is very pro-Thatcher but says she is faced with, if not a conspiracy, a hotbed of dissent within her ranks from what he terms 'the Whites boys', who deeply resent being led by a woman. I asked who were loyal to her. Pym?‡ No, he said. He does not much like Pym. Nor Whitelaw,§ who is waffly. Keith Joseph¶

---

* This was not the first time J.L.-M. had been amused by the Duke's assumption that the Countess of Albany must have been the wife of an English earl: see *Ancient as the Hills*, 14 February 1973.

† Charles Douglas-Home (1937–85); journalist, on staff of *The Times* from 1965 (deputy editor, 1981–2; editor, 1982–5); m. 1966 Jessica Gwynne, artist and stage designer.

‡ Francis Pym (b. 1922); Foreign Secretary, 1982–83 (appointed on resignation of Lord Carrington after Argentine invasion of Falkland Islands); backbench critic of Mrs Thatcher in 1983–87 parliament; cr. life peer, 1987.

§ William Whitelaw (1918–1999); Home Secretary, 1979–83; Conservative elder statesman, loyal to Mrs Thatcher though often disagreeing with her; cr. Viscount, 1983.

¶ Sir Keith Joseph, 2nd Bt (1918–94); ally of Mrs Thatcher, known as 'the mad monk'; Education Secretary, 1981–86; cr. life peer, 1987.

and Howe* are thoroughly loyal. He evidently has much admiration
for Murdoch,† as might be expected. He says Michael Ratcliffe‡ is
going. They can't afford to keep him on for he takes a fortnight to
write a review, reading all the other books on the subject of the book
he is writing about, like Raymond [Mortimer].§ Charlie is much
concerned by the Falklands trouble. He has written all the leaders on
the subject himself. I asked him how long it took him to write a
leader. He said he does them very quickly. He has a reliable woman
secretary who advises him by confirming or questioning the clearness
of his message to the average reader. He is a most sympathetic, jolly
and charming fellow, very simple, but quick. He has an awfully
responsible task. I hope he sticks it out. When we arrived they were
listening to the news and thought we might be about to invade the
islands. He thinks that, if Mrs Thatcher wins, she will be more persecuted by colleagues than ever. This does not speak highly for Tory
ministers.

Charlie wore an old pair of nondescript trousers and torn woolly
jersey. Not the least vain. He has rather lost his looks, but is still
charming. Jessica is dark, inscrutable, very fascinating and attractive,
her face obscured beneath a fringe of black hair and wide summery
hat. Two scruffy little boys, natural and affectionate with parents,
playing together with the lock gate of the mill race. Looking at these
underfledged chicks I thought of my Rupert. Must make him fifteen,
I think, not fourteen.

Tuesday, 11th May

Called on Rosamond [Lehmann]¶ before dinner. She is terribly upset
by a letter from A. abusing her for being a treacherous friend. In a way
this is my fault, because when A. admitted to me that she had written
to M. threatening him two years ago,‖ I stupidly said that I knew of

---

* Sir Geoffrey Howe (b. 1926); Chancellor of the Exchequer, 1979–83; considered a
Thatcher loyalist at this time, but a contributer to her downfall in 1990; cr. life peer, 1992.
† Rupert Murdoch (b. 1931); Australian media tycoon, whose group had bought *The
Times* in 1981.
‡ Literary editor of *The Times*, 1967–72 (b. 1935).
§ Literary reviewer (1895–1980) (see *Deep Romantic Chasm*, 12 January 1980).
¶ Novelist (1901–90); m. 1st 1923 (diss. 1928) Walter Runciman (later 2nd Viscount), 2nd
1928 (diss. 1944) Wogan Philipps (later 2nd Baron Milford).
‖ See *Deep Romantic Chasm*, 29 November 1981.

this and did not wish to discuss it. A. instantly jumped to the conclusion that Ros had told me, which indeed she had in an unguarded moment. Most unfortunate, and I hate being involved in this sort of thing and causing R. distress. Afterwards M. dined with me at Brooks's and I stayed with J.K.-B. who was in one of his black moods, his tenants absconding, etc.

Wednesday, 12th May

Lunched with the Bamber Gascoignes* at Richmond. Such a nice terrace house right on the river, with only a footway between house and river, and that sunk below their terrace. Facing them an island of willow trees and birds. House bare and carpetless, floors cleverly painted to resemble carpets. We lunched out-of-doors beneath a wisteria in full flower. Salad luncheon, adequate. Afterwards I signed nearly two hundred copies of *Images of Bath*. It took well over an hour. Bamber is extremely methodical, carrying stacks of these heavy books onto a table, providing blotting papers. I am disappointed by the quality of the prints, which is muzzy. The original photographs were very good. The type is excellent, and the layout, but for so high a price I think there may well be criticism.

Am finding the index of my silly little anthology taking much time. For the names are legion, and I have to look up in peerages (extinct and non-extinct), landed gentries, *DNB* volumes, et cetera, to find out whether the Duke of This and That is the fifth, sixth or seventh; worse still, who the wives were.

Collins have now written wanting to discuss book projects. Possibly W. J. Bankes would do.

Thursday, 13th May

A. and I motor to Kingston Lacy for day. I look through some of the Bankes papers, but still the Trust has not been given permission to enter the Muniment Room. Unless there are more papers there of a personal nature or about Bankes's travels, I doubt whether I could make much out of accounts and payments for works of art he bought.

---

* Arthur Bamber Gascoigne (b. 1935); author, broadcaster and publisher; m. 1965 Christina Ditchburn; son of J.L.-M's old friend Midi Gascoigne.

Saturday, 15th May

Darling Diana [Westmorland]* is not well. I called at Lyegrove after work and found June and Jeremy [Hutchinson]. June told me Diana was in bed. She has trouble with her aorta, brought about by the curvature of her spine and back. Her breathing is very quick and short, even when she is asleep. June believes she may die quite suddenly and painlessly when the aorta bursts. I feel very sad.

Sunday, 16th May

June and Jeremy came over to tea in the kitchen. I accompanied Jeremy on foot nearly to Lyegrove down the verge, with the dogs on a lead. I said how lucky he was to have known Virginia Woolf, for I have been reading about her friendship with his parents in the latest volume of her diaries. He said he was too young to know her properly. She was very fond of children, who loved her because she was such a tease and so funny. Always seemed cheerful to them. Bloomsbury struck him and Barbara as a great joke. They imitated their exaggerated voices with deep emphasis on adjectives, particularly Roger Fry's. Jeremy a most sympathetic man, but I was a bit distressed by his obvious dislike, if not resentment, of Diana, who he thinks fags June unmercifully. He says D. is very exacting and not good with servants – very Edwardian, in other words. Jeremy hates the aristocracy and is horribly left-wing. At tea, A. refused to discuss Argentina because of their dislike of Mrs Thatcher. 'Let's change the subject,' she said. 'We shall never agree.'

Chiquita [Astor]† and Sally [Westminster]‡ lunched. Chiquita is curiously shy of telephoning her friends in case they don't want to see her, she being Argentinian. She has just returned from there via Madrid. Says Galtieri is not a clever man and is a mere figurehead. The presidency of the country lasts only two years. Nor is the Government the least Fascist. It is however a bulwark against

---

* Diana Lister (1893–1983), dau. of 4th and last Baron Ribblesdale; m. (3rd) 14th Earl of Westmorland (d. 1948); regarded by J.L.-M. as 'far and away my closest friend down here' (4 December 1983).
† Ana Inez Carcano, m. 1944–72 Hon. John Jacob Astor (d. 2000), 4th son of 2nd Viscount Astor.
‡ Sally Perry (1911–91), half-sister of the writer Joe Ackerley; widow of Gerald Grosvenor, 4th Duke of Westminster (d. 1967).

Communism, and she is sure the whole Falklands crisis has been engineered by Russia.

Sunday, 23rd May

Never has there been a better year for Queen Anne's lace. The verges of the lanes are dense and tall with these delicate flowers. They impart a lusciousness to the spring and give an impression of remoteness, as though the old country of my youth was returned to me. One can get lost in them. An indifferent bluebell year, however. And not a single cuckoo have I heard since I got back to England.

Watched Horowitz* playing in his first concert in England for over thirty years. His fingers turn up at the ends, like a pig's nose.

Wednesday, 26th May

Went to old Mrs Anthony's funeral at Alderley. The tiny coffin was pushed into the aisle on a sort of pram. None of that shoving, heaving and lifting. Church quite full, for this eighty-nine-year-old had lived here a long while. The parson's intoning about worms consuming the body cannot have been palatable to the son and daughter. He referred to 'Mother in that box', which I found unacceptable. Said the physical resurrection of the body was 'difficult for us to apprehend' – difficult indeed. In reference to the South Atlantic War, we sang the hymn for those in peril on the seas, which she would have liked, being a general's daughter and deep-dyed Tory and patriot.

In the novel I have brought about the temporary exit of Rupert, gone back to school. M. who has read Part I says it needs to be crisper. I now have to face Amy's seduction by Ernst.

Thursday, 27th May

To London for the day in order to lunch with Norah and Jeremy Lewis† to meet David Roberts, bright, affable, handsome Old Etonian representing Rainbird's. He is keen to take the Stuarts and all now depends on the Americans being willing. He seems sanguine, but I am not so sure. Says Rainbird's would print fifteen to twenty thousand copies, and

---

* Vladimir Horowitz, Russian-born pianist (1903–89).
† Publisher and author (b. 1942).

showed me a comparable book by Jan Morris* on the Venetian Empire. I am not in favour of the long lines of small print, which make the text unreadable.

The alternative is to have a decently produced, non-glossy, serious book which may receive reviews. I fancy Rainbird books don't, unless by Nancy [Mitford].†

Whitsunday, 30th May

Selina Hastings‡ and M. came for three nights. A. had to provide food for every meal despite suffering from a bad bronchial cold that made her feel rotten. We both found Selina perfect – amusing, clever, appreciative, getting on with everyone. Each morning she worked in her bedroom on the children's books she writes for Sebastian Walker.§ M. says he enjoyed himself very much. I took him and Selina to see Eliza Wansbrough,¶ who showed us a photograph of Sibyl [Colefax],‖ which is a rarity. And Selina went off with my Eton photograph of Tom [Mitford] for her Nancy biography. A. tells me how much she likes M., but I don't think she finds him wholly her cup of tea. He is too nervous of her. And no wonder.

Tuesday, 1st June

To London for night at Eardley's. Taken by Burnet** to *Simon Boccanegra* at Covent Garden. Enjoyed it, but the heat so terrific it spoilt full enjoyment. Kiri [te Kanawa] the New Zealand girl is perfection in voice and

---

* Writer (b. 1926), known as James Morris prior to a much-publicised sex change in 1973.

† Eldest of the Mitford sisters (1904–73), who lived in Paris after 1945; novelist and author of historical works; m. 1933 Hon. Peter Rodd.

‡ Lady Selina Hastings (b. 1945), dau. of 15th Earl of Huntingdon; author and journalist, then writing a biography of Nancy Mitford.

§ Publisher, philanthropist and art collector (1942–91); founder of Walker Books, which revolutionised publishing for children.

¶ Dau. of Sir George Lewis, 2nd Bt, and granddau. of famous late Victorian solicitor of that name; m. 1928–38 George Wansbrough.

‖ Sibyl Halsey (1874–1950); m. 1901 Sir Arthur Colefax, QC (d. 1936); London hostess, famed for her 'lion hunting'; founder (1931) of a firm of decorators (later Colefax & Fowler).

**Burnet Pavitt (b. 1908); businessman and music lover, trustee of Royal Opera House; friend of J.L.-M. since 1948.

looks. Burnet says she is as good a voice as he has heard since he joined the Board. Heat in E's flat also oppressive. No windows open. Went to his exhibition and bought a small still life for £100, which I don't really want but felt I ought to buy to encourage my oldest friend. I think E. has improved – more substantial; more confident; and he has developed his own distinctive style, got away from the Vanessa [Bell]–Duncan [Grant] influence.

Monday, 14th June

Was motored by new N.T. Representative for Severn Region to Kingston Lacy. Tony Mitchell[*] brought the Francis Haskells[†] from Bath. She a Red Russian intellectual lady, surprisingly nice and friendly. Lucky woman to have escaped. Did a little browsing through Bankes material, but am not sure whether I can or should do this biography. So many experts are looking into his artistic activities that it might be a mistake to tackle his life before they have drawn their conclusions. But I shall wait until I have access to the Muniment Room and know what papers exist there. Meanwhile I am besieged with requests to write books from literary agents and publishers.

Tuesday, 15th June

To London. For several days have been in a state over the few words I am to deliver at tomorrow's prize award. Indeed, the prospect upsets me to the point of taking all the savour out of life. I have written out my few words and learnt them by heart.

Went to Graham Sutherland[‡] exhibition at Tate after leaving my upper plate at the dentist's for the day. Don't like Graham's work of the 1940s and 50s. Think those twisted, spiky, inflated thorns were, if not fraudulent, then an affectation. But there can be no doubt at all that his portraits were masterly.

Dined with Elizabeth and John Betj[eman]. Noticeable declension since my last visit. J. barely spoke. Must have had another little stroke

---

[*] Anthony Mitchell (b. 1931); N.T. Historic Buildings Representative 1956–96 (for Wessex Region 1981–96); m. 1972 Brigitte de Soye.
[†] Francis Haskell, FBA (b. 1928); Professor of Art History, Oxford University and Fellow of Trinity College, Oxford from 1967; m. 1965 Larissa Salmina.
[‡] Artist (1903–80); m. 1927 Kathleen Barry.

by the slipped look of his face on right-hand side. Enormous blown-up stomach. Movement from his chair to dinner table most painful. Was told not to help. Nice friendly old Anglican monk staying. While Elizabeth supported J's shoulders the monk gently kicked J's feet. Thus they dragged him, bent sideways like a telephone pole half blown over, to the table. I sat beside him. Tried to tease him into amusement. Barely succeeded. Yet yesterday, he was televised sitting in his chair. I said, 'I suppose you were talking about yourself as usual?' He laughed in the old way. He said, 'No. I was catty.' Strange reaction. Asked him how his biography was getting on. He said it was awkward. I have since learnt that Feeble does not like Bevis Hillier* and won't co-operate with him. Left feeling very sad. Cannot believe he will survive the year.

Wednesday, 16th June

The dreaded day. Lunched at Collins with Christopher Maclehose,† Mark Bonham Carter and my co-prize winner, Jonathan Raban,‡ youngish man with charming smile. Did not enjoy it. Mark charmless and embittered. Loathes Mrs Thatcher, of course. After meal, C.M. talked about the book they want me to do: to take ten houses of the world (no less) which survive untouched since built. All travelling paid for. I to discuss their creators and intentions. They say the BBC will do a programme on each house in turn, but only if I am the author. I don't altogether trust these people. I don't know how much I want to do such a book.

Then came the Royal Society of Literature. I walked from Brooks's. Sat through annual meeting, C. M. Woodhouse§ in chair. Awful tea afterwards. Hundreds of people came up and congratulated. Helen Dashwood¶ embraced me. Joanna Richardson‖ like a

---

* Author, journalist and critic (b. 1940); Antiques Correspondent of *The Times*, 1970–84.

† Publisher (b. 1940).

‡ Novelist, travel writer and critic (b. 1942).

§ Hon. C. Montague Woodhouse (1917–2001); academic and politician, sometime MP (C) for Oxford; author of works on modem Greek history; s. brother as 5th Baron Terrington, 1998.

¶ Widow of Sir John Dashwood, 10th Bt (1896–1966) of West Wycombe Park, Buckinghamshire, wartime headquarters of N.T., whose foibles J.L.-M. had (to her indignation) described in his wartime diaries (she d. 1989).

‖ Author of historical and literary biographies (see entry for 21 August 1982); FRSL, 1959.

huge man-of-war in full sail. The hall was full to the brim. I came first. Woodhouse read out some words about the book, called upon me, presented me with envelope, made me sign a book. Then I turned round and delivered my words. Was not good, but did not disgrace myself. A. sitting below me said it was all right. So did M. who was present, but I don't think they were impressed. Relief that all was over. Then I gave a small dinner at Brooks's – Nigel [Nicolson],* Sheila Birkenhead,† Charlotte Bonham Carter, A. and M. Ordered champagne. Enjoyed it because I am fond of Charlotte and dearly love Sheila. She told me that she has lost the use of her right hand and cannot write, but she doesn't seem to mind. I cut up her duck for her. Charlotte's head sideways in the plate.

Thursday, 17th June

Lunched alone with M. at his club. We talked of his future projects and mine. In spite of my severe remonstrances I doubt whether he will get Sibyl [Colefax] off the ground.‡

On the way home A. and I went to garden party given for Mollie Buccleuch§ in Caroline Gilmour's¶ garden at Syon. Lovely house on bend of the Thames, next door to Wyatt boathouse in which Diana Daly lived. Hundreds of antiquated persons. Did not enjoy it at all. Mollie's slender looks all gone, poor darling. Face big and wide. Alan Pryce-Jones‖ whom I met in the Burlington Arcade yesterday told me Mollie was wretched and interested in nothing and longed to die.

---

* Politician, author and journalist (b. 1917), who in recent years had edited the letters of Virginia Woolf in six volumes; yr. s. of Harold Nicolson and Vita Sackville-West; in 1976 he had invited J.L.-M. to write his father's biography; resident at Sissinghurst Castle, Kent.
† Hon. Sheila Berry, dau. of 1st Viscount Camrose; m. 1935 Frederick Smith, 2nd Earl of Birkenhead (1907–75) (who as Viscount Furneaux had been an Eton and Oxford friend of J.L.-M.).
‡ See entry for 5 December 1984.
§ Vreda Esther Mary Lascelles (1900–93); m. 1921 Walter Montagu-Douglas-Scott (1894–1973) who in 1935 s. his father as 8th Duke of Buccleuch and 10th Duke of Queensberry.
¶ Lady Caroline Montagu Douglas Scott (b. 1927), yr dau. of Mollie Buccleuch; m. 1951 Sir Ian Gilmour, 3rd Bt, MP (Lord Privy Seal, 1979–81).
‖ Author and journalist (1908–2000); editor *Times Literary Supplement*, 1948–59; contemporary of J.L.-M. at Eton and Magdalen College, Oxford; cousin of Mollie Buccleuch.

Sunday, 20th June

George Dix* who saw my little picture by E. remarked, 'These rich amateurs of painting ought to give their beastly pictures away to their friends instead of asking inflated prices for their trash.'

Thursday, 24th June

Successful day in London. Terrible [traffic] queues near Heathrow owing to tube strike. Streets crowded. Norah Smallwood let me park in her yard at Vincent Square, from where I walked. Not raining for once, nor too hot. M. lunched at Brooks's, off to Paris tomorrow. He accompanied me to Rainbird's in Park Street, where I was greeted by that charmer David Roberts. Left with him my photographs for Stuart book, if it materialises. Don't much care if it doesn't, for then Chatto's will publish it as an ordinary book. It depends on the Americans. I looked over jackets of their latest books, the same glossy reproductions of Canalettos, Guardis, etc., commonplace and boring. Later wrote to Roberts suggesting an oval display of silver Stuart medals on a simple blue ground. Then to Norah's for tea to discuss endpapers of *Caves of Ice*. Found her rather muddly and dense. Poor woman, she is ill, and fearfully jealous of her writers: was not pleased when I told her about Maclehose's designs for me at Collins. Dined with Eardley to meet his nephew and niece the Hudsons, and Fanny Partridge.† Motored home at 10.45, arriving 1 a.m.

Saturday, 26th June

We dine with the Somersets.‡ Ali Forbes§ staying. He is splendid value, possessing the facility of story-telling and joking which I entirely lack. I feel tireder and tireder these days. It must be the heart I think.

---

* Friend of J.L.-M. since 1945, at which time he was a US naval officer.
† Frances Marshall (b. 1900), diarist and critic; m. 1933 Ralph Partridge (d. 1960).
‡ David Somerset (b. 1928), art dealer; cousin and heir of 10th Duke of Beaufort (whom he succeeded, 1984); m. 1st 1950 Lady Caroline Thynne (1928–1995), dau. of 6th Marquess of Bath, 2nd 2000 Miranda Morley; then living at The Cottage, Badminton.
§ Alastair Forbes (b. 1918), literary critic resident in Switzerland.

Friday, 2nd July

Terrible fork luncheon at Alderley Grange* after meeting of [N.T.] Regional Committee there. Lots of old colleagues. I escaped early and stopped car on the hill of the Tresham road. Walked the dogs in Foxholes Wood. Never have I seen a more beautiful landscape. These combes on the edge of the Cotswolds surpass everything. Passed through a field of barley sprinkled with red poppies. Glimpsed through the trees, very decayed and Constablesque, the winding yellow lane to the farmstead, and the prospect of the vale. Just like a Jane Austen drive which phaetons would take for picnics. The Grange is full of lovely things, but too expensive, like a Bond Street antique dealer's. One imagines a price ticket discreetly tied to the back of each piece of furniture. Garden lush and much grown since we left. A. complained as we went round that the dear Acloques had made some mistakes in replanting. I could not see this, but regretted some of the garden statuary. But what a joy that this is now a family home with children being born and brought up there. They will love it.

Saturday, 10th July

On Thursday Bamber [Gascoigne] gave a party in my Bath library for subscribers to the morocco-bound volumes of *Images of Bath*. Beautiful they are, splashed with gold too. An extraordinary collection of subscribers turned up. No one I had ever seen before, and not rich-seeming. Yet why do they buy these volumes? For Bamber says the leather people, as he calls them, are generally the same for all the volumes in the series. There are two butcher brothers in Richmond who buy two copies of each issue, at £600 a time. Extraordinary.

M. goes to Spain today, having been two nights in London. Says Maître Blum† has consented to appear with him on television in October when he is confronted with opponents to his Duke of

---

* Georgian country house at Wotton-under-Edge, Gloucestershire, where the L.-Ms lived from 1961 to 1974. They left with regret, A.L.-M. (who had created a celebrated garden there) selling the property to Guy Acloque (m. 1971 Hon. Camilla, dau. of 9th Baron Howard de Walden).
† Maître Suzanne Blum (1898–1994), the formidable Paris lawyer of the Duchess of Windsor, for whom Michael Bloch had been working since 1979.

Windsor theories. This splendid octogenarian lady says she cannot leave him to their mercies. Then she had a long talk with him about homosexuality, telling him most of her male friends had been so. M. thrilled by these confidences.

A. and I lunched today with Patricia Hambleden* at Ewelme. David H.† staying, much aged and not so ebullient as usual. Lovely to be with them. We lunched out-of-doors under a lime tree, from the branches of which starlings dropped pellets onto A's head. David and I were born within two months of each other.

Yesterday I motored to Kingston Lacy to glance through some more papers of W. J. Bankes. Found one or two personal papers relating to his outlawry, but suspect recent members of family may have destroyed compromising letters. Anyway, I have decided to defer tackling this subject, and to do the Rome anthology for Nick [Robinson]‡ when I have finished my novel.

Monday, 12th July

Yesterday morning I rang up Nick and told him that I had finally decided to do the Rome anthology for him. Then in the evening A. and I went to the Hollands'§ annual concert in their barn in aid of the National Art Collections Fund. Before the concert I saw Lionel Esher,¶ who said to me, 'You remember that a year ago I told you I had engaged another writer to do my grandfather's biography? It was

---

* Lady Patricia Herbert (d. 1994), dau. of 15th Earl of Pembroke; m. 1928 3rd Viscount Hambleden.

† Hon. David Herbert (1908–95), yr s. of 15th Earl of Pembroke; Eton contemporary of J.L.-M.; resident of Tangier.

‡ J.L.-M's favourite great-nephew (b. 1955), second of the three Robinson brothers (sons of J.L.-M's sister Audrey's daughter Prudence), who had recently established his own publishing firm.

§ Sir Guy Holland, 3rd Bt (b. 1918); farmer and art dealer; m. 1945 Joan Street.

¶ Lionel Brett, 4th Viscount Esher (b. 1913), architect; m. 1935 Christian Pike, artist. His father, Oliver Brett, 3rd Viscount (1881–1963), had chaired the Country Houses (later Historic Buildings) Committee of the N.T. when J.L.-M. was its Secretary during the 1940s. It was Lionel's grandfather, Reginald ('Regy') Brett, 2nd Viscount Esher (1852–1930), the shadowy figure who advised monarchs and prime ministers while refusing high office and leading a secret homosexual life, who was to be the subject of J.L.-M's next biography. (J.L.-M. had already expressed interest in writing this book a year earlier – see *Deep Romantic Chasm*, July–August 1981 – but had been discouraged by Lionel.)

Max Egremont.* He has now backed out, so if you are free I will offer it to you.' I was struck all of a heap, and during the first half of the concert, Howard Shelley playing Schubert and Rachmaninov, could think of nothing else. During the interval I had a further talk with Lionel, who said he didn't want a fourth chucker after Philip Magnus,† Michael Howard‡ and Egremont. Lionel wonders what it was about his grandfather that put these eminent people off. Each made a different excuse, Egremont's being that he had decided to concentrate on writing novels. I wonder if the reason was that Esher was too stuffy, for the volumes of his letters which M. gave me for Christmas I found extremely boring. Lionel says they were heavily expurgated. Says his grandfather was too grand by half, an outrageous snob. L's father Oliver took against his father because he opposed Oliver's marriage to Antoinette, who was not only American but un-grand. When, going through his father's papers on his death, Oliver discovered the truth about his father, he wrote a short but bitter book about him which he decided not to publish. I asked if I might be allowed to read it, but Lionel thought not. I must form my own opinion. No M. to discuss.

Today the Berkeleys lunched on their way from the Cheltenham Festival to Berkeley Castle. Lennox very detached, Freda complaining in front of us that he paid no heed to two things which were worrying her, the dissolute conduct of their youngest son and the notice from their landlords that 8 Warwick Avenue must be sold in a few years for £130,000, which they have not got. Lennox just smiled blandly and seemed not to take it in. After luncheon I strolled with him in the park. Conversation proved difficult until I said, 'Lennox, you must have bad days when you can't compose. I have bad days when I can't write, which make me suppose I may never write again. This depresses me inordinately.' This awakened him and he became quite animated. 'Yes,' he said, 'I do have these days and I have these same fears. And it is awful, awful.' He lives in a world of his own,

---

* Max Wyndham (b. 1948); s. father 1972 as 2nd Baron Egremont and 7th Baron Leconfield; of Petworth House, Sussex (which after negotiations largely conducted through J.L.-M. had been donated to the N.T. by his great-uncle, 1947); writer; m. 1978 Caroline Nelson.

† Sir Philip Magnus-Allcroft, 2nd Bt (1906–88); historian; m. 1943 Jewel Allcroft of Stokesay Court, Shropshire; formally assumed surname of Allcroft in addition to that of Magnus, 1951.

‡ Michael Eliot Howard (b. 1922); Regius Professor of Modern History, Oxford, 1980–9; kt, 1986.

music, at which he is as good as formerly. But he shrugs off every other consideration. Lives in a cloud.

Tuesday, 13th July

Motored to London with A. last night. She stayed with Midi,* I with Eardley, whom I found low, muddled and losing things. Took my car round to Norah's yard in the morning and was leaving keys at her office when Dirk Bogarde† and a friend walked in. A short, well-preserved, still youthful man with dark hair, looking like Angus Menzies.‡ I said, 'I saw you three evenings ago in the best film in the world.' He asked what film that was, and whether I had not mistaken him for Humphrey Bogart. '*Death in Venice*,' I said. 'I've never seen it,' he said. 'You're like me, then, I never read my own books.' 'I read mine all the time,' he said. There is something rather camp about him.

At Properties Committee, the N.T. Librarian told me he had taken the mediaeval parchment sheets we found at Kingston Lacy last week to the [British] Museum, where they were identified as the earliest known English manuscripts, being part of an Old Testament dating from AD 690–760. They had been used for wrapping a sixteenth-century lease. Museum people thrilled.

Sunday, 18th July

A. and I motored to Calke Abbey [Derbyshire] on Friday to join a small party of members of the Properties Committee to determine whether this property with its large estate, lovely park and the 1703 house is worthy of acceptance through the Treasury in lieu of death duties. A. and I have no doubts whatever of its worthiness. I was last here twenty-eight years ago with Rupert Gunnis§ and Hugh Euston.¶ Exterior totally untouched, except for Wilkins's portico which is an improvement, and balustrade. Fine staircase and upstairs saloon, heightened by

---

* Hon. Mary O'Neill (1905–91), m. 1934 Frederick ('Derick') Gascoigne (d. 1974); friend of J.L.-M. since 1920s.
† Professional name of Derek van den Bogaerde (1921–2000), film actor, becoming known at this time for his novels and autobiographical writings.
‡ Charismatic bachelor cousin of A.L.-M. (1910–73).
§ Author of *The Dictionary of British Sculptors, 1660–1851* (1953).
¶ 11th Duke of Grafton.

Wilkins. No great works of art, perhaps, but every stick of furniture, every content covetable. Nothing thrown away. I opened a trunk in the cook's room over the kitchen, and found it full to the brim with sailor suits and other Edwardian children's clothes. We saw photographs taken in 1880 of rooms which look exactly the same today. Quite extraordinary. The family has been eccentric for 150 years, the late owner and present owner (his brother) no exception. By tradition each owner leaves his predecessor's apartments intact and moves on to the next suite of rooms. In the Gothic church in the park, a late eighteenth-century tablet praises a Mrs Harpur Crewe in these terms: 'Though she was placed far above want herself yet Affluence could never abate her Humanity.' Howard Colvin* who has nursed this house ever since Rupert's death was present to receive us. He said that he had peeped into a box which contained Caroline of Anspach's[†] unpacked bed, its hangings still in pristine condition.

Marion Brudenell present. We went on to Deene to stay with the Brudenells.[‡] Large house party. Twenty every meal. Table covered with silver, and delicious food. A very fine house within. Great hall with open roof superb. Excellent collection of family portraits, many bought back by Edmund. The twin sons came on Saturday night, dark, saturnine, well-mannered youths. On Sunday, service was held in a chapel made in the house since we were last there, for the church has been closed down, and memorial busts, one by Pierce very good indeed, removed by Edmund into the house. One of the twins read the lesson. Fellow guests included George Lane[§] and wife, daughter of Lord Heald. He is a Hungarian with great contempt for the Poles, the Pope and the Church. David Scott[¶] came to luncheon on Sunday, aet. 95 and not well. Francis Egerton[‖] and I walked from Deene to Kirby

---

* Howard Colvin (b. 1919), architectural historian (kt, 1995).

[†] Queen (d. 1737) of King George II.

[‡] Edmund Brudenell (b. 1924) of Deene Park, Norhamptonshire; m. 1955 Marion, dau. of Reginald Manningham-Buller, later 1st Viscount Dilhorne; descendant of 2nd Marquess of Ailesbury, who inherited Deene Park from his kinsman, the 7th Earl of Cardigan of Crimean War fame.

[§] George Lanyi (b. 1915); war hero, farmer and businessman; m. (2nd) 1963 Elizabeth Heald.

[¶] Sir David Montagu-Douglas-Scott (1887–1986), diplomatist; cousin of 7th Duke of Buccleuch; m. 1st 1918 Dorothy Drummond (d. 1965), 2nd 1970 Valerie Finnis, VMH, horticulturist and writer.

[‖] Chairman of Mallett & Son, antique dealers (b. 1917); lived on Crichel Estate, Dorset.

Hall, almost getting lost. Impressive ruins but Ministry-kept gardens atrocious. We left after luncheon today and drove to Northampton to visit Gervase Jackson-Stops, who has broken several limbs in a motor smash. Sitting in bed with one leg on a pulley. Totally naked and looking like a boy of ten, were the top of his head not bald. Even this gives him a baby look, with his fair, smooth skin.

Tuesday, 20th July

Motoring in the dark I ran over a hedgehog and killed it flat. Very distressed. Had seen the poor little thing scuttling across the road. Tried to avoid it so that it might pass under the car between the wheels, but no. A. says its babies would wonder why it had not returned and would die of starvation. I loathe killing things. Could only kill IRA members willingly.

Friday, 23rd July

Met Mary Beaufort walking through the gates of the big house. She was wearing blue bedroom slippers, white cotton trousers too short in the leg and a peasant shawl over her head. I asked her where she was going. 'I am going to the Agent to apologise for not keeping an appointment this morning.' Then she said, 'Do you like living in this little cottage?' I said Yes, we did. 'We must arrange for you to come to dinner one night, or do you dislike dining out?' 'Not with you,' I said gallantly. 'Snob!' she replied. A. vastly amused when I told her. I said I hope to God she doesn't invite us, it is such torture. A. said, 'She may say to Master, "Who are those people who live at the lodge?" and he will reply, "I wouldn't bother about them if I were you."'

Saturday, 24th July

Wrote to Marcus Worsley* recording my strong favour of Calke Abbey; corrected *TLS* proof of my review of Debo's† Chatsworth

---

* Sir Marcus Worsley, 5th Bt (b. 1925), of Hovingham Hall, Yorkshire; MP (C) Chelsea, 1966–74; Chairman of N.T. Properties Committee since 1980; m. 1955 Hon. Bridget Assheton.

† Hon. Deborah Mitford, youngest of the Mitford sisters (b. 1920); m. 1941 Lord Andrew Cavendish, who s. as 11th Duke of Devonshire 1950; châtelaine of Chatsworth, Derbyshire.

book; typed out A's article on this garden for R[oyal] H[orticultural] S[ociety] *Journal*. Then walked with dogs round Cherry Orchard. A dull day till then but a gauzy sun came out. In hedgerows meadow-sweet, fire-weed of both sorts, still some tatty geraniums; convolvulus trailing over nut trees; some butterflies, undersized, meadow browns I think. Height of summer. Slumberous landscape of park. Group under a large tree picnicking, blobs of yellow and blue like Impressionist painting in jiggling haze. Fishermen bent over lake under outsize umbrellas, other figures standing languidly doing nothing.

I virtually finished my novel yesterday. When I killed Rupert on his bicycle, I wept. Probably a bad sign of sentimental twaddle. M. thinks Part II brilliant, thinks less of Part I, and will think less still of Part III.

Sunday, 25th July

Have finished Berthoud's life of Graham Sutherland.[*] Dullish but fair and not eulogistic. Reading this biography reminded me how little I cared for Graham. A. and I saw a lot of him and Cathy in the 1950s when we lived at Roquebrune. There was a period of a few years when we constantly met at restaurants in the winter and they would dine with us at La Méridienne, never we with them that I remember. There was something smug about him. Disingenuous. The trouble about both of them was their worldliness. Towards the end of his life Graham could not bear to be among people who were not famous. And his judgement of those famous people he considered worthwhile was faulty. He was easily impressed by businessmen millionaires. Cathy was very mischievous. She thought it smart to be bitchy. Our relations with them were never the same after a row they manufactured between us and the K. Clarks.[†] Cathy told Jane that we had criticised their upbringing of their children – quite fatuous. She apologised and we got over that trouble. Then one night when Eddy Sackville-West[‡] was staying with us and the Sutherlands dining, Eddy criticised their

---

[*] Roger Berthoud, *Graham Sutherland: A Biography* (Faber & Faber, 1982).
[†] Kenneth Clark (1903–84), art historian; Surveyor of the King's Pictures (1934–44); m. 1st 1927 Elizabeth ('Jane') Martin, 2nd 1977 Comtesse Nolwen de Janzé (1925–90); cr. life peer as Lord Clark of Saltwood, 1969.
[‡] Hon. Edward Sackville-West (cousin of Vita), writer and music critic (1901–65); s. father as 5th Baron Sackville, 1962.

new friends, mentioning by name Lord Beaverbrook, Aneurin Bevan and Douglas Cooper.* Cathy at once repeated this to that swine Cooper, but stated that it was A. and I who had made the remark, not Eddy. Result was that Cooper, who until then had been civil, cut us, not that that was a great loss. A. made me tax the Sutherlands with this mischief in a restaurant in San Remo where we had been lunching. Graham took it badly when I accused Cathy of having made this *potin*, which she did not deny. He looked daggers and went very red. After this incident we did not see the Sutherlands again except on neutral territory.† Nevertheless, I do consider his portraits works of genius. His landscapes so-so, and his theories of art pretty good nonsense.

Monday, 2nd August

The discovery of the Kingston Lacy parchment sheets is a direct link with the Reformation. They must have been torn from some library in the early sixteenth century, when the monasteries were despoiled, to be used as wrapping paper for a farm lease, and remained serving this ignoble purpose for 550 years, undisturbed.

A. and I motored back from Glyndebourne last night after *Don Giovanni*. A terrible journey through the suburbs of London – Reigate, Crawley, Byfleet, Cobham, Staines, Windsor – and on to the M4. Never again, we agreed. But the opera magnificent. A black, misty, thunderous production. No fun and games. All deadly serious. The first chord established the doom-laden atmosphere. We stayed two nights at Firle, probably for the last time as Diana‡ is leaving for Lancashire. Very sad situation. Her stepson Sammy, the new Lord Gage, is not coping well with his inheritance, but refuses to surrender rights to his younger brother Nicky, married with two little boys.

On Friday we lunched at Nymans with Anne Rosse.§ Large party.

---

* Art collector and patron, heir to an Australian fortune (1911–84); restorer of Château de Castille in south-eastern France (purchased 1949).
† See entry for 13 May 1984.
‡ Diana, *née* Cavendish (Hon. Mrs Campbell-Gray) m. (2nd) 1971 6th Viscount Gage (1895–1982) as his 2nd wife.
§ Anne Armstrong-Jones (*née* Messel), m. (2nd) 1935 Michael Parsons, 6th Earl of Rosse (d. 1979).

A. walked round garden, by which she was impressed, but it is not her sort of garden. Anne has given me a tiny sixteenth-century Spanish or Italian crucifix, to keep her and Michael [Rosse] in mind. Very sweet thought.

Took train to London for seventy-fifth birthday dinner given for Alec Clifton-Taylor* at the Savile Club. Walked from Bond Street Station to Savile with my bag. One of those summer London dog days, stiflingly hot. But dinner in large cool room at head of grand double-flight staircase in this pomposo building, once the London house of the Harcourts, all Frenchified Edwardian and rather splendid.† About thirty guests at three tables joined to form a U. Alec protested that he had known nothing of the feast until he arrived, having been bidden by two old friends and expecting their company only. I was honoured to be put at the top table, between John Julius Norwich and Jasper More,‡ one away from Alec. Jasper made usual witty speech with jokes at which we laughed. Said Alec had achieved immortality, a thing few of us could claim, with his book on building materials. Alec replied listing the prerequisites for leading a happy life. (1) Health. (2) Money, enough to satisfy modest needs. (3) Interest in and dedication to one's work. (4) Ability to control and come to terms with one's sexual urges. (Surprising, coming from him. I never supposed he had any. Turn away from the thought.) (5) Friendships, which to him meant everything. To which he added (6) being able to recognise one's own limitations, stretch them to the utmost, and never to envy the superior ability of others. Rather charmingly put. The moment the meal was over I slipped off to take underground to Islington to stay at Jack Rathbone's.§

---

* Writer and broadcaster on architectural subjects (1907–85).

† The house (69 Brook Street) was designed by the Paris architect Bouwens in 1891 for the American banker Walter H. Burns and his wife, sister of J. Pierpont Morgan. The Burnses' daughter married the politician Lewis (later 1st Viscount) Harcourt, who moved there with his family after Mrs Burns's death in 1918. The Viscount committed suicide there in 1922 after a scandal involving J.L.-M's Eton contemporary Edward James (then aged thirteen), and his wife and children left soon afterwards; the Savile acquired it as their clubhouse in 1927.

‡ Sir Jasper More (1907–87); author of travel books on Mediterranean countries; Conservative MP for Ludlow, 1960–79; Eton contemporary of J.L.-M.

§ John Francis Warre Rathbone (1909–95); Secretary of N.T., 1949–68.

Tuesday, 3rd August

Max Egremont lunched with me at Boodle's. Delightful man, what I would call young middle-aged, with looks of a less handsome Nick Robinson. Yet strange to learn he was born after the war, in 1948. We discussed Reginald Esher. What put him off the book were the mass of papers and the unsympathetic character of the man. But was not put off by his sexual deviations, not at all. I liked Egremont much. Have since read his *Balfour*, which lacks sparkle. Went to tea with Ros [Lehmann]. She is very upset by the illness of her granddaughter Anna, paralysed from waist down. Also upset by her row with A. and wants me to put things right, but A. will not listen and regards the subject as closed.

Wednesday, 11th August

Listened last night on the wireless to the Glyndebourne production of *Orfeo*. Deeply moved, especially by the glorious aria when Orpheus recognises he has lost Euridice. This was Janet Baker's very last operatic performance, with her warm, unaffected voice. My favourite opera, to the music of which I would like to die.

M. has told me that he considers the ending of my novel bad, trite and unacceptable. Am rather put out by this, though pleased by his candour. I had a misgiving that the death of Rupert was too sentimental. I would now like someone else to advise me. M. sees silliness in a 1920s boy's serious attitude towards sexual deviation, and thinks the end should be a *ménage-à-trois* between Rupert, Ernst and Amy. He does not realise, I tell him, how we had to conceal, be evasive, were fearful.

Friday, 13th August

Ian McCallum* said that rats in winter snuggle together to keep warm. Often their tails get tied in a mysterious knot which no scientist has been able to explain. The poor things starve to death because the harder they pull the tighter their tails get knotted.

Hansel Pless† told me this evening that when he was a small boy the Kaiser and retinue came to stay at his father's house in Poland. The

---

* Curator of American Museum at Claverton near Bath (1919–87).
† Henry, Prince of Pless (d. 1984); m. (1958–71) Mary Minchin (see entry for 1 February 1984).

men of the house, including Hansel, awaited the Kaiser with their hats in their hands; after His arrival, they put them on again. The Kaiser went up to Hansel and crushed his top hat over his nose and chin. Not only did it hurt, but the boy was deeply offended. The Kaiser roared with laughter, as of course did the courtiers. When I told Pless Diana Mosley's story of how the Kaiser requested the Headmaster of Eton to have a boy swished in front of Him for His benefit, he said that this was another example of His peculiar sense of humour. Pless said the Poles were hopeless, like the Irish. They had charm, and liked to tell you what they thought you wanted to hear, but were inefficient and untrustworthy. The Plesses always employed Germans to run their Polish estates.

Monday, 16th August

On Sunday I motored to stay the night with the Droghedas.* Garrett full of charm and most welcoming. Joan subdued and memory extremely bad. One has to help her along, reminding her of names and trying to think ahead for her. Barbara Ghika and her husband staying.† A very intelligent, liberal-minded, equable woman abounding in good sense, like Fanny Partridge without the political fanaticism. After breakfast I left for Windsor Castle.

   Arrived at Henry VIII entrance gate. Police asked me my business. Before admitting me they telephoned the Library. Were given OK and let me through. Then I walked to what is called the Side Door. Police inside. Again they telephone Miss Langton,‡ who looks after the Archives. An official in morning coat, long tails, took a huge bunch of keys on the end of a long chain and opened the entrance door of the Round Tower. I climbed straight long flights of steps. Smiling Miss Langton at head of stairs. Charming, efficient, helpful spinster. I was shown card catalogue of Stuart documents, of which there are about 150,000 in 552 bound files or boxes. Quite impossible to go through all these, but I found the catalogue most useful because the

---

* Garrett Moore, 11th Earl of Drogheda (1910–89); businessman, publisher and Chairman (1958–74) of Royal Opera House; m. 1935 Joan Carr, pianist (she d. 1989).
† Barbara Hutchinson (sister of Jeremy, Baron Hutchinson); m. 1st (1933–46) 3rd Baron Rothschild, 2nd 1949 Rex Warner, 3rd 1961 Nico Hadjikyriakou-Ghika, painter (she d. 1989).
‡ Jane Langton, Registrar of the Royal Archives.

name of the writer and recipient of each letter is listed, with a short description of who each correspondent was. I managed to get through five of the fourteen drawers between 10 a.m. and 5 p.m., with a break (to be polite) for coffee with three ladies on the staff and two other researchers, one of whom 'knew my books'. I calculate that I can complete the work in two more visits. Am always happy working in a library of this sort, being waited on by kindly, helpful people in the quiet of a scholarly atmosphere. No sign of Sir Robin* which is rather a relief, he being in Australia. I only looked at three files. One rather interesting letter of 1751 from a Roman tailor to the Cardinal Duke† gives estimates for the stuff of liveries, enclosing a sample about four inches square – of rose silk velvet with silver braid border, in mint condition.

Clarissa [Luke] told me that her grandmother Gwladys Chaplin,‡ when talking of death, would say: 'I am told they come to one with jinglin' bells.'

Saturday, 21st August

The one hundredth birthday of my uncle Robert Bailey.§ When I remarked on this to A. at breakfast, she said that her father would probably be a hundred and ten if alive today, so what? But I remember my Uncle Robert with reverence and affection, for I was brought up to believe him to have been the gentlest, most saintly scholar and sportsman, the ideal of a pre-1914 English gentleman, adored by his colleagues among the House of Commons clerks, by his friends, by his two sisters, my Mama and Aunt Doreen, and by the working men at whose clubs he taught. I have one memory of him, like a muzzy, rapid shot of an old cinematograph film, chasing me around the yard at Wickhamford. This must have been during his last leave in the First War. He was wearing a black-and-white check suit and stiff collar,

---

* Sir Robert ('Robin') Mackworth-Young (1920–2000); Royal Librarian at Windsor Castle and Assistant Keeper of Queen's Archives, 1958–85; m. 1953 Rosemary Aue.
† Henry, Duke of York (1725–1807), grandson and last legitimate descendant of James II; created a cardinal by Pope Benedict XIV in 1747; considered by Jacobites to reign as Henry IX after the death of his elder brother, Prince Charles Edward Stuart, in 1788.
‡ Hon. Gwladys Wilson, dau. of 1st Baron Nunburnholme; m. 1905 Eric Chaplin (1877–1949), who s. father as 2nd Viscount, 1923.
§ Only brother (1882–1917) of J.L.-M's mother; a clerk to the House of Commons; killed in action.

with his short hair parted at the side and a smooth, youthful, not quite handsome face. He was in his mid thirties. As a boy I rejoiced when told I resembled him. I feel more in accord with him than with any of my relations.

Last Wednesday I motored from Badminton to Windsor to pay a second visit to the Royal Library. The servitor who admitted me to the Round Tower wore a scarlet waistcoat. Friendly, talked about the weather. On admitting me and retiring he banged the door so hard that the echo reverberated along the stone vaulting of the staircase. I counted the steps – 102 – before reaching the Archives; then I mount a further floor, and there are two more floors above the one I work in. It is very *gemütlich* up here. I hear the distant sounds of commands from the sentries drilling below, and rejoice that it is not me who is being drilled.

Sunday, 22nd August

Joanna Richardson wrote to A. out of the blue to say she is writing a book about Colette.* A. asked her to stay and she accepted with alacrity. A big woman with huge brow and sandy hair. Typical product of an Oxford women's college. Professional author who pours out books. Writes well. Agreeable, if too earnest. Has a poor opinion of other writers, particularly the female. I found I had made a record in my diary of my only meeting with Colette,† which I sent her after her visit.

Wednesday, 25th August

Joined J.K.-B. at Kenwood to see Pompeo Batoni exhibition. When I advocated an exhibition of this important Rome portrait painter of English milords years ago, no one paid any heed. This is a good one, with splendid catalogue. I observed how many of the subjects wore jackets with fur fringes. J. thought they were fur-lined. Much *embonpoint* visible, even on the youngest milords. Was this too much swigging of ale, or was it a foible of the artist who found the convex curve aesthetic?

---

* French novelist (1873–1962); protégée, like A.L.-M., of Princesse Edmond de Polignac (see note to entry for 23 October 1983).
† See *A Mingled Measure*, 19 February 1953.

Friday, 27th August

My third visit to the Royal Archives in the Round Tower at Windsor. Managed to complete my rapid survey of Stuart catalogue entries. I noticed nervousness on the part of Miss Langton. When I mentioned that I saw four boxes of letters labelled *Lord Esher's Correspondence*, she said, charmingly but firmly, 'You would have to get Sir Robin's permission before I could let you see these.' When her back was turned I took one down from the shelf, and tried quickly to open it just to see what was inside. Like Peeping Tom. Discovered folder fastened by press buttons. Opened one, saw nothing inside but a blank sheet of paper, couldn't do up the button and hastily thrust it, not properly shut, back on the shelf.

Monday, 30th August

Alice Witts invited us and Audrey to her eightieth birthday party at Upper Slaughter. A very young octogenarian. Lots of old and more new faces. Alice had a small display of family photographs. Our great-grandfather Joseph Lees in top hat looked very distinguished. His wife good-looking, though sad. We were shown her engagement ring. Ravishing.

Have corrected proofs of *Caves of Ice* and have to face up to index when I return from Venice. I left with Norah the draft of my novel, provisionally entitled *Innocence*. She reports that it is too short for a novel and too long for a short story. I must add 15,000 words at least. Claims not to be shocked by the story, but says I need to be 'more subtle with seduction scenes' – which means she does find it too porn-like, I fear.

Am dreading Mount Athos, for the temperature in Greece is 90 degrees. I shall die of it. Every now and then I have sharp pains around the heart. I quite expect to be stricken soon with another coronary.

On 5 September I flew to Salonika, and with Derek paid my last visit to the Holy Mountain. Wrote a day-to-day diary in a little red notebook – what Derek calls 'the disloyalty notebook', imagining it contains disparaging references to himself.* I returned to London for one

---

* Not found. The diaries kept by J.L.-M. on his three previous visits to Mount Athos with Derek Hill – in 1977, 1979 and 1980 – are included in *Through Wood and Dale* and *Deep Romantic Chasm*.

night, and next day set forth with A. to Venice, where we stayed at Hotel Luna until the 23rd.[*] The object was to spend my £1,000 literary award, which object was attained, and more. Sad to say my Venetian enthusiasms have waned.[†] Is it that Venice is over-familiar to me, without my really knowing it? Is it that my interest in architecture has evaporated? Or is it age and general lack of enthusiasm?

Thursday, 7th October

M. lunched with me at Brooks's yesterday. He is having much advance publicity with his *Duke of Windsor's War*. Appeared on television pitted against one Cannadine,[‡] a charmless and aggressive young don. M. rebutted the man's charges with righteous indignation. Then appeared on Radio 2 between pop music recitals and again came out well. Meanwhile my wretched little anthology is about to appear. John Saumarez Smith[§] says it will sell well, and M. says it will be seen in every middle-class lavatory. Alvilde's *The Englishman's Garden* is also out next week.

Friday, 8th October

A. and I motor to Norfolk. Stayed two nights with Billa [Harrod] at Holt. Ostensible reason is for me to look at some of the many letters Roy received from people I knew at Oxford. As a young don at the House, Roy was very much liked and became the confidant of numerous undergraduates, all the bright ones in fact, like Michael Rosse, Henry Green, Basil Ava,[¶] Freddie Furneaux, Randolph [Churchill],[‖]

---

[*] J.L.-M. wrote from there to the editor on 22 September: 'We have had rather more society than I relish – luncheons with Anna-Maria Cicogna, dinners with the Duc & Duchesse Decazes, drinks with the Ashley Clarks, and seeing my old friend John Sutro & wife, whose visit coincided with ours.'

[†] He was nevertheless suffciently inspired to write *Venetian Evenings* (1988).

[‡] David Cannadine (b. 1950); Fellow of Christ's College, Cambridge, 1977–88, and University Lecturer in History, 1980–8; author of works on the influence of the British aristocracy.

[§] Managing director of G. Heywood Hill Ltd, booksellers in Curzon Street.

[¶] Basil Blackwood, 4th Marquess of Dufferin and Ava, killed on active service in Burma 1945; an exact contemporary of J.L.-M. at preparatory school, Eton and Oxford.

[‖] Journalist and politician (1911–68), only son of Sir Winston Churchill (see entry for 5 May 1984).

Quintin Hogg,[*] Robert [Byron], Christopher Sykes.[†] Several letters too from Desmond [Parsons], who evidently relied on Roy for advice as to his future. Many too from Harold Acton.[‡] I was never myself drawn to Roy, but there must have been certain qualities which bound these young men to him with hoops of steel, he being not the least bit homo. He kept every single letter he received for over sixty years, tying them in bundles labelled by the year. From these Billa has already extracted correspondence with Maynard Keynes and others about his subjects, viz. economics and philosophy, which she has put in the hands of an agent. He tells her she may get as much as £100,000 for these alone from Japan or USA. Apparently the Japanese venerate him.

I knew Billa wanted me alone for this visit, and the fact that poor A. accompanied me made her cross. She made remarks like, 'It nearly kills me to have to cook and arrange your bedrooms.' A: 'Then we had better not come another time.' B: 'No, for goodness sake, don't.'

On Sunday we went to Orford and lunched with Tom Bridges[§] and wife. He is the son of Edward, smaller, very quick and intelligent, with the same schoolmasterly manner. I liked him, and his wife who is also very intelligent. But they are somehow not on our beam. Nice house in the village, but awful taste. He disclosed that he is to be sent to Rome as Ambassador next year, but it is still a secret. We called at Snape for a cup of tea with Heywood and Anne [Hill],[¶] just returned from Italy where Anne almost choked to death on a peanut. Much hilarity.

On to Bramfield to stay a night with the Gladwyns.[‖] Enjoyed this. Charming old red brick house. Very cold. Smoking fire in large room.

---

[*] Conservative politician (b. 1907); MP for Oxford, 1938–50; s. father as 2nd Viscount Hailsham 1950 but disclaimed title, 1963, becoming MP for St Marylebone; cr. life peer, 1970, as Lord Hailsham of St Marylebone; Lord Chancellor, 1970–74 and 1979–87; Eton contemporary of J.L.-M.

[†] Author, journalist and broadcaster (1907–86).

[‡] Sir Harold Acton (1904–94); author and aesthete; owner of Villa La Pietra, Florence.

[§] 2nd Baron Bridges (b. 1927); diplomatist; Ambassador to Italy, 1983–7; m. 1953 Rachel Bunbury. His father Edward Bridges (1892–1969), Cabinet Secretary and Permanent Secretary to the Treasury, ennobled on retirement, was only son of Robert Bridges the Poet Laureate, and A.L.-M's second cousin.

[¶] George Heywood Hill (d. 1986), founder of the bookshop; m. 1938 Lady Anne Gathorne-Hardy (b. 1911), o. dau. of 3rd Earl of Cranbrook, who had been engaged to J.L.-M. in 1935–6.

[‖] Gladwyn Jebb, 1st Baron Gladwyn (1900–97), diplomatist; Ambassador to France, 1954–60; subsequently Liberal spokesman in the House of Lords; m. 1929 Cynthia Noble (she d. 1990).

Cynthia dressed in tight red one-piece, short skirt, *décolletée*. She is good-natured, gossipy and sympathetic. Gladwyn stern, abrupt, deaf, knowing his mind, yet good to talk to and enjoying jokes. Excellent dinner produced by local lady who cooked and served. Champagne before dinner; good claret. They would insist on giving us fishcakes for breakfast, whereas neither of us eats cooked food then. Gladwyn very opposed to Mrs Thatcher, whose refusal to negotiate with anyone he thinks a disaster. Thinks the Liberal–SDP Alliance may lead to a coalition with the Tories after the next election. His lot will join with the Tories provided they adopt proportional representation. Cynthia says that Nancy [Mitford] had a miscarriage by a Frenchman called Le Roy, but denies that Palewski[*] could be the father of Marc de Beauveau:[†] he was too young, too little known, and 'not in society' at the time of Beauveau's birth.

Sunday, 17th October

If I didn't know the Vicar[‡] and merely attended his services I would be an unconditional admirer. He has a splendid, bold voice, and his sermons are superb. Today he spoke about the Church expressing views on unilateral nuclear disarmament. Roundly condemned it for interference in matters it could not judge. We must leave these tricky matters to the Government which receives expert advice. Introduced St Luke, whose feast day tomorrow, as the Intellectual Evangelist. Easy to distinguish his gospel from the others by his keen observation of detail, for he paints a background which the other Es neglect. But the Vicar *will* nobble me in church. This evening at Acton Turville he regaled me with long story of misbehaviour at Eddie Somerset's wedding,[§] where one of his most respectable parishioners on going to the loo found two young people 'at it'. Parishioner deeply shocked; Vicar pretended to be also; and so did I, but half-heartedly.

---

[*] Colonel Gaston Paleswski (1901–84), principal wartime aide of General de Gaulle; a great seducer of women (m. 1969 Violette de Talleyrand-Périgord) and love of Nancy Mitford's life.
[†] Prince de Beauveau-Craon (1921–82), Free French soldier and friend of Gaston Palewski. In the course of her Nancy Mitford researches, Selina Hastings had been investigating the rumour that he might have been Palewski's son.
[‡] Revd Thomas Gibson (b. 1923), Vicar of Badminton, 1974–93.
[§] Edward Alexander (b. 1958), yr s. of David and Lady Caroline Somerset; m. 1982 Hon. Caroline Davidson.

I don't think I really mind in the least – good luck to them – but they might have locked the door. Everything is permissible behind locked doors.

Accompanied A. to London, for she leaves tomorrow on Serenissima cruise to the Near East, from Venice. Was sad and moved on parting from her after dinner in her new club near Sloane Square.

Wednesday, 20th October

Felt obliged to attend cocktail party given by Hatchard's for a book by Isaiah Berlin,* also my rotten little anthology out the following day I gather. So in pouring rain, carrying luggage, helped by kind John Jolliffe, I staggered there at 6.30. Found shop crammed and very hot. Couldn't hear a word said to me by Frankie Donaldson,† and after quarter of an hour left. Staggered to King's Cross by underground. Was met at Cambridge station by M., who gave me cosy supper in his room at 9 King's Parade, in front of the gas fire. Memories of Oxford *circa* 1930. M. has got me a room in St John's.

Friday, 22nd October

All yesterday and today it poured with rain from dawn to dusk and dusk to dawn. Got soaked walking under umbrella to Churchill College, down the main road to Bedford. Beastly building, like enormous public lavatory. Nothing to recommend it except its inhabitants, all nice to me. Charming and helpful archivist, Miss Marion Stewart. They begged me to write Regy Esher's life. Spent from 9.30 to 5 both days glancing at his papers. Appalled by the quantity, but have decided to go ahead, provided the College and Lionel will allow to me to take the papers away. Otherwise impossible. Miss Stewart said she would be glad to get rid of papers until the biography is written. Could easily be sent to me by Securicor van. I suppose I could house the 129 boxes in Bath. It would be my last literary enterprise. I only wish I liked Regy more. Don't positively dislike: am mystified, and interested. Had

---

* Sir Isaiah Berlin (1909–99); Russian-born historian and writer, noted for his works on political philosophy.
† Frances Lonsdale (1907–94), writer; m. 1935 'Jack' Donaldson (1907–98, cr. Baron Donaldson of Kingsbridge, 1967), Labour Party politician, Minister for the Arts, 1976–9.

a talk with Dadie [Rylands]* in King's and discussed the question with him. Dear Dadie will be eighty tomorrow. He was very intelligent and wise, and strongly advised me to take it on. So does M.

Saturday, 23rd October

Stayed on till afternoon because M. had a luncheon party for me. Included Warwick McKean, nice New Zealand law don whose guest in college I have technically been, and a couple of handsome but tiny postgraduate students, boy and girl living together. Mrs Barnett, M's devoted landlady, cooked what she called a nursery luncheon for my benefit. M. accompanied me to station. Has been angelic.

Much enjoyed staying in St John's. A cloistered existence suits me. But Churchill College is a beastly building. Surely Churchill would have been even more appalled by the college named after him than he was by Graham [Sutherland]'s portrait of him.

Sunday, 24th October

A splendid review of M's book in *Sunday Telegraph*. Had to telephone. He of course in bed asleep. Came half-comatose to telephone. When I said, 'Congratulations on having written "a classic of its kind",' he was thrilled, not yet having seen it. Am so glad, because he has been a little disappointed by the slowness of reviews. *The Times* yesterday also carried an appreciative notice of old Mrs Loch,† who died in Ouranopolis on the 8th, just three weeks after Derek and I last saw her.

Tuesday, 26th October

This week alone in Bath. Have corrected the Index to *Caves of Ice*, the best and most complete index I have ever done. Now that book is off my chest. Have written a long letter to Lionel saying I will write

---

* George Rylands (1902–99), Shakespearean scholar and Fellow of King's College, Cambridge.
† Australian widow of the author of a book on Mount Athos, who lived in a tower at the foot of the Holy Mountain where she dispensed hospitality to many pilgrims – including J.L.-M. and Derek Hill (as described in *Through Wood and Dale* and *Deep Romantic Chasm*).

Regy's life subject to conditions, the chief one being that I must be allowed to have the papers in Bath. Am now revising my novel. Each time I read through it I find something to correct; but apart from adding or deleting an extra line or two, I have done nothing to 'fluff out' Part I or to make it more subtle. M. agreed it was not subtle enough. How to remedy this I do not know.

Wednesday, 27th October

Rather relieved to hear from Nick [Robinson] that he can't find a publisher for his Rome anthology project. This lets me off to attend to Regy, once I have done the introduction to Gervase Jackson-Stops's book on *Writers at Home*.

Dined with Alex [Moulton] last night. A faithful friend who always gives me a hearty welcome and dinner. We gossip about his projects and mine. He is inventing a new bicycle. Tried to explain to me the differences between it and the previous Moulton bicycle, which I failed to understand. When I told him about Regy, he expressed disapproval, saying that I ought to write what he calls books of the imagination. Nice of him, but I haven't any imagination, as recent struggles with novel testify.

All Saints' Day, Monday, 1 November

When I had tea with Diana Westmorland at Lyegrove on Thursday, she was dreadfully upset by the Dodington* débâcle. Simon Codrington's[†] last desperate fling at letting part of the park for a funfair has been turned down by the local authorities. On Sunday Eardley, staying with me, and I dined with the Francis Burnes.[‡] Rosalind Ward[§] and Simon Codrington also present. Lady C. did not come, being I gathered in bed recovering from a nervous breakdown. I liked Simon for the first time. Clearly not bright, but gentle and sympathetic. Seemed sad and left before we finished dinner. Before he

---

* Dodington Park near Bath, once described by J.L.-M. as a 'disappointing' house constructed of 'shoddy' materials and gone to seed (*A Mingled Measure*, 10 May 1953).

[†] Sir Simon Codrington, 3rd Bt (b. 1923); m. (3rd) 1980 Sally Gaze (m. diss. 1988).

[‡] Of Wick Manor, Avon; friends of Eardley Knollys.

[§] Rosalind Lygon (b. 1946), heiress to Madresfield Court, Worcestershire; m. 1st Gerald John Ward, 2nd (1984) Sir Charles Morrison, MP (C) for Devizes.

left Francis lent across me and gave him advice for a critical meeting to take place next day with the funfair people, who are turning nasty. I did not join in conversation beyond saying how sorry I was and wishing him luck. After he had gone Francis told us he owed £400,000, had creditors all round him, could not pay his staff, was utterly broke, without money to buy milk or petrol. Francis had some extraordinary scheme to save Dodington. But Peggy* this morning says, 'Did you see Dodington on telly last night?' Apparently the news is all out. The place is to be put into liquidation. Very tragic. This important house is Wyatt's last and best classical country house and has the most beautiful park in these parts. Codringtons have lived there for centuries. It is like an eighteenth-century ending, as though an owner gambled away his wife and estate at Brooks's in a night. Landowners go broke all around us, and have to leave or sell; but seldom is the owner driven to live in the kitchen by a paraffin stove.

Much enjoyed having Eardley, almost like old times. At first I fancied visit might be sticky, for there is about E. these days a slight air of disapproval. That soon melted and gave way to jokes, if not quite the jokes of yore. I was amazed and flattered to hear him say at dinner with the Burnes that he has kept every letter I have written him.

All Souls' Day, Tuesday, 2nd November

Drove with dogs all the way to Stokesay Court near Craven Arms [Shropshire] to lunch with Philip Magnus, some ninety miles. Beastly dank and grey day, with fog patches. Lady Magnus-Allcroft did not appear. Has had two strokes and lives with a female keeper upstairs in a separate wing, from which Philip is happy to descend I fancy. We lunched alone, good country fare, mutton chops with currant jelly and claret. He is a nice old boy, two years my senior and looks eighty-six. Purpose of this visit to discuss Regy [Esher], for he had intimated that I should not write this biography. As it was we talked about the project, but I derived little that was useful. However, he did warn that the task would be formidable because of the quantity of material; that I would find the papers on Army and Navy Reform very boring; and lastly, that I would be so fascinated by the private life that I would concentrate on this to the exclusion of all else. He added, 'It is not a good

---

* The L.-Ms' daily help, Peggy Bird.

thing for people with your tastes and mine to write about such matters.' I replied that being seventy-four I no longer cared what people thought or said about me. He asked if I saw M. still. Such a nice, good-looking boy. I remarked that Regy liked a good-looking boy. 'Who doesn't?' he said. There is something sad about this ageing man with *non compos* sick wife living in huge, mid Victorian house which should be full of children and life. I find it fascinating, and would like to browse around on my own.

Wednesday, 3rd November

I had just got to Bath rather later than usual, having called on Dr King, when the telephone rang. There was a 'Hold on, please', from which I deduced a foreign call. Not M. Then a voice said, 'I am John Julius [Norwich] speaking from Jerusalem.' My heart sank to my knees. I thought, Alvilde is ill, or dead. He said, 'You are not to be alarmed. Alvilde has had an accident. She fell into a hole while sight-seeing at some monument. She has had to have stitches in her head and has injured the bottom of her spine. Luckily the cruise doctor was present.' She is to fly back with the others on Sunday, will stay the night at the hotel at Gatwick, and I am to meet her there on Monday with a large car in which she can stretch out. J. J. admitted she was in considerable pain. I hardly knew what to say, was so shocked. I asked if I should come out. He said on no account. For the rest of the day I was unable to work or concentrate on anything. Felt deeply concerned. Caroline [Somerset] offered to lend me her car.

Thursday, 4th November

Telephoned Sally [Westminster] this morning. Am dining with her tonight. She said at once she would drive me to Gatwick on Monday. I protested, but am immensely pleased. My only fear is that Sally is so vague, she may find she has some uncancellable engagement which will prevent her.

This afternoon I have had my four remaining front teeth out. I dreaded the operation. Local anaesthetic. At first I felt the digging and begged him to give me some more. Felt like the Duke of Monmouth being executed, begging the executioner to finish him off properly. As it was, the digging, the wrenching, the crunching, the hammering, the explosions of broken teeth as of rocks, were very disturbing.

I felt quite faint and tearful for a minute. Then I walked to the car, went shopping, and took the dogs for the usual walk around the golf course. So can't be too bad. Sally had promised me slops for dinner but it turned out to be pheasant, not minced but shredded.

M. sent me a notice by Kenneth de Courcy* about his book, curiously phrased but hitting the point – that neither of the Windsors had a purpose in life after the war.

Friday, 5th November

Dick's and Elaine's† friends the Blackwoods telephoned to say they had a sponge for me, and asked me to fetch it and have a drink. I was about to demur when she, Doreen, said something which made me realise they thought we snubbed them by never accepting their invitations. So, A. being away, I thought I had better go, and accepted invitation to dine. Delicious meal but teeth more painful than last night. Another couple present called Sands,‡ who have a large apartment at the newly converted Charlton.§ They told me they owned Gainsboroughs, a Cézanne portrait, and countless other important paintings.

Sunday, 7th November

Lunched yesterday with the Loewensteins.¶ I sometimes feel that I get on better at friends' meals without A., which is horrid of me. I motored today to lunch with Tony and Violet Powell to meet Clarissa Avon.‖ Tony talked about Asquith's letters to Venetia Stanley, which he says are fascinating. Clarissa remembered her as one of her mother's best friends. C. is extremely bright, clever and sharp. Much faded since the days when I saw a lot of her, her angular features becoming witch-like.

---

* Journalist and intriguer (1909–2000).

† J.L.-M's younger brother (b. 1910) and sister-in-law, residents of Cyprus.

‡ Christopher Sands (d. 2000), nephew of the painter and art collector Ethel Sands.

§ Charlton Park, a seventeenth-century 'prodigy' house near Malmesbury, Wiltshire; converted into flats *c.* 1975.

¶ Prince Rupert zu Loewenstein (b. 1930), financial adviser; m. 1957 Josephine Lowry-Corry.

‖ Clarissa Churchill (b. 1920); sister of J.L.-M's friend Johnnie Churchill; m. 1952 Sir Anthony Eden, later 1st Earl of Avon (1897–1977).

Monday, 8th November

Caroline lends me her car, which is large enough for A. to stretch out in, and Sally arranges for Bob Parsons* to drive me in it to Gatwick. We find A. in Hilton Hotel at midday. She looks tense and stiff but is shuffling round the foyer. Sits in the back seat curled up which she says is more comfortable than stretched out. Full of aches and pains but nothing broken, thank God. We drive there and back in torrential rain.

Monday, 15th November

My stepdaughter Clarissa came to stay from Tuesday till Sunday, a great help. I have never liked her more. She is full of chat and laughter, a radiant personality, makes light of all adversity.

I have had constant visitations to the dentist, which will cost me hundreds. Long, painful and awkward business. I cannot now bite, only chew. Had never thought of this predicament.

I went to church yesterday, Armistice Sunday. Full panoply. Mrs Punter dressed in uniform holding British Legion banner at the altar rails. Mary Beaufort submerged by pew. Only when she stands up is her tiny head visible. When the service is over the Beauforts and David Westmorland† leave first, just as in eighteenth century, David Somerset follows, politely opening doors of pews behind theirs for *hoi polloi* like me and the farmers. Reminds me of Cardinals washing the feet of the poor.

I have written to congratulate Brian Masters‡ on his excellent book *Great Hostesses*. It is very well-written and readable, a most charitable, perceptive book. He never derides these women, some of whom might have seemed preposterous to a man of his generation and origins. I really think he is a remarkable young man. He has got Emerald [Cunard] perfectly, her gossamer quality and sense of the ludicrous. Many quotations from my published diaries.

---

* American architect (1920–2000); tenant and repairer of Newark Park, Gloucestershire, N.T. property.

† David Fane, 15th Earl of Westmorland (1924–93); son of Diana, Countess of Westmorland; Master of the Horse, 1978–93; m. 1950 Jane Findlay.

‡ Author (b. 1939), subsequently celebrated for psychological studies of mass murderers (see *Deep Romantic Chasm*, 19 August and 30 November 1981).

Thursday, 18th November

I received an ambiguously worded letter from Lionel [Esher]. He says Churchill College wish to know if I will accept an honorary and temporary fellowship. This would not necessitate my having to look through the Esher papers there. The archivist in charge has confirmed that I may have them in Bath on loan. Yet I have received no invitation from the College. I have told Lionel that I suppose I ought to accept what is intended as an honour. He sees no point in acceptance. Anyway, the die seems cast. I have written to Sir Robin Mackworth-Young asking for permission to see the 'royal' papers, both those in Lionel's possession at Churchill, and those at Windsor. I am not absolutely confident that this reserved, suspicious, correct man will say Yes, particularly in view of M's tribute to me in *The Duke of Windsor's War*. I have also written to Sidgwick & Jackson asking if they are still interested in publishing the book, and to Lady Phipps,* practically the last person still alive who knew Lord E. Lionel asks if I really want to write the book. I have said Yes. I hope to God I still feel the same in six months' time. Meanwhile I still have to write the preface for Gervase [Jackson-Stops], with whom I lunch in London tomorrow.

Victoria Glendinning† has sent A. the final chapters of her biography of Vita [Sackville-West], in which A's relations with V. are referred to. A. handed them to me at breakfast this morning, asking me to read them with a view to discussing them with her this evening. They have come as something of a shock, for although I always supposed V. and A. had a *Schwärmerei*, I did not realise until now how passionately V. was in love with A. Vita was not entirely honest, for in her correspondence with Harold she consistently belittles A., whereas he of course expresses positive dislike of A. Victoria G. expresses no opinion as to A's reciprocation, but the reader must assume she did reciprocate. Indeed, why not – for there was I, an inattentive husband. But our friends will undoubtedly think badly of A. for having made such a tremendous fuss over my affair with J[ohn

---

* Frances Ward; m. 1911 (as his 2nd wife) Sir Eric Phipps, diplomatist (1875–1945), Ambassador to Berlin (1933–7) and Paris (1937–40).
† Hon. Victoria Seebohm (b. 1937), author and journalist; daughter of Baron Seebohm; m. 1st 1958 Professor Nigel Glendinning, 2nd 1982 Terence de Vere White (1912–94), solicitor, writer and sometime literary editor of *Irish Times*, 3rd Kevin O'Sullivan.

Kenworthy-Browne], which began after hers with Vita, about which I had remained quite mum. I don't take credit for my attitude because I didn't mind, or rather was never as jealous of A. as she was of me. I suppose that, when I was writing Harold's biography, Nigel [Nicolson] deliberately withheld Vita's diaries for this period. I have always refused to read V's letters to A., though A. has often asked me to do so. Although I am all for honesty, somehow I don't relish these revelations in our lifetime.[*]

Wednesday, 24th November

We dined with Joanie Altrincham[†] who had staying the widow of Ed Murrow, the American broadcaster and commentator, a frail, gentle, well-educated little lady who was with A. on her cruise. A. manages to go short distances by car and can sit propped by special cushions at a stranger's table for half an hour without discomfort. Joanie is not charitable about her children. Grumbled about both her sons. I only know John, who strikes me as a saintly character. When I asked her how many volumes of Lloyd George's life John [Grigg] was writing, she professed not to know, saying she had not read those already published. Why is not this intelligent woman proud of her clever elder son's brilliant biography? On the other hand, she is keen on the book *White Mischief*,[‡] just out, about those rotten people, Broughtons, Kinnouls, living in Kenya during the 1930s. She vouchsafed that the then Prince of Wales was the worst guest she and her husband, when Governor, had to stay. He was demanding, displeased, totally philistine and interested in nothing they were prepared to show him. Also that Asquith tried to 'get off' with her when she was an unmarried girl, in the back of a motor car. Nasty old man, she affirmed.

---

[*] At A.L.-M's request, Victoria Glendinning subsequently cut much of what she had originally written about V.S.-W. and A.L.-M.

[†] Hon. Joan Dickson-Poynder (1897–1987), o. c. of 1st Baron Islington; m. 1923 Sir Edward Grigg, MP (1879–1955), formerly private secretary to HRH The Prince of Wales and David Lloyd George, later Governor of Kenya (1925–31), cr. Baron Altrincham, 1945; she lived at Tormarton near Badminton.

[‡] James Fox's best-selling book, later made into a film, was an attempt to solve the mystery of Lord Erroll's wartime murder in Kenya, and especially admired for its authentic evocation of the hedonistic expatriate world of 'the Happy Valley'.

Thursday, 25th November

To Widcote near Pewsey to lunch with Lady Phipps. She lives quite alone in a dear cottage on the bank of a canal, full of pretty things. Is herself pretty, with well-tended, glossy white hair. She is ninety, stone deaf, blind (cannot read even the headlines or letters written to her) and halt. Struggles round the house on two sticks. She knew old Lady Esher — Nellie — well and was devoted to her, a dumpy little woman with sad brown eyes like a spaniel. But could tell me little about Lord E. beyond the fact that in Paris, when her husband was First Secretary at the British Embassy during the First World War, he would appear in a khaki uniform covered with ribbons, a distinguished figure. But as she denied he was bald, she cannot have seen him with his military cap off. Proceeded to London, where M. and Eardley dined with me at Brooks's. Was conscious of being very boring.

Friday, 26th November

I showed Norah [Smallwood] my little portrait of Bonnie Prince Charlie, which she agreed would do nicely for the jacket of my Stuart book. Went to two exhibitions. First, Neapolitan paintings at Burlington House. All blood and volcanoes. The blood I suppose from the Spanish influence on that cruel city. Then Van Dyck at National Portrait Gallery. After gazing at fifty court ladies they begin to pall. Obviously Van Dyck was too popular and painted too much, pot-boiling. Two things struck me. Where did the women get those enormous drop pearls, the size of pears, from? Can they have been real? And the men's stockings all look as though they are falling down the calf. I suppose no suspenders. Even Charles I's legs have creases in them. Lunched with Margaret Willes [of Sidgwick & Jackson] at a superior wine shop in Museum Street to talk about the Esher book. A sweet girl, very easy to converse with. Did not feel a bore with her, or with Norah. How is it that at times one cannot click even with the friends one loves most?

Tuesday, 30th November

Am in a state of depression, not relieved by anxiety about Mackworth-Young. Having received no answer to my letter written almost three weeks ago, I telephoned Miss Langton at Windsor. She told me that Sir Robin received my letter but has had to write to or consult the

Queen before he can give me permission to see royal papers. Why couldn't he at least have acknowledged my letter? It amazes me that the Queen has to be consulted personally. Since she will not have a clue as to who I am (she had no idea at the Hatchard's party when I was presented), and presumably has not heard of Lord Esher either, I suppose she will be guided either by Mackworth-Young or her private secretaries. They may well say I am a *louche* or flippant writer who has published some questionable diaries and appears in the acknowledgements of an embarrassing book about the Duke of Windsor. I rang up Lionel, who was a pillar of calm. He says he will write a line to Mackworth-Young backing me. He confirms I have the consent of Churchill College to have the papers here, and advises me to proceed with my researches and not to worry.

Friday, 3rd December

Everything happens at once. I had been feeling miserable after struggling for three days with a review of two architectural books for the *Burlington* [*Magazine*], when this morning I received a letter from Miss Langton to say that the Queen has granted me permission to see the Esher papers at Windsor. A great relief. Also a letter from Nicholas Hill asking to do an article on me for *Tatler*. And a message from Chatto's that *Harper's* will publish extracts of *Caves of Ice*. Then an invitation from Rainbird's to do a book on Florence, and one from Oxford University Press asking me to write one on changes in manners (both not on). And I have been asked to write the *DNB* entry on Cecil Beaton.*

Sunday, 5th December

Went to see A. J. Sylvester,† suggested by John Grigg. He lives in a cottage at Rudloe near Corsham. Wonderful old boy of ninety-three who remembers Regy Esher. Had highest opinion of him for his power of organisation and rapier-like mind. He (Sylvester) worked for Hankey on Committee of Imperial Defence and later became Private Secretary

---

* Sir Cecil Beaton (1904–80); artist, stage designer and photographer (see *Deep Romantic Chasm*, 19 January 1980).

† Albert James Sylvester, CBE (1889–1989); Private Secretary to Lloyd George during and after his premiership, and author of works about him.

to Lloyd George. Says L.G. undoubtedly the greatest man he ever came across, greater than Churchill, who was a man of war whereas L.G. a man of peace. Was best man at his wedding to Frances Stevenson and present at his death-bed, where Frances held one hand and Megan, who hated her stepmother, the other. Sylvester a farmer's son from Staffordshire. Began work at fourteen as a clerk in a brewery. Became adept at shorthand and typing and entered Civil Service as an ordinary secretary, rising to important heights. He was the first secretary to be present at a cabinet meeting. In 1914 his wages were £3 5s. a week. He talked for two and a half hours without stopping, mostly about Lloyd George. Lives on his own, taking the bus to Corsham once a week to buy food which he cooks himself. Wife died twenty years ago. Likes solitude. His work is to sort his papers and tell the truth about L.G., about whom he has already published a book. A really splendid old man.

Sunday, 19th December

There's no pleasure like looking a gift-horse in the mouth. For my fifteen years of service as Paul Methuen's* trustee, involving train journeys to London for which I forewent payment and hours spent wrangling with solicitors, John Methuen† has presented me with half a dozen sherry glasses from Woolworth, the sort that any cottage dweller in Badminton would consider in cheap taste. And to use another proverb, it's an ill wind that blows no good. The hideous lamp standard which the estate here has allowed the local authority to erect at the bottom of our garden has an orange globe, which in the early morning after rain casts a light like coins of gold upon the lozenge-shaped flags which A. has laid from the statue of Orpheus to the central parterre.

All this month I have been working on my 15,000-word Introduction to Gervase's National Trust book *Writers at Home*. Despite help from Gervase, who supplied a synopsis, it has caused me much agony and sweat. I hope to finish it before 6 January, when the Esher papers are due to be delivered to me from Cambridge.

---

* Artist (1886–1974) who succeeded as 4th Baron Methuen in 1932 and devoted much of his life to the conservation and management of the Corsham estate in Wiltshire; subject of a portrait by J.L.-M. in *Fourteen Friends*.
† Paul Methuen's nephew (1925–94), who succeeded in 1975 as 6th Baron and owner of Corsham.

Yesterday was a bad day. Nicholas Hill came with two assistants from the *Tatler*, including a photographer who took a picture of A. and me, she sprawling on my bed, I sitting on a small chair at the foot with Honey on my knee. I thought this was for an article on us alone, but it turned out to be about four couples, the other three unknown to us and I dare say everyone else. N. Hill is Derek's and Heywood's nephew.* He knew nothing about either of us but borrowed Freda Berkeley's copy of *Ancestral Voices*, which he read on the way down. We did our best to be friendly, and put ourselves out to the extent of giving them a sandwich luncheon. By the time they left, my working day had been ruined, so I went to Westonbirt Arboretum with the dogs, who ran away. I waited an hour and a half in perishing cold with no book to read. When Honey returned at dusk I picked up some twigs and beat her as hard as I could.† She yelled. A busybody lady came up and said, 'What is going on? No wonder the little dog is too frightened to get into your car.' I was in a furious temper and drove off, only to realise it had been Georgina Harford.‡ Doubtless my choler and cruelty to animals will be the talk of Beaufortshire. Returned home, still angry, to find the Lukes had come to stay, and was too put out to be nice. Then had a row with the horrid steward of the village club, this time induced by A., who made me go and complain that he had parked his car so that she could not drive into her motor house. He was very impertinent, which made me angrier still. I hate this place. I loathe Badminton and always have.

Thursday, 23rd December

No carol singers these days. Formerly there used to be at least one group an evening before Christmas. In a way it was a bore, having to listen at the door in the cold, or invite them in, and find money, half a crown. This year we have only had the Marshfield Players, who came this evening and played one dreary tune on their brass band outside the village club. A. said, 'Go and give them something.' I went

---

* His father was the brother of the artist Derek Hill and his mother the sister of the book-seller Heywood Hill, the two families being otherwise unrelated.
† Marginal note added by J.L.-M. on 16 March 1988: 'Poor darling little dead Honey. I hate myself now for what I did.'
‡ Wife of 'Ben' Harford of Ashcroft, Gloucestershire (whose parents had been neighbours and friends of the L.-Ms at Alderley).

to the gate but they did not approach me. Instead they all trooped into the club for a drink. As they do this for charity I thought their efforts distinctly half-hearted. When we were children at Wickhamford the great excitement on Christmas Eve was the bell-ringers. Numb with cold they came into the hall and to our amazement and admiration six of them played 'Good King Wenceslas'. Then we gave them beer.

I read Bruce Chatwin's* novel *On the Black Hill* – reluctantly, because I did not think much of his previous, highly-acclaimed book on Patagonia. This novel is excellent. Bruce has identified himself with these strange Welsh border folk and their rough, reclusive ways. His keen observation of their manners and of the landscape are both matter-of-fact and poetic.

Saturday, 25th December

Christmas at Parkside† as usual. Only Burnet [Pavitt] staying. We were made rather sad by Joan's loss of memory. Almost impossible to have a conversation with her now. Not only does she forget names, as we all do, but when one reminds her of a name she cannot attach it to a person.

We went to St George's Chapel this morning, pews in the Garter Stalls. I sat in Lord Kitchener's. Facing me was Sir Robin Mackworth-Young, looking saturnine and alarmed. Glorious richness of windows. 'Richly dight' comes to mind. We waited. The organ voluntary stopped, and a voice from the clouds announced through an amplifier: 'You are welcome to St George's Chapel. When the Royal Family enter the Chapel, please will the congregation not stand on pews; and will no one offer a present to Her Majesty. Happy Christmas.' Most of the Royals dressed in mousse pink, unbecoming. Princess Alexandra as always the sweetest, in black with blue Garter bow in front. One handsome son and daughter, pretty, sandy-haired, frail, resembling mother but less beautiful, but with the same twisted smile that Princess Marina had and was so attractive. No Queen Mother. On our last day at luncheon, a letter came from Royal Lodge for the Droghedas, by special messenger. Joan read it and passed it to Garrett down the table. 'Dearest Joan', I could not avoid reading.

---

* Travel writer and novelist (1940–89), formerly a neighbour of the L.-Ms at Alderley.
† The Droghedas' house near Windsor.

The [Derry] Moores came for Sunday night, hot from lunching at Chequers – forty guests at no tables, balancing disgusting food on knees. Derry says Mrs T. is going mad. She never stopped talking and never allowed anyone to get a word in edgeways. Took them round the house and addressed them as if from the despatch box of the House of Commons. Made such idiotic remarks as, 'Of course we had to have the Titian removed to the basement, because one cannot show a bird in a cage these days.' Alexandra due to have a baby in March. Great excitement. Hope desperately it will be a boy,* otherwise the Drogheda title will become extinct.

Friday, 31st December

Last night the Somersets and Daphne Fielding† dined. Alone they are enchanting. One can talk about anything to David, who is an intelligent as well as an amusing man. He told his mother-in-law and me that when he was a boy he had a tutor to coach him in the holidays. David would sit on the sofa with his legs stretched out and the tutor would stroke his thighs, an experience he found delicious. This from the ardently heterosexual David. He also said that Bobby Shaw, Nancy Astor's son, once told him that he had first been seduced by Lord Kitchener.

Today I finished my long introduction to *Writers at Home* and posted it to Gervase. It has taken me a month, and was a great struggle. I was determined to finish it by the end of the year, to clear the decks for Lord Esher in 1983.

---

* It was: see entry for 27 August 1983.
† Caroline Somerset's mother, Hon. Daphne Vivian (1904–97); novelist and fellow resident of Badminton estate; m. 1st 1926 Henry Thynne, later 6th Marquess of Bath, 2nd 1953 Xan Fielding, war hero and author.

1983

I dislike having my photograph taken very much. It makes me feel horribly self-conscious. Why, then, having been photographed last month for Nicholas Hill's silly article in *Tatler*, do I now allow myself to be taken again for *Harper's*? Is it vanity? A. reproaches me for consenting. I reply, with less than total conviction, that it is a good advertisement for my book, as the *Harper's* picture is to accompany their publication of extracts of *Caves of Ice*. Derry [Moore] came with the editor and sub-editor of *Harper's* last week, photographed us together and gave us an expensive luncheon at the Royal Crescent Hotel. We were five and the meal cost £17.50 per head. We had three bottles of wine, so the bill must have come to about £120. The food was not all that good.

The sympathetic Hungarian drunk who lives in the village and used to be employed in the stables calls me Sir, which rather embarrasses me these days. Yet I would not object if everyone called everyone else Sir or Madam, as they do in France and Italy.

The Powells and Zita and Baby Jungman* lunched yesterday. Tony told me that, in bed every night, before turning to whatever book he is reading, he spends the first twenty minutes on Shakespeare or Fletcher. Zita and Teresa lead a strange existence. They go to bed at 4 a.m., have breakfast in bed, lunch at 4 p.m. and dine at 10 p.m. I asked Zita if she belonged to a public library. No, she said, she bought quantities of books but seldom read them. Instead she reads old newspapers. Has stacks of them never thrown away. An extraordinary waste of time it seems to me. Both sisters say they dislike meeting people younger than themselves, except for the young who come to question them about their 1920s heyday. Both are devout papists and, although they were once leading Bright Young Things, claim never

---

* Teresa ('Baby') Cuthbertson and Zita James, daughters of the rich socialite Mrs Richard Guinness by her first husband, the Dutch-born artist Nico Jungman. As girls in the 1920s, the sisters attracted attention through their ribald antics, and started a craze for masquerades and treasure hunts at country house parties. Evelyn Waugh was in love with 'Baby' in the early 1930s, but she refused to marry him on account of his divorce.

to have had extra-marital love affairs. Zita said she only learnt her husband was dead when a friend told her weeks after the event. I asked how she missed the announcement in the papers. She said she had not got beyond the papers of 1980 yet.

Tuesday, 18th January

Midi [Gascoigne], to whom I confided that I was writing the biography of Regy, now asks everyone she meets if they know anyone alive who met him. Very sweet of her, although I don't particularly want it discussed by all and sundry. I had thought that perhaps her aunt Lady Celia Coats, now ninety-seven, might have remembered him; but Midi says she is too far gone to be asked. Today she telephoned to say that Roger Sherfield* has spoken to Lord Adeane,† the Queen's late Private Secretary, who does remember him and is willing to talk to me. His mother was a Bigge, daughter of Lord Stamfordham,‡ so undoubtedly he is my man, and may be usefully communicative.

Wednesday, 19th January

The Beits gave a dinner party of sixty guests in the Subscription Room at Brooks's for Alfred's eightieth birthday. Masses of old friends, all the women except for Caroline Somerset dressed up to the nines. Pamela Egremont and Anne Tennant the stars. The first wore a stomacher of diamonds in sprays, splashing up to her bosom and down to her waist – a Leconfield heirloom which needed airing, she told A. The last a real beauty, clothed in white samite. I found it very trying to hear above the hubbub. Poor Helen Dashwood looked dazed. She told me she was eighty-three. Juts her lower jaw forward like many old people – false teeth I suppose. I sat next to Joan Drogheda, with whom I merely had to smile and make the ghost of a joke and press her hand in sympathy.

---

* Roger Makins (1904–96), diplomatist; Ambassador to USA, 1953–6; cr. Baron Sherfield, 1964.
† Lieut.-Col. Sir Michael Adeane (1910–84), Private Secretary to HM The Queen and Keeper of Royal Archives, 1953–72; m. 1939 Helen Chetwynd-Stapylton; cr. life peer, 1972.
‡ Arthur Bigge, 1st Baron Stamfordham (1849–1931), Private Secretary for thirty years to George V as Prince of Wales and King.

My other neighbour Lady Airlie,* a very remarkable woman. Not a beauty, but bright face with greying hair. Is a daughter of Nin Ryan and granddaughter of Otto Kahn.† Clever as a monkey. As well as being a Lady-in-Waiting to the Queen, she is a member of the Fine Arts Commission. Admitted to giving her approval to the ghastly shit-coloured tin building on St James's Street; agreed the finished thing is a horror, but said the design was 'interesting on paper'. Has six children. Very intellectual woman.

Thursday, 20th January

Went to see Rosamond [Lehmann]. She reproached me for not communicating with her. Complained that it was always she who had to get in touch with me these days, and assumed I wanted to avoid her because of the incident with A. I tried to assure the dear old thing that this was nonsense. Women like to be aggrieved. She has Diana Mosley coming to see her to talk about Mrs Hammersley.‡ Ros sits in the most ungainly manner, on a low armchair, her legs spread-eagled, displaying her not very attractive knickers up to the fork. Strange no one has told her about this. She *will* wear skirts which are too short and too tight. Diana when placed in the visitor's chair facing Ros will be horrified by this apparition. She is the most fastidious person I know.

I gave a small dinner party at Brooks's for M. Consisted of Derek [Hill], Kenneth Rose,§ recovering from shingles and yellow-visaged, Peter Hesketh,¶ and Hugh Massingberd,‖ who failed to turn up. Successful. Kenneth got on well with M. and told me he little

* Virginia Fortune Ryan, m. 1952 David Ogilvy, later 13th Earl of Airlie (b. 1926; Lord Chamberlain, 1984–97); Lady-in-Waiting to HM The Queen from 1973.

† German-born financier and art patron (1867–1934), emigrated (1893) to New York via London.

‡ Violet Hammersley (d. 1963), rich and eccentric widow who had been a friend of Diana Mosley's mother, and godmother to Rosamond Lehmann's brother John. The Mitford sisters found her an endless source of amusement, and Lady Mosley was currently writing a piece on her for inclusion in her forthcoming book of biographical essays, *Loved Ones* (1985).

§ Historian and journalist (b. 1924); writer of *Albany* column of *Sunday Telegraph*, and about to publish a biography of King George V.

¶ Peter Fleetwood Hesketh (1905–85), of the Manor House, Hale, Liverpool; architect, author and illustrator; Hon. District Representative of N.T., 1947–68; m. 1940 Monica Assheton (d. 1982).

‖ Hugh Montgomery-Massingberd (b. 1946); author, journalist, publisher and genealogist.

expected so abrasive a writer to be so gentle. Poor Peter has become
a bore. Conversation exclusively about people he knew in the past.
Looks very extraordinary now. In his case too false teeth have altered
the expression, giving him a predatory look. He has become smaller
and curiously dapper, wearing pale fancy waistcoat with brass buttons
and huge gold watch chain, tight jacket and trousers. Looks like Harry
Melvill* or Lord Carisbrooke,† an old queen, which he emphatically
is not. But very lonely without his Mo.

Saturday, 22nd January

I dined with Sally [Westminster] last night, A. not invited since Sally
desperately over-femaled. Nan Bernays brought her friends, the sisters
Lady Wakehurst‡ and Lady Elliot,§ charming and clever old ladies in
their eighties who are aunts of Diana Westmorland, aged ninety. Their
father Sir Charles Tennant¶ was born in 1823, and walked with his
father (born 1780s) in a 'demo' march in favour of the Reform Bill in
1832. Lady Elliot is known as 'The Happy Hippo'.

Sunday, 30th January

Reading Regy's correspondence with his Eton mentor William
Cory,‖ I was surprised to find that my great-uncle Fred Lees was a fre-

---

* Edwardian man-about-town and raconteur.
† Alexander Mountbatten, 1st and last Marquess of Carisbrooke (1886–1960); o. s. of
Prince Henry of Battenberg and Princess Beatrice, 5th dau. of Queen Victoria;
renounced German titles, assumed Mountbatten surname and received UK peerage,
1917. Visiting him at Kew on 13 July 1947 J.L.-M. wrote (*Caves of Ice*): 'He reminded me
of an old spruce hen . . . a typical old queen.'
‡ Margaret Tennant (1899–94); m. 1920 John de Vere Loder, later 2nd Baron Wakehurst;
DBE, 1965.
§ Katharine Tennant (1903–94); m. 1934 as his 2nd wife Sir Walter Elliot (d. 1958);
created life peeress (among the first batch, 1958) as Baroness Elliot of Harwood.
¶ Sir Charles Tennant, 1st Bt (1823–1906), Scottish industrialist and politician; m. 1st
1849 Emma Winsloe, by whom his many children included Edward (cr. Baron
Glenconner), Charlotte (m. 4th Baron Ribblesdale, father of Diana Westmorland) and
Margot (m. H. H. Asquith, Prime Minister); m. 2nd 1898 Marguerite Miles, mother of
Lady Wakehurst and Lady Elliot.
‖ William Johnson (1823–92), Eton master and poet; assumed grandmother's maiden
name of Cory after he left Eton under a cloud, 1872; a great influence on many Eton
boys, including the future 2nd Viscount Esher.

quent visitor to Halsdon, Cory's Devon house. Cory states that 'dear Fred' was not intellectual and not much of a reader, but very good with animals and an excellent shot. I do not suppose Cory was sexually attracted by him, although I see from a photograph I have of Uncle Fred in the 1860s, wearing an Eton scug cap,* that he had a merry, alert face. I have written to his grandson John Poë to enquire if he has any letters written to Uncle Fred from Cory.

Last night on the Third Programme there was an interesting talk by a don about the literature of Russian émigrés in America. They prefer America to England because there is a Russian colony there and the severe winters and hot summers remind them of Russia. Various dissident authors spoke and made evident how serious they were about their writing. Because they are so patriotic and desirous of keeping their native language pure, and because they are writing for fellow Russians (their works being smuggled into the Soviet Union and read by millions), their literature, according to this sagacious don, is better than anything comparable produced by the West.

Tuesday, 1st February

Day in Oxford. Drove through snow blizzards to Oxford University Press. Was taken out to lunch by Judith Luna and two directors, all young and charming. We discussed their proposal that I should write a book on the changes in manners which have taken place this century. I warned that I did not know when I would be able to begin. Then they said they wanted to publish a one-volume abridgement of my *Harold Nicolson*. I said I could not be bothered to do the abridging myself but was happy for some editor to do it, provided I was able to approve the excisions. They were delightful, earnest and sympathetic. I called on my cousin Jamie Fergusson† in his bookshop, but this visit not a success. Can't converse with someone who is on call, and busy. A clever, shrewd young man now, with real bibliographical knowledge.

---

* Until the 1950s or 60s an Eton boy going into the town out of uniform wore a cap, in school or house 'colours' if he had won any; boys who had not thus distinguished themselves were known as 'scugs', and wore a plain cap.
† Antiquarian bookseller (b. 1953), later founding Obituaries Editor of the *Independent*, whose father was a second cousin of J.L.-M.

Saturday, 5th February

Jessica Douglas-Home is inscrutable, sharp, very intelligent, sluttish, mysterious and extremely attractive. She is frank, and saying little, makes no silly remarks; when she does speak, her point of view is always original. Her encapsulated personality and her sudden affection, for I believe she likes me, excites me. I feel drawn to her. I would say she is not a happy character, but very fond of that dear man, her husband Charlie, who is unwell with a mysterious disease.

Wednesday, 9th February

To London by train for the day. Did a little research on Regy in London Library. Then to Burlington House to Murillo exhibition. Wonderful artist, underestimated by me hitherto. Brilliant colours, like Poussins. Then to Cecil Beaton exhibition. For all his sophistication, I am more than ever struck by Cecil's meretriciousness and superficiality. Two clever but horribly cruel caricatures of Violet Trefusis, one of her stubbing a cigarette in a pat of butter. Then Michael Adeane, Queen's late Private Secretary, lunched with me at Brooks's. Just as I remember him at Eton in the distance – round head, small frame. Kind and helpful, though couldn't tell me much about Regy that I didn't already know. Stayed with him as a boy in Scotland, where Regy helped him fish. Told me that his mother remarked on how Regy painted his face, which meant nothing at the time to the young Adeane. He is Stamfordham's grandson, and his own son is currently Prince Charles's Private Secretary. These Court posts are hereditary, and all the better for it. He explained that the Private Secretary is also Keeper of the Royal Archives, Mackworth-Young being only his deputy, and confirmed that the Queen would certainly have been consulted about my request to see Esher papers. Like all English gentleman, Adeane is extraordinarily modest and apparently simple, whereas if one looks him up in *Who's Who* one sees that he has every honour, and even got a First at university. I suppose shrewd. Said that travelling overseas with the Queen he was always aware that persons they met were sucking up to him because of his position. Nice little man. Liked him much. He advised me to see Regy's granddaughters by Zena Dare.

In the afternoon I was interviewed on Radio Four by Frank Delaney*

---

* Irish-born author and broadcaster (b. 1942).

in a programme called *Bookshelf*. I was not very good, but not too bad. When asked who was the most brilliant person I had ever met, I could only think of Oliver Esher, not a good choice. *Caves of Ice* is having some advance publicity. Apart from this wireless interview, there is the serialisation in *Harper's*, the *Tatler* article, a visit from a young lady on a Bristol paper, and an interview in 'Atticus'.

M., who has been ill in Paris with a kidney stone, called for me at Brooks's at six. Affectionate as ever. We looked at Derek Hill's caricature of Sibyl Colefax which he offers to M. for reproduction in his book. Not wholly like, but two lines show S's predatory look. He gives her a beaky nose. M. and I joined Brian Masters for dinner at restaurant near Paddington. When I left to catch 9.40 train home, M. accompanied me to the station and kissed me farewell. He goes to America on Saturday, A. and I to South Africa. I am sad getting out of touch with him, although without worrying, for I have faith in his constancy.

J.L.-M. mentions that he 'recorded a day-to-day account of our experiences [in South Africa] in a little notebook'. This has not been found among his papers. His letters to the editor, however, convey some of his impressions.

> *c/o The Hon. Mrs O'Neill,*
> *Broadlands Stud,*
> *Somerset West,*
> *Cape Province.*
> *Wednesday, 16th February*

. . . We had an extraordinary flight non-stop all the way from London to the Cape. No refuelling *en route* and no flying over other countries. The plane sweeps round the Bay of Biscay over the Atlantic in a curve. Which shows how hated this country is. And yet a first impression made is of universal affluence and content. How deep below the surface is hatred one may or may not discover. All the seven indoor coloured servants seem content and are polite and cheerful without a touch of subservience. They address one as Master, and refer to me as Master Jim, just as the servants at home did in my youth. This house is a large, low, spreading bungalow crammed with fine French furniture, choice china, pictures and bibelots. There is no space anywhere in my huge bedroom to put a pin down. I have had to clear an open space among a forest of Dresden porcelain shepherdesses in which to put my book, spectacles and few toys.

There are three hundred horses large and small in de luxe stables looked after by coloured boys wearing scarlet bonnets. There are twenty dogs, thirty cats (which make the place stink), two marmosets, three enormous parrots which perch on one's shoulders at meals, snatch grapes as one puts them into one's mouth, and bite chunks off one's ear and lip if one thwarts them. Very alarming. There are strange hangers-on, as in Tolstoy households, ladies of unidentifiable extraction and purpose: always twelve to thirty people at each meal. I see little chance of work, alas, and there is too much company. But we have been taken to several beautiful eighteenth-century Dutch Colonial houses lived in by the fourth and fifth generation of owners, some the descendants of their builders. A. is thrilled by the gardens and exotic plants. We are here for two and a half weeks, then have to leave – we know not whither – when the offspring of Lord Mountbatten occupy our rooms when they unveil a memorial window to Ld M. in Cape Town Cathedral.

We see no newspapers and have no news of Blighty. People here are not interested in Europe and the Civil Servant chopper-up of thirteen corpses.* I am wondering how I can survive a whole month away. The Beits are being very kind and take us on excursions. The country is extremely beautiful – mountains like spinal cords, knotted and twisted, which turn amethyst at sunset; lush pasture lands and some enormous camphor trees. There is a wind. When it abates it is very hot, but bearable being a dry heat . . .

Friday, 18th February

. . . the temperature well in nineties when not reduced by a roaring wind . . . Of course we eat out every meal, feasting on crayfish and mangoes. This household is so dotty as to be indescribable. I manage to do a certain amount of reading – all Wm Cory's unpublished letters which are those of an extremely erudite sage, really the best-educated man of the nineteenth century . . .

Yesterday we motored eighty miles inland to lunch with a sweet woman of English descent – the Anglos and the Afrikaans mix but

---

* The social security clerk Dennis Nilsen had just been arrested and charged with murder after the drains of his house in North London were found to be blocked with dismembered corpses (which turned out to be the remains of young men he had befriended in homosexual pubs).

little, yet do not hate one another. They regard themselves equally as the aborigines, and all the coloureds as illegal immigrants whose passage 'home', wherever that may be, they gladly will pay. Mrs Southey, our hostess of yesterday, lives in an old Dutch homestead, as opposed to manor house, not coming of wealthy stock. Until her parents' day the floors indoors were strewn with dung and in winter they all huddled in the capacious kitchen which contains the only fire-place . . .

I think the Cape Coloureds (as distinct from blacks) are divine – handsome and intelligent and sympathetic. The apartheid is not pronounced in the country. (We have not yet been to Cape Town.) Nevertheless, the accepted untouchability of the coloureds makes me uncomfortable. It is assumed that they are fit for the lower grades of service and nothing else.

The mountains are everywhere, craggy, Wagnerian, devoid of all life, animal, bird or vegetable – but haunted by the spirits of the Hottentots who were done to death like vermin by the early settlers. They had Hottentot hunts . . .

Friday, 25th February

. . . The course of existence here has continued fairly uneventfully. We have been on day expeditions to local 'monuments', i.e., nice little Victorian villages, Dutch homesteads, and gardens galore. Have entertained and been entertained by members of the cosmopolitan jet set and by locals to endless meals of indigestible NAAFI food in dinky little suburban houses of indescribable bedintness. But these last folk are preferable. Weather continues to be about perfect, always sunshine, v. hot at midday, cool in mornings and evenings. Wear open shirt (my craggy neck) and thinnest pants.

Yesterday we went to top of Table Mountain by funicular. Alarming experience, for the cabin, into which thirty people are pushed to stand sardine-wise as in rush-hour tube, is pulled up perpendicular rock face by slender wire for 5,000 feet. I shut my eyes until we reached the top. Descent even more alarming. But the flat summit is remarkable and what the moon ought to be but isn't, made of bumpy grey boulders like pigs' backs with ferns and strange exotic flowers growing from the cracks. Ascent made exciting by group of wounded white soldiers on crutches, shirtless in shorts, jammed against one. In Cape Town one sees many very young men who have been wounded in battle with SWAPO* terrorists fortified by Cuban 'volunteers'. The feeling against the West is very hostile. The South Africans are bitter. There is no communication with West, which supplies none of their needs. Not a single British car to be seen, yet French and German galore. No English paper can be bought and there is minimum mention of news from Britain in papers here, except about Lord Linley going naked to the Bath theatre. They think us hypocrites, unaware of their problems . . .

Tomorrow the four of us (i.e., our hostess Pat O'Neill, [her brother] Rory [Cameron], A. and I) motor inland for four nights, returning here on the 2nd. On the 6th A. and I leave for safari in the Transvaal, returning on the 10th to Beits for two nights, and Home on the 11th. Am only fairly enjoying myself. Truth is, I don't enjoy staying away. I think I may enjoy this trip in retrospect. But positively dread safari, with no desire for close quarters with giraffes and hippopotami at 4 a.m. in tropics . . .

Lake Pleasant Hotel
Monday, 28th February

. . . This country evinces a strong pre-1939 nostalgia in spite of the strong Afrikaans element which predominates. They are to a man anti-black, whereas the Anglos with whom we have most consorted are liberal-minded, sensible yet sympathetic to the coloureds. They point out, with truth I think, that apartheid diminishes annually and you cannot be in too much of a hurry in giving them the same privileges as the whites. Indeed, the blacks here are utterly irresponsible even when engaging. The Cape Coloureds quite different, and rather bright. Moreover the blacks in South Africa enjoy far better living conditions than in any black-governed state in Africa . . .

. . . We are on a tour inland. It is so interesting. Oddly, it is less hot inland and the Kooloo Desert where we are tonight is positively cooloo. We drove a hundred kilometres through what is called The Valley of Desolation, ravishingly beautiful plain of gold sand and scrub surrounded by blue Lear-like mountains that never seem far away. They all look flat like Table Mountain, by some mysterious geological freak which I wish someone would explain.

We were in ostrich country this morning – fields and fields of them.

---

* South West Africa People's Organisation.

I bought an egg. Couldn't resist it. Is considered unlucky – and since purchasing we had first a breakdown of the engine of Pat's Mercedes and then a burst tyre. The affluence of the Ostrich Palaces, all built at height of the feather boom *circa* 1900, has to be seen to be believed for vulgarity. Yet the people speak of them with veneration. Only money is respected in this world, I have deduced. Regy [Esher] would not have been pleased to meet one of the owners at the Devonshire House Ball.

I love some of the towns, with their demure little stucco early Victorian houses with verandas and churches like wedding cakes . . . We leave at dawn and arrive at dusk. *Daniel Deronda* will never be finished . . . We had tea with a lady (Anglo) living alone in a farmhouse surrounded by leopards and baboons. She has twenty dogs which chase the baboons out of the house, to get eaten by the leopards . . .

> *117 Beach Road, Gordon's Bay*
> *Friday, 11th March*

. . . You may be surprised to learn that the safari I dreaded turned out a treat. It was thrilling seeing giraffes, elephants, hyenas, zebras, baboons, et cetera – and ravishing sunbirds – and rhinos in their natural state, being amongst them driven in a jeep by a butch tracker, a rifle across his golden hairy sunburnt naked knees. The heat was terrific, over a hundred degrees [fahrenheit] the last day. We went out twice daily – at 5.30 a.m. and again 5.30 p.m., returning in the dark, the black boy on the bonnet of the Land Rover swinging to left and right a huge torch with wide beam and picking out strange nocturnal animals like leopards and civet cats.

Today we lunched with charming lady MP called Helen Suzman[*] who is a Progressive and passionately anti-Government, as indeed Clementine Beit is. I don't know what I ought to think, having listened to both Progressives and Nationalists. I only know what I do think.

Today we motored to the actual Cape, which is thirty miles south of Cape Town. Wonderfully romantic. The actual projection is a high, craggy, windy wedge-shaped rock cleaving the Atlantic and Indian Oceans. Silver sands and high-breasting surf, no habitations, no humans, only cormorants and baboons. Nothing between one and the South Pole. I wonder if Cape Horn is even more impressive and terrifying.

---

[*] Helen Gavronsky (b. 1917) m. Dr M. Suzman; South African economist and politician.

... Have heard no news of *Caves* beyond a mere glance at a review in an old *Times* of last week found here . . .

The diaries resume.

Sunday, 20th March

On 12 February we left for South Africa and we returned on the 12th of this month. In retrospect I enjoyed it all, and the safari. Returned to a pile of letters reporting good reviews of *Caves of Ice*, none of which I have yet seen. Weather here balmy. Was surprised and uplifted to find a bank of primroses in Somerset Place garden when I took the dogs for their matutinal pee. Crocuses and small daffodils to rejoice the heart.

An awful number of friends have died during my month's absence. First Charles Robertson,* who only a few weeks ago took me to look at the new property on the outskirts of Bath on Sham Castle side. He was so charming and gentle that I regretted having fallen out with him over the Bath [Preservation] Trust rows of a year or so ago, and said to A. that we must ask him and his wife to lunch when we got back. Heart failure, I believe. Then Alan Lennox-Boyd,[†] run over and killed. Boofy Arran[‡] gone. Jock Balfour.[§] And now Leigh Ashton,[¶] who had been shut up in St Andrew's loony bin for the past twenty-five years, so I cannot lament his departure. Boofy not seen for ages. A nervous, jumpy, sharp little man like a bird. Very intelligent and quick, with a staccato

---

* Businessman and philanthropist, head of the jam-making firm; m. Barbara Fry (sister of Jeremy Fry, inventor and resident of Bath), sometime Chairman of Bath Preservation Trust.

[†] Alan Lennox-Boyd (1904–83), politician; MP (C) Mid-Bedfordshire, 1931–60; Secretary of State for Colonies, 1954–9; cr. Viscount Boyd of Merton, 1960 (after it was pointed out to the Prime Minister, Harold Macmillan, that he would make an unsuitable Foreign Secretary on account of his homosexual proclivities); m. 1938 Lady Patricia Guinness.

[‡] Arthur Gore, 8th Earl of Arran (1910–83); journalist and broadcaster; m. 1937 Fiona Colquhoun; known to history as the heterosexual peer who introduced the Sexual Offences Bill which decriminalised homosexual acts between consenting adults in private and became law in July 1967.

[§] Sir John Balfour (1894–1983), m. 1933 Frances van Millingen; diplomatist, Ambassador to Spain, 1951–54; known to J.L.-M. as a friend of Harold Nicolson.

[¶] Sir Leigh Ashton (1897–1983); expert on Chinese art; Director of Victoria and Albert Museum, 1945–55.

voice like David Cecil's* and Andrew Devonshire's, he being related to them both. He was a friend at Oxford and used to make long-distance train journeys in order to write his essays, the only way he could manage them, and had fast motor cars. He once made advances to me when I lived in Norfolk Street off Park Lane, after we had wined and dined, and jumped into bed. It was not a success and neither of us ever referred to the incident again. I had not seen Alan either for some years and suspected he might have been offended by something I wrote in my diaries about him or Chips.† With him too I slept more than once, as indeed with his brother George, but they were not romantic occasions. I knew all four Lennox-Boyd brothers, Francis the youngest being the most mysterious and charming. Elegant, slim and willowy, and addicted to soft clothing and a soft life, he became a parachutist in the war and was shot on landing behind enemy lines. Donald was murdered by the Nazis before the outbreak of war and his ashes handed over to Alan in a little box on his being summoned to Berlin. I suppose a British spy. Altogether a good bunch of brothers. Some mystery about their origins.

Wednesday, 23rd March

To London for two nights. Stayed the first with John [Kenworthy-Browne]. We dined at Brooks's and saw *Heat and Dust* at Curzon Cinema. Good film about India, contrasting a great-aunt's affair with Indian prince in 1930s with that of great-niece today with Indian servant. The first elegant and at least romantic, the second squalid and purely physical. J. complains that I don't introduce him to my high and mighty friends. I spoke rather sharply about his self-pity, which alienates people.

Lunched with Kenneth Rae‡ in his pleasant house off Ladbroke Grove. A ghost of his former self, eighty-one and suffering from palsy,

---

* Lord David Cecil (1902–86), yr son of 4th Marquess of Salisbury; historian and author; Goldsmiths' Professor of English Literature, Oxford, 1948–69; m. 1932 Rachel MacCarthy.

† In *Ancestral Voices*, J.L.-M. describes the unreciprocated passion of Lennox-Boyd ('X.-B.') for the American soldier Stuart Preston in 1943, and the fruitless efforts of Lennox-Boyd's brother-in-law, Henry 'Chips' Channon, MP, to encourage the affair.

‡ At the time J.L.-M. was the N.T's Historic Buildings Secretary, Rae was Secretary to the Old Vic – both of them being responsible to committees chaired by Oliver, Viscount Esher.

but mind unimpaired. He reminded me of the occasion when Oliver Esher, with whom we were both lunching at Brooks's, complained that so many people were asking for salary rises, both Kenneth and I working for charities at the time and being very poor. So Kenneth replied, 'It's all very fine for you, who were born with a silver spoon in your mouth and married a woman with a gold canteen in hers.' Oliver was amused. He also recalled that, when Miriam Wansbrough* married, he had made for her a very pretty pair of pearl and diamond earrings. He showed these to Antoinette Esher, who produced a very ordinary, cheap compact she had bought for Miriam. She said, 'Will you swap the earrings for my compact? It is more suitable that I should give the earrings.'

Humphrey Whitbread† had tea with me at Brooks's. He had little to tell me about his father's friendship with Regy, yet was very charming. Was most distressed by death of Lanning [Roper],‡ but did not tell me what I later heard from Freda [Berkeley], that he sat for hours with Lanning as he lay dying.

At 7.30 I went to Broadcasting House to be interviewed about *Caves of Ice* for that night's *Round Midnight* programme. I didn't acquit myself too badly and hoped to hear the broadcast later, but Eardley's ancient wireless set could not get Radio Two. Next morning did another broadcast, this time at the flat of a man in Harcourt Terrace. Not a success. Sitting on the edge of the man's bed, for the front room was on the noisy street, with a waving toast-rack thrust into my face and the interviewer's misting eyes a foot from mine, I felt ill at ease. He asked me about eccentric people I had known, so I found myself trotting out the tale of Lord Berwick and Lady Sybil Grant.§ It was a great effort for him and a worse one for me. I shall never hear this programme, which is put out for the Third World, just as I have not heard the previous ones for the First and Second. People will talk to me about *Caves*, assuring me how much they are enjoying it. I endeavour

---

* Only dau. (b. 1932) of J.L.-M's friend Eliza Wansbrough.

† Of the brewing dynasty; a young friend of the old age of A. E. Housman, and having other interesting associations.

‡ American landscape gardener and writer (1912–83).

§ Lord Berwick (of Attingham Park) and Lady Sybil, elder dau. of 5th Earl of Rosebery, were neighbours in Shropshire and fellow spiritualists, who corresponded about advice they were receiving from friendly ghosts. Lord Berwick told J.L.-M. that they never exchanged such information by telephone 'for fear of the spirits overhearing and taking offence', but J.L.-M. suspected it was 'more likely for fear of Lady Berwick overhearing and strongly disapproving' (*Ancestral Voices*, 8 July 1943).

not to read the reviews. Each time I do so I am affronted by some observation. The incident in the Boboli Gardens, for instance, embarrasses me.* Then why mention it at all? Why indeed.

I was told by Josephine Loewenstein who had been told by Lady Leicester that the trouble with the Princess of Wales is her abysmal stupidity. She is also obstinate, wilful and sulky. Pity, for she has charm, beauty and chic.

Monday, 28th March

Christopher Chancellor† asked himself to lunch. Rang up rather pathetically, saying he was feeling so old that he did not suppose he would live long and would like to talk to me again. So I bade him come to Bath where I heated up a quiche and opened a bottle of wine. He told me that Edward, Prince of Wales fell in love with his [Christopher's] mother when he visited Southern Rhodesia, of which Christopher's father was then Governor. His mother fell in love back, but platonically, feeling drawn to this wayward, motherless, sad and pretty youth. Christopher asked his daughter Susanna [Johnston] if she would take her mother, Sylvia, to live in her village when her mother-in-law died, the former being a mere eighty-three while the latter is eighty-seven. Susanna agreed with alacrity, saying, 'I will go and shoot my mother-in-law at once.' Christopher replied in his humourless way, 'I am not dead yet.'

Monday, 4th April

The Vereys‡ came. While Rosemary and A. were in the garden, David told me he believed he had been cured of his cancer. As well as taking pills from his doctor he visits the ex-Bishop Bardsley and undergoes faith-healing. Bishop, who believes, as does David, in the apostolic

---

* 16 October 1947: 'On my return on foot along the Arno I met the handsome young Italian . . . Very sweet he was . . . [We] walked arm-in-arm towards the pitch darkness of the Boboli Gardens, which were shut now. "But I know a way in," he said, "and we shall have it entirely to ourselves." We did . . . I salute his evanescent youth and beauty.'
† Sir Christopher Chancellor (1904–89); on staff of Reuters, 1930–59; subsequently chairman of companies and charities, including Bath Preservation Trust; m. 1926 Sylvia Paget. His daughter Susanna m. 1958 the architect Nicholas Johnston (b. 1929).
‡ David Verey (1913–84), architectural historian, of Barnsley House near Circencester; m. 1939 Rosemary Sandilands (b. 1918), garden designer and co-editor of books on gardening with A.L.-M.

succession of bishops of the Church of England, puts his hands on David's head – the hands are cool – and on his arms – the hands are hot. Since a year ago, when he believed that he was dying, David has lived a spiritual life. Told me he was now quite impotent, and that this deprivation has helped in removing him from the material plane.

Thursday, 7th April

Map in hand, I drove to look round the Sherborne estate [near Cheltenham, Glos.] which has been bequeathed to the N.T. by the late Charlie Sherborne.* It was just like the old days when I so often made these inspections. Went first to Lodge Park, not visited by me since 1938, now inhabited by the Sherbornes' housekeeper and husband, nice people. I found myself automatically exercising that old manner which used to endear me to owners.† They have been given the right to live in the Lodge if they want to. I was amazed that the Sherbornes, who were very rich indeed, lived in such drab surroundings. Lord S. died only three months ago and the rooms are down-at-heel, paper peeling off walls in bedrooms and bathrooms. Very little furniture or pictures of interest. In one bedroom a stack of portraits, nothing very good I guess. They had a sale about a year ago. Allowed services of porcelain to go piecemeal, some still remaining at Lodge Park. The housekeeper's husband told me they didn't take the slightest interest in their possessions. And Audrey‡ with whom I had tea, said that he never went round the estate for years before his death. Estate very broken down. Altogether a depressing property and I don't find the land beautiful. The part on the hill is flat and dreary, the Sherborne brook vale prettier. The large house was sold and is being turned into flats. Ugly car park with asphalt and concrete curb.

Sunday, 10th April

A. had been due to accompany me to lunch with the Eshers today. Instead she was summoned by Rupert Loewenstein to fly in David

---

* Charles Dutton, 7th Baron Sherborne (1911–82), m. 1943 Joan Jenkinson. The heir to the barony was his distant cousin Ralph Dutton, friend of J.L.-M., on whose death in 1985 it became extinct.

† Marginal note added by J.L.-M. in 1988: 'Some pretension.'

‡ J.L.-M's sister Audrey Stevens, a tenant of the Sherborne estate at Windrush Mill.

Somerset's plane with hired pilot to France. Mick Jagger,* the Rolling Stone, having read *The Englishman's Garden*, told Rupert that he wanted Mrs L.-M. to lay out the garden of his château near Tours. So she chucked the Eshers today and I went alone.

Arrived punctually at one o'clock at the tower Lionel has built for himself on Christmas Common, just inside the drive gates to Watlington [Park, Oxfordshire]. Very nice inside. Outside gloomy and without charm. Not strictly speaking a tower, though built on four levels. More like a London town house. Gloomy dusky brick and ugly pitched roof. Pretty wooden ceilings exposed, and much wainscot. Picture windows. View from top bedroom (Christian's) splendid. No garden, some rides cut through the trees. Elms, once thick, now dead and gone. Oaks, both old and seedlings. I returned Oliver's 'secret life' of his father and another book lent me by Lionel. His sister Nancy there along with husband Evelyn Shuckburgh,† retired ambassador with beard. Also his cousin Mary Cheyne, daughter of Maurice Brett and Zena Dare.‡ During luncheon we talked of Regy. Evident that Mrs Cheyne devoted to him. Wouldn't hear a word of criticism by Lionel. As children, after the death of their father, she and her sister lived with their grandmother, Nellie Esher. Said her grandmother was less sympathetic than her grandfather, whom she could tease; he had a sense of humour and was gentle with children.

When the other guests left, Lionel and Christian and I walked across park to the big house where Christopher Brett lives with second wife and seven children. Wife very friendly little thing with pointed red nose. The Brett boy has lost the good looks I remember. They fished down from top shelf four further volumes of correspondence for me to take away. Oliver Esher kept every single letter he received, and at the end of each year had them all bound in rich morocco. He did not omit any item, whether from the tailor or the gas company.

---

* Michael Philip 'Mick' Jagger (b. 1943); singer and songwriter, co-founder of Rolling Stones, 1962.
† Sir Evelyn Shuckburgh (1909–94), diplomatist; close aide of Sir Anthony Eden as Foreign Secretary and Prime Minister; Ambassador to Italy, 1966–9; m. 1937 Hon. Nancy Brett.
‡ As J.L.-M. was to describe in his biography, Reginald Esher had an unusual relationship with his younger son Maurice Brett (1882–1934), whom he bombarded with love letters and whose marriage (1911) to the actress Zena Dare he arranged. Marie (b. 1916), youngest of three children of that marriage, m. 1938 Commander Archibald Cheyne.

Heavenly Christian talked about Regy's daughter Dorothy Brett,*
known as 'Doll' or 'Brett', whom she and Lionel saw in New Mexico
where she lived the greater part of her life, having gone there with
D. H. Lawrence and Frieda [in 1924]. Showed me one of Brett's pictures, full of dancing movement. Christian would like to organise an
exhibition to coincide with the publication of her biography this
autumn. I suggested she contact Richard Shone.† Regy violently disapproved of his daughter's painting. When the Tate acquired some of
her work, she said, 'Poor Pupsie must be turning in his grave at the
thought of me hanging there.' Through the library window of the
big house, I watched Christian's slim dark figure, like an apostrophe
in the grey-green landscape, receding as she walked back to the
Tower. Seductive.

Sir Evelyn told a story of a young foreigner in the 1930s staying for
the first time in a grand English country house. He told the son of the
house that he did not think he could keep up with the tradition of
drinking quantities of port after dinner. The son said, 'Oh, that's all
right. As soon as you feel you've had enough, just slip under the table.'
He drank one glass, which satisfied him, then slowly sank under the
table. He waited seemingly for hours in an uncomfortable position
while the other men continued talking. Then he felt a pair of hands
clutching his throat. 'Who are you?' he whispered in horror. A small
voice replied, 'Only the boy employed to loosen the collars.' Can that
be true? Of Regency times, perhaps.

Tuesday, 12th April

A. greatly enjoyed her visit to Mick Jagger. He is charming with a
huge smiling mouth. Quite unspoilt. Rather touching in that he reads
voraciously and has taste and a desire to accumulate beautiful objects.
The château he has bought near Amboise is ravishing and she is eager
to lay out and plant the garden for him. House still very uncomfortable. Jagger offered to put her and Rupert up in a hotel, but A. said
No, she preferred to stay with him. Given a room with no running
water and slept on the floor, after a good French dinner with wine.
Jagger drinks little. Speaks good French. Has read my book on

---

* Artist (1883–1977).
† Art historian (b. 1949); author of *Bloomsbury Portraits* (1976); associate editor of
Burlington Magazine from 1979.

Beckford. Told her he came from Lees, Lancashire, where his father was church organist. So we have the same origins. Whenever he buys an antique his mother complains, 'But Mick, you can afford to buy something really nice. That's second-hand.'

Wednesday, 13th April

Motored to Ascot to lunch with Angela Thornton,* daughter of Maurice Brett and Zena Dare. Sweet and pretty woman in her seventies. Lent me a packet of letters written to her by her grandfather Regy who loved her, I guess because she was pretty and lively. The letters are very disloyal about his other children and grandchildren. Wrote that the Brookes were all untrustworthy, and sneered at the Watlington children. Her nice sister Marie Cheyne, whom I met with the Eshers on Sunday, came over after luncheon, and they both talked at length about their grandfather whom they adored. Not a hint that they knew of his peccadilloes.

On leaving them I drove to Eton, which owing to the holidays was empty. Wandered round the schoolyard and fields and into the Chapel. While looking at Uncle Robert's and William Leveson-Gower's tablets in the ante-chapel, my eye was caught by the adjoining tablet. It was to Thomas Lister, brother of Diana Westmorland, killed in Africa.† Also saw the list of the boys' seating arrangements for the last Half, pinned on a board. Noticed that they still call an Honourable 'Mr'. Among the Johnson ma., Smith mi., Lord Selborne, etc., there is *Mr* Fortescue. I wonder whence this custom derives. It is rather nice.

Thursday, 14th April

Had tea alone with Diana Westmorland and mentioned her brother's memorial tablet in Eton Chapel. She remembered when the terrible news of his death arrived. Her parents had followed him throughout the South African campaign, staying behind the lines, as civilians did at Waterloo. He was shot soon after their return. This greatly upset her father Lord Ribblesdale, and the death of his younger son

---

* Born 1911, m. 1934 Kenneth Thornton.
† Captain The Hon. Thomas Lister (1878–1904), eldest son of 4th Baron Ribblesdale; won DSO in Boer War; subsequently killed in Somaliland.

Charles* in 1915 broke him completely. She said [her father] should never have married Ava Astor, a horrid woman.† He left his comfortable rooms in the Cavendish Hotel for her big house in Grosvenor Square, and was miserable. He was a very simple man who did not care for the social life. Adored by Diana.

Sunday, 17th April

I find visitors staying here an increasing strain unless they are intimate friends. For Badminton weekend‡ we have the Keffers again.§ Perfectly agreeable, but not on our beam. Very anxious to return our hospitality at Glyndebourne or wherever we wish. He orders all my books and even advertises for those out of print. Today Nick and Henry [Robinson]¶ came to luncheon. Very jolly they were, full of chat and argument, teasing one another and us. After luncheon, A. and I went with the two Keffers to watch the final ceremony of the Event, the jumping of the winning competitors. The beauty of these glossy, well-groomed, well-trained horses, so delicate, with their little raised feet and straining curved necks and nervous flanks.

Monday, 18th April

Stayed with Eardley in London. Arrived in time for dinner with him, Richard Shone and Mattei.‖ I brought some pudding and wine. A *froideur* between the two young men, and only after Mattei left did we three talk easily. Richard said Anthony Blunt's** omnipresence at the *Burlington Magazine* has been an embarrassment to the staff. He confirmed that Blunt was not altogether straight in his art opinions. Had

---

* Hon. Charles Lister (1887–1915), whose death doomed the Ribblesdale barony to extinction.

† Mary Ava Willing of Philadelphia, former wife of John Jacob Astor, who married 4th Baron Ribblesdale (d. 1925) in 1919 as his 2nd wife.

‡ The Badminton Three-Day Event was then held in April, usually the second weekend; later moved to May, after a succession of disastrously wet springs.

§ John Keffer, Chairman of Trustees of American Museum at Claverton.

¶ Henry Robinson (b. 1953), farmer, Nick's elder brother.

‖ Mattei Radev (b. 1927), Bulgarian-born picture framer and gilder.

** The recently deceased Blunt (1907–83), art historian and Surveyor of the Royal Pictures 1945–72, had been officially disgraced in 1979 following the exposure of his former career as a Soviet agent.

more than once been known to boost pictures which were not genuine for the benefit of dealers. Horrid, snake-like man.[*]

Tuesday, 19th April

Lunched with David Lloyd[†] at Franco's in Jermyn Street. He had come up from Hertfordshire for the occasion in spite of illness. His wife Jean had telephoned me at Eardley's last night warning he might not be able to make it; but he did. Luckily he arrived at the restaurant first and waved to me from a table, otherwise I should not have recognised him. An old man supported by a stick. Face shape altered, eyes large and watery, yet unseeing. Only his teeth when he smiled were recognisable. Suffers from emphysema owing to smoking fifty cigarettes a day, also from excessive drinking. I always picture David as a boy at Eton, then young man at Cambridge, in perpetual trouble for small peccadilloes, who would come to my room in Portman Square and sit on my writing table, begging me to get him out of some scrape, such as having driven his father's car into a ditch when he should have been attending a lecture. He is now very ill. He had asked to see me ostensibly to talk about the future of his father's papers, which are in fact safely lodged at Churchill College. What he really wants is for me to write the biography, but I told him some years ago that I cannot. Today I exhorted him to undertake it himself, knowing that he will not have either the energy, ability or length of life to do so, but feeling it would give him occupation and interest. He was very pitiful, and talked so much that by the time I left for N.T. meeting we had decided nothing. He showed me a letter from a woman who runs 'the Box', ending, 'I wonder if you have had a serious shock within recent years?' David marvelled at this, saying she could not have known how the suicide of his son Charlie had knocked him edgeways. But of course she could have known it. He asked me directly whether his father was homosexual, 'not that I mind a scrap', et cetera. I said he surely was so by nature, but did not practise that I knew. He told me that Alan Lennox-Boyd, whose junior minister he had been at the Colonial

---

[*] J.L.-M. was not so damning at the time of Blunt's disgrace, describing him (*Deep Romantic Chasm*, 17 November 1979) as a 'shy, courteous, withdrawn figure'.
[†] Alexander David, 2nd Baron Lloyd of Dolobran (1912–85), son of the proconsul and Conservative politician George, 1st Baron, for whom J.L.-M. had worked as private secretary, 1931–5; m. 1942 Lady Jean Ogilvy; Under Secretary for the Colonies, 1954–7.

Office, could often not be found at moments of crisis, having gone off with, as David called him, 'Sweetie'. He suggested that homosexuals were unreliable in that respect. (Indeed, they do seem to have less control over their emotions than other men. Why is this?) I left David feeling sad, and later wrote telling him I would do anything to help with the biography short of writing it.

Wednesday, 20th April

I suffer less from angst these days and more from worry and fuss. Less too from spring fever or restlessness, due to impotence, I suppose. I think how hateful it will be to leave my possessions which I love and cherish. No one will treat them with the affection I do.

Friday, 22nd April

Alex Moulton called for me at ten in his beautiful Rolls. Drove to Devon. Main object of exercise to visit Halsdon House, William Cory's, where Regy and his friends stayed in the 1870s. We found it in the evening, before sunset. It was just as I imagined, and as it must have looked when Cory was living there. Still very remote, approached down high-banked, primrose-studded lanes. We followed the route they must have taken on foot or by wagonette from Eggesford station. Left car in lane and walked through white gate. Smoke rising from a bonfire. No one about. The house seemed empty, except for a Georgian bookcase and a Regency couch which we espied through a cobwebbed window. Building in state of slight decay, garden being attended to just as it would have been by the young men staying with Cory. I thought of Chat,* Uncle Fred Lees and others in this compact, unimportant small squire's seat in the depths of Devon. Forgot to look for Regy's and Chat's carved names on the window sill. Next morning visited an estate agent in Great Torrington who informed me that the house had just been bought, presumably from the Furse family who have owned it since the seventeenth century, by of all people the drummer of the Rolling Stones.† Curious coincidence in view of A's new alliance with Mick Jagger.

---

* Charles Williamson, Regy Brett's great love at Eton, who later became a Catholic priest but remained a close friend.
† Charlie Watts.

Motored to Penzance. Such a storm, the sea so rough we could not cross to St Michael's Mount. Had tea with Lady St Levan.* Gave her a copy of *Some People*,† just out in paperback. She did not talk a word about Harold. Remarkably fit for eighty-seven. Might be sixty. Not deaf or decrepit, but cold. Don't suppose my visit gave her much pleasure. Alex on the other hand a great success, talking about his new bicycle which interested her much. On return to Badminton I felt so exhausted that I slept for three hours in the afternoon and woke still feeling tired. Alex a sweet companion, taking an interest in all things. His sole fault is a tendency to over-emphasise and pontificate, using long words which he often gets wrong.

Saturday, 30th April

Delicious day, sun and storm, but the ground is drenched. Took dogs for the usual weekend walk – Cherry Orchard round. It takes me exactly one hour and thirty-five minutes, and I am quite tired after it. Heard my first and probably last cuckoo in the distance. Of all bird calls it still moves me most, more so than the nightingale's, for it truly recalls far-off things and battles long ago. Primroses along the banks of the lane less conspicuous than a fortnight ago because the grass and other foliage has sprung up. Indeed, the green has burst, still only into loose bud, not full flower. This is the one moment when I do want to be in England – this and the October moment.

Have just finished Rupert [Hart-Davis]'s fifth volume of correspondence with George Lyttelton.‡ I can hardly bear the knowledge that there can be but one more, for Lyttelton died in 1962 and we have now reached 1960. He complains of increasing deafness and pains, yet is never self-pitying. Rupert's spryness is a slight irritant, only very slight to me, but definitely to Diana Mosley who complained of the

---

* Hon. Gwendolen Nicolson (1896–1995), only sister of Harold Nicolson, m. 1916 Francis ('Sam') St Aubyn who succeeded (1940) as 3rd Baron St Levan. Her cool reception of J.L.-M. may have owed something to the fact that in his biography of her brother, published in 1981, he had indicated that in the 1930s she had conducted a lesbian affair with her sister-in-law, Vita Sackville-West.

† Harold Nicolson's celebrated work of semi-fictionalised autobiography, first published in 1927.

‡ Sir Rupert Hart-Davis (1907–99), publisher, editor, writer, and friend of J.L.-M. since Eton, was editing his correspondence with his old Eton housemaster Hon. George Lyttelton (1883–1962), published by John Murray in six volumes, 1978–84.

last volume in this respect. Lyttelton's letters are the more fascinating. Yet he complains that, whereas Rupert has so much to tell about the million things he is doing and distinguished folk he is seeing, he has so little, as a retired schoolmaster living in Suffolk. It merely proves my theory that the best diarists and letter-writers are those who see *nobody* and have *nothing* to write about. The learning of both staggers me. I have written to Rupert today suggesting spending a night at the end of May after lunching with Roger Fulford,* whose condition is extremely sad.

A. told me that, at the opera three days ago, Loelia Lindsay† approached her with loud complaints of my *Caves*. A. groaned. Loelia said she might be old-fashioned, but she was disgusted by my reference to having caught crabs during the war. This upset me because I had wondered whether to leave the incident out, but in the end my determination to be honest decided me to leave it in. Anyway, when I got to Bath I began tearing up several pages of unpublished diaries; then desisted.

Wednesday, 4th May

Today I was surprised to receive a request from Loelia, via Hugo Vickers,‡ for permission to quote a passage from my diaries – about Send Grove§ – in some absurd album she is publishing.

Nigel Nicolson stayed last night on the way to lecture at Chippenham, then to stay at Alfoxton because he wants to walk where Wordsworth and Southey and Coleridge walked, a commendable thing. He abounds in energy and enthusiasm. Has wisely abandoned his book on Napoleon and intends to write about his Russian Campaign only. An excellent idea, for Nigel is an expert on battles, having written the history of the Grenadiers and Life of Lord Alexander [of Tunis]. He amazed me by saying that a huge portrait of Ben [Nicolson] by Rodrigo Moynihan is now hanging in the

---

* Sir Roger Fulford (1902–83) of Barbon Manor, Carnforth, Lancashire; historian; President of Liberal Party, 1964–5; m. 1937 Sibell *née* Lyttelton (whose son by her earlier marriage succeeded as 4th Baron Shuttleworth, 1942).
† Hon. Loelia Ponsonby (1902–93), dau. of 1st Baron Sysonby, m. 1st (1930–47) 2nd Duke of Westminster ('Bendor'); 2nd 1969 Sir Martin Lindsay of Dowhill, 1st Bt (1905–81).
‡ Author (b. 1951); see entry for 5 November 1983.
§ Her house near Woking.

National Portrait Gallery. Odd to think of Ben next to establishment figures like Lord Redcliffe-Maude.

Nigel has just returned from a fortnight in the United States, during which he sold all Harold's and Vita's correspondence to the University of Bloomington, Indiana for $100,000. Is slightly fussed at having 'sold', and thinks Vita would not have disapproved but Harold might have. I am sure he is justified, for the letters were badly deteriorating at Sissinghurst and N. was constantly being asked to allow access to scholars, a dreadful bore for him. Now they will be cherished. Says the boys and girls of this university are incredibly beautiful, owing to the climate. They lead an outdoor life, airing and sunning their bodies to the neglect of their minds. The dons who teach them are constantly falling in love with them.

Wednesday, 11th May

Motored to London to dine with M. and Charles Orwin* at Oxford and Cambridge Club. M. is off tomorrow to Spain and Portugal for a month.† Delicious evening. Charles full of engaging chaff, caustic and affectionate. M. on these occasions goes into a slouching daze, speaks little, and then, aroused by some remark, delivers himself of a devastating rejoinder. Charles deprecates his wasting his talent on the Windsors. Alas, I agree. As we parted on the pavement at Pall Mall, C. kissed me on both cheeks, M. on the lips. M. said, 'Ring me up tomorrow morning, please.' I motored off to stay with Eardley, happy. Found E. suffering from lumbago and somewhat depressed. I fear age is affecting his natural gaiety.

Driving from Oxford to London, I marvelled at the beauty of the spring struggling against the desecrations of man. At a new road junction near High Wycombe, bulldozers were tearing up acres of meadows and woods. Amid the chaos, the mangled, torn earth and the exposed chalk, a few remaining hedges of may in blossom and two weeping willows somehow managed to survive. One must now seek beauty no longer in the mass but in the little, and thank God for the diminishing oases of untouched nature. Plants are the only form of life devoid of evil.

---

* Publisher (b. 1951).

† In connection with a book he was writing on the Duke of Windsor's adventures there in the summer of 1940.

Thursday, 12th May

A profitable morning in the London Library. But could not find my
little black notebook later, and unless it turns up, my labours will
have been in vain. Then to a ghastly stand-up snack luncheon at the
Royal Festival Hall to honour Lennox [Berkeley] on his eightieth
birthday. I always vow not to attend these ceremonies, and always
find myself at them. Standing with a glass of lemonade in one hand,
a plate containing mouldy cubes of cheese with toothpicks through
them in the other, yelling platitudes to people I haven't seen for years
and whose worn purple faces arouse disgust rather than compassion
(a sentiment doubtless reciprocated by them) – how I hate it.
Speeches made, and poor Lennox supported by Freda obliged to
thank, not finding words, not knowing whom he was addressing, all
muddled, his memory in flight, pathetic. Then an orchestra struck
up and played several movements of Lennox's dry sonatas from an
adjoining room, while we continued to balance glasses and empty
plates, standing on one foot, then the other. At two I escaped back
to the London Library. At four a pretty young man called George
Plumptre* came to Brooks's for a cup of tea to discuss a book on
country houses which Collins want him to write with my assistance.
I made it clear I would not visit, research or write. So don't see that
I can be of much use beyond approving the nice boy's choice of
houses and vetting what he writes. It will probably come to nothing,
and I don't care.

Having left my car all day in Burlington House courtyard – my only
privilege as a Fellow of the Antiquaries – joined Rosamond
[Lehmann] at the Royal Society of Literature. We listened to one of
the best lectures I have heard, by youngish don A. N. Wilson† on
Hilaire Belloc.‡ Wilson made him out to be an object of compassion,
his life ruined by early death of his beloved wife. He would kiss her
bedroom door every time he passed it for the remaining forty years of
his life. I used to meet Belloc at Pixton, staying with Mary

---

* Hon. George Plumptre (b. 1956), yr s. of 21st Baron FitzWalter; m. 1984 Princess
Alexandra Cantacuzene; later worked for Sotheby's, and wrote books on gardening and
cricket.
† Andrew Norman Wilson (b. 1950); journalist and author of works of fiction and non-
fiction; lecturer at Oxford, 1976–81; literary editor of *Spectator*, 1981–4, *Evening Standard*,
1990–7.
‡ Writer, poet, Liberal politician and Catholic propagandist (1870–1953).

Herbert.* In old age he was a great nuisance. He expected his hosts to provide him with quantities of wine, even during the war when it was hard to come by. He was a provocative, aggressive, contrary old man, enunciating his theories in clipped tones as though they were papal encyclicals. Wore a black cloak, tattered and spotted. He once set fire to himself in the middle of the night and Mary and I had to extinguish the flames by rolling him on the bathroom floor.† His Catholicism was of that provincial, aggressive-defensive sort which alienates Protestants. No one relishes the assumption that he is a totally philistine outsider, which is what Belloc made one feel. Yet I liked his life of James II, giving a refreshingly contrary view to that taught in schoolbooks, and his satirical verse. Immensely enjoyed dining with Ros afterwards. She said, 'Can't we make a pact to meet once a month?'

Sunday, 15th May

We have Oenone‡ staying in the attic bedroom with her lover, a charming young man of thirty who works at Faber & Faber. Bright, easy, intelligent and extremely handsome, with glossy raven hair and an eagle-like face. What I imagine my Ernst§ to be like. I wonder how he can tolerate the silliness of O. I suppose – indeed hope – he is infatuated.

Fanny Partridge said to me at the RSL lecture that I had a distinctive back view. Yes, I said, the back of my head is like an empty bird's nest.

Sunday, 22nd May

Received a postcard from Lady Shuttleworth on Monday to say it would be impossible to come to lunch with Roger Fulford on the 27th as arranged because he was so ill. Next morning his death

---

* Hon. Mary Vesey (1889–1972), dau. of 4th Viscount de Vesci; m. 1910 Hon. Aubrey Herbert (1880–1923), yr s. of 3rd Earl of Carnarvon; mother of Evelyn Waugh's wife Laura; châtelaine of Pixton Park, Dulverton, Somerset.
† J.L.-M. gave a slightly different version of this incident in *A Mingled Measure*, 14 August 1953.
‡ Oenone Luke (b. 1960), second of J.L.-M's three step-granddaughters.
§ The seducing German count in J.L.-M's recent novel.

announced in *The Times*. So once again I have left undone the task of
seeing a dear old friend for a final goodbye. One of the dearest of men.
I must have met him in the early 1930s, and in those days thought he
looked eighty, the age at which he has died. But always whimsical,
humorous, pedantic in the sweetest way. Would never snub, yet had a
passion for accuracy. Regarded me as a wayward child; thought my
political views more funny than deplorable. Was a nineteenth-century
Whig with absorbing interest in the Royal Family, their vagaries and
comicalities. Yet a serious historian and editor. I always enjoyed
staying with them at Barbon. With Sibell made the perfect couple.
She an angelic woman, who rose above a lifetime of tragedies. He
radiated affection.

Yesterday A. and I motored to Simon and Tricia [Lees-Milne]'s
newly acquired house by Clifton-on-Teme. Far larger and nicer than
the one at Alfrick. In the heart of old, unspoilt Worcestershire; indeed
the most lovely country in England, and on approaching it my heart
gave a leap – though not as high as it would have been ten years ago,
the spring in it having slackened, I fear, like all my emotions. Odd that
Simon, who was brought up in Oldham, where we Leeses sprang from,
should have made his life and home in Worcestershire, where Dick and
I were reared. The house they have bought is a rather basic version of
Wickhamford – half-timbered wing, but with tall eighteenth-century
brick attachment at one end. All steep little staircases and ups and
downs. A. said she would rather live in a villa in Worcester. Poor
things, they have absolutely no taste. But they are so happy and proud
of their acquisition that it is delicious. A happy pair. Gave us excellent
luncheon, roast chicken tenderly cooked, and oranges sliced in ginger.
A view of Jones's folly at Abberley* would have been visible from the
house had it not poured with rain all day. Indeed, it has rained every
day this year. Worst spring ever. Land waterlogged.

On the news this evening announcement of K. Clark's death. Now,
I have always regarded him as about the greatest man of my generation. I have never known him intimately. Few men have. He did not
care for men, and greatly loved women. Was a proud, aloof man with
a gracious manner that did not put one at ease. But whenever he gave
praise one felt that God Almighty had himself conferred a benedic-
tion. I think he may be classed with Ruskin as an interpreter of the

---

* A clock tower built for John Joseph Jones of Abberley Hall in memory of his father by
J.P. St Aubyn in 1883.

arts. He would also have made an admirable dictator, had he turned his talents to politics.

Sunday, 22nd May

To the Hollands' annual concert at Sheepridge Barn. Freezing. Nearly died of cold eating our snacks in the cloister. I perched on a chair next to Liz Longman, balancing plate and glass, and was photographed by an inquisitive press man. Joan Holland, dressed and painted to kill, swathed in canary silk rustling dress (with, she explained, tweeds underneath), swept A. and me into a tent where Princess Margaret, guest of the evening, was drinking whisky out of a large tumbler. We were presented. She, possibly distracted by meeting so many people within a small enclosed space, was not gracious and a little brash. Said to me, 'Had I known you were a contributor to the Picnic Book, I would not have written my piece.' How does one take this sort of remark? I smiled wryly and said, 'Oh Ma'am, but I so enjoyed yours.' 'Do you like the book?' she asked. 'I liked the jacket,' I said untruthfully. 'I hate picnics,' she said, 'but did you like the book?' – this time to A. as much as me. That was as far as our contact went. How I hate meeting royalty. One gets absolutely nowhere.

Wednesday, 25th May

Attended my first Foyle's Literary Luncheon as a Guest of Honour, to celebrate Fleur Cowles' garden book and Lady Cottesloe's *Duchess of Beaufort's Flower Book*. Master was incongruously in the chair.* I sat between Sally Westminster and Christina Foyle[†] at the top table. Liked Miss Foyle. Sympathetic woman, slightly bedint which makes for cosiness. Must have been pretty. Told me about her father who started the bookshop in 1904. She has a mass of papers. Has known all the literary people of her time. She entered the shop at nineteen. I said she ought to write her memoirs and the history of Foyle's. Fleur Cowles,[‡] wearing dark spectacles to give herself confidence, read her

---

* Lady Cottesloe was an intimate friend of the Duke of Beaufort (see *Deep Romantic Chasm*, 8 July 1981), as was Sally, Duchess of Westminster.

[†] 1911–99; Managing Director of W. & G. Foyle Ltd, booksellers (founded by her father); started Foyle's Literary Luncheons, 1930; m. 1938 Ronald Batty.

[‡] American writer and artist, author of *The Flower Game* (1983); m. (1946–55) Tom Meyer.

speech. Mrs Callaghan, wife of former PM, gave vote of thanks. Whereas Master and Miss Cowles began their speeches 'Your Serene Highnesses, My Lords, Ladies and Gentlemen' (don't know who the SHs were), Mrs Callaghan, with what seemed like some deliberateness, began, 'Ladies and Gentlemen, at short notice I have been asked by Lord Beaufort . . .' Was this meant to take the Duke down a peg according to socialist principles?

In the street afterwards I was accosted by an old man, shabbily dressed, who said, 'You won't remember me. We were at Magdalen together. My name is Greenham.'* 'Yes, of course,' I replied, 'the eminent painter who did that masterly portrait of Charlotte [Bonham Carter].' He in turn praised my books. This sort of thing happens so often that I almost take it as a Good Morning.

Friday, 27th May

Today was to have been my luncheon with poor old Roger Fulford. Instead I drove straight to Marske-in-Swaledale to stay the night with Rupert and June Hart-Davis. Nearly three hundred miles in my small car, all on motorway and A1 on which there were several dreadful road blocks owing to Bank Holiday traffic. Rupert older in looks. Walks hesitatingly, and slightly bent. Face and nose longer. But mind alert as ever. His pipe-smoking, and tweed jacket with leather patches on elbows, still lend him a military air. We compared our disabilities. He is stone deaf in one ear and forgets recent events. This year is producing four books. We talked incessantly. He approves of my undertaking Regy. Gave me a copy of his precious Max Beerbohm catalogue, and wrote in it. Asked me to write in his copy of *Caves of Ice*. We found we had both written the same dedication, each naming the other as his oldest and dearest friend. Rupert said he is besieged by young thesis and biography writers. I said how clever and well-informed I found them. 'Yes,' he said, 'but bear in mind that they only know about their subject. They have no knowledge of and no interest in anything else. For example, they never remark on the prettiness or ugliness of the house. Never look at or comment on my pictures, which are not uninteresting. They do not read poetry, attend concerts or visit picture galleries. At least the literary ones don't. I'm sure the

---

* Peter George Greenham (1909–92); RA, 1960; Keeper of Royal Academy Schools, 1964–85; m. 1964 Jane Dowling.

architectural ones don't look at gardens or listen to music, and have
never heard of Max Beerbohm or W. H. Hudson.'

Saturday, 28th May

In drizzling rain, greyness and death-like cold I motored to
Hovingham, stopping at Escrick to look at pretty Yorkshire town.
Marcus Worsley not present for luncheon but I was received very
kindly by Lady Worsley. Two sons, a daughter and other charming
people there. They made me feel old and shy. Eldest son William very
attractive, dressed in tight purple corduroy trousers and dark red open-
neck jersey; younger son Giles, budding architectural historian, less
handsome, but gentle, attentive and kind. Took me round the house.
An ungainly pile, but curious with arched Palladian entry to riding
school and some interesting ground floor rooms with stone groined
vaulting. Filled-in colonnades on park side. An amateur's house,
Thomas Worsley's, in 1750. Paintings not in good trim. Marcus
arrived at two and continued the tour. Very kind they all were, yet I
felt not wholly at ease.

Drove on to Chatsworth. The purpose of this visit to read Regy's
letters to Lord Hartington,* all put out for me in the old dining room
on ground floor at north-west angle of house. I worked hard all next
day, and walked in the garden with Debo [Devonshire] and Elizabeth
Winn.† Party consisted of the usual young; Lady Petre, separated wife
of Lord Petre; and Fanny [Partridge]'s friend Stanley Olson,‡ now
writing the life of Sargent and commissioned to write Rebecca
West's – dark, squat, no legs, good-looking face, indulgent, normal,
clever. Also extraordinary American called Tom Vail, who owns and
edits a Cleveland newspaper. After dinner the first night, when the
ladies left the room, he talked about his intimacy with various
Presidents of the United States, press barons such as himself being
regarded by the White House as informers of public opinion. Had
reservations about Kennedy's cleverness. Admired Nixon who had a
genius for negotiation and getting on with foreign heads of state, but

---

* 8th Duke of Devonshire (1833–1903); Liberal (later Liberal Unionist) statesman, whom
Reginald Brett had served as private secretary, 1878–85.
† Interior designer (b. 1925); niece of Nancy Lancaster; social figure and renowned
mimic.
‡ Scholar and aesthete (1947–89); biographer of Elinor Wylie and John Singer Sargent.

was obsessed by money and tended to judge people he met by their
wealth. Asked by Andrew [Devonshire] why Nixon did not destroy
the Watergate tapes, he said because Nixon intended to sell them at
a later stage. Lyndon Johnson a barbaric bear who would steal up
behind him and lift him off his feet. Reagan sends for him at all hours
of the night. I thought Vail a bit of a bounder, but Andrew greatly
impressed and flattering.

Andrew said David Cecil had recovered wonderfully from
Rachel's death. Their marriage was so perfect that her death was
almost a consummation of their mutual bliss. They knew it was
impending. One afternoon they were resting together on the bed,
holding hands. David dozed off. When he woke up, still holding her
hand, she was dead. Andrew also expatiated on his theory that the
most abandoned rogues are venerated if they live to a great age. Gave
as example the late Lord Rosebery (Harry to him), who as a young
man was a crook and involved in some scandal connected with racing
which got him expelled from the Jockey Club. Each decade he was
more respected, finally becoming a Grand Old Man of the turf and
public life.*

Thursday, 2nd June

Eardley, who shared a snack with me in Bath, remarked that politicians' brows become furrowed through constant denunciation of
their opponents, whereas artists have smooth, contented brows. I
thought this theory confirmed in watching Georg Solti† conducting
a Mozart piano concerto on the telly with three violinists and a cellist.
Solti's face was as serene and smooth as those of the young men,
though he must be in his sixties.

Saturday, 4th June

Gervase Jackson-Stops, who is staying the weekend, came with me to
Sudeley Castle [Gloucestershire] and Broadway [Worcestershire]. We

---

* Harry Primrose, 6th Earl of Rosebery (1882–1974); son of 5th Earl (Prime Minister
1894–5); Steward of Jockey Club, 1929–32 and 1945–48; Regional Commissioner for
Scotland, 1941–45; m. 1st 1909 Lady Dorothy Grosvenor, 2nd 1924 Eva, Lady Belper
(d. 1987).
† Sir Georg Solti (1912–97), Hungarian-born conductor.

visited Dorothy de Navarro* at the Court Farm. Garden delicious,
with topiary laid out by Alfred Parsons† and the rolling view to the
Tower on top of the hill. Dorothy older and more bent, but gentle
and sweet. Took us to see Gertrude Caton-Thompson‡ sitting upright
in her little oak-panelled room, aged ninety-five. Very spry, only a
little deaf, dressed immaculately in tweed coat and skirt. Hair silvery
and swept back just like that of Mamie de Navarro in Sargent's splendid drawing of her in the big room. Was overcome by the goodness
of these two old ladies, like china goddesses. Have they ever had an
evil thought in their heads? Had Toty?

Wednesday, 8th June

M. telephones from Madrid that he is returning home tomorrow in
order to vote, which shows a sense of responsibility. Whereas Eardley
is leaving for Paris regardless of the election – typical of him, who has
always been an evader of issues.§

A. saw Evelyn Woolriche today who told her she was reading *Caves*
and asked if I could possibly have a friend left in the world after the
things I wrote about them; or were they all dead? Then this evening
A. and I planned our trip to Scotland in September, and thought it
would be nice to invite ourselves to stay at Tyninghame with the
Haddingtons.¶ Then I remembered that I had written some rather
cheeky things about Lady Binning, who was the mother of Lord
Haddington.‖ We both read them through, and agreed that in the

---

* Dorothy MacKenzie Hoare (1901–87), Fellow of Newnham College, Cambridge,
m. 1940 José Maria 'Toty' de Navarro (1896–1979), archaeologist and Fellow of Trinity
College, Cambridge. They settled at Court Farm, Broadway, Worcestershire, where
J.L.-M. was often entertained by Toty's parents, devout Roman Catholics, after his
conversion to Catholicism in 1934 (see *Deep Romantic Chasm*, 22 and 25 February
1979).
† Victorian water-colourist and pioneer of the Arts and Crafts style in gardens, especially
in the Broadway area (1847–1920).
‡ Former fellow of Newnham College, Cambridge; anthropologist and archaeologist.
§ The Election returned Mrs Thatcher to power with a landslide majority of 144.
¶ George Baillie-Hamilton, 12th Earl of Haddington (1894–1986), of Tyninghame,
Haddingtonshire, son of Brig.-Gen. Lord Binning (d. 1917); m. 1923 Sarah Cook.
‖ J.L.-M. first met Lady Binning (*née* Katharine Salting; d. 1952) in December 1944 and
saw her often during the next three years to discuss her bequest of Fenton House,
Hampstead to the N.T. He depicted her as a rather ridiculous old lady, expressing vio-
lently pro-Nazi views, but agreeably infatuated with himself.

circumstances we could not possibly ask ourselves to stay. At times I am overcome with embarrassment at my foolish and impertinent anecdotes and criticisms. Wish I had never published these bloody diaries. Can't think what came over me.

Tuesday, 14th June

Had an appointment with Pat Trevor-Roper[*] this morning. Took him an offering of three bottles of whisky as he refuses to send me a bill. He gave me a prescription for new spectacle lenses, my left eye now being almost blind. M. lunched, full of Iberian news. Has lost that gazelle, El Greco look. Then to N.T. Properties Committee. Terence Morrison-Scott,[†] who like me reaches retiring age in the autumn, said he would not attend any further meetings. He cannot concentrate on the long memoranda we are given, which mean little unless one visits the properties.

Wednesday, 15th June

Motored Audrey to Bretforton for Harry Ashwin's memorial service in the village church. He died a week ago after being a cabbage in bed for two years.[‡] Was a wraith of his former plump self, and barked at visitors, who had to be kept away. We strolled in the churchyard and looked at Ashwin headstones dated 1680. Were told later that the family has been here since the 1530s, 450 years in direct descent. Harry the last, no children. His niece, Ruth's daughter, inherits, and will sell the estate. That is the end of an ancient line of small Worcestershire squires of little distinction, the house of no great distinction either. Yet sadness envelops me when I cast back my memory nets to their furthest limits. For we children adored the Ashwins, the only friends we had. In the school holidays we saw them most days, either at Bretforton or Wickhamford. Rode over on our ponies, or

---

[*] Opthalmic surgeon (b. 1916); co-tenant with Desmond Shawe-Taylor of Long Crichel, Dorset.

[†] Sir Terence Morrison-Scott (1908–91); Director, Science Museum (1956–60) and Natural History Museum (1960–68); Eton contemporary of J.L.-M.

[‡] J.L.-M's last visit to Harry Ashwin is described in *Deep Romantic Chasm*, 6 January 1980. Bretforton was the Worcestershire estate neighbouring Wickhamford.

drove in the trap, or bicycled, motor-scooted, motor-cycled or motored. In summer played tennis on the lawn before scrumptious teas, in winter hide-and-seek upstairs in the gloomy passages and bed-rooms. My favourite was Clare, tall and plain with a dry sense of humour; she died in 1945 of consumption brought on by war work. Harry always deadly dull, a lump. Mrs Ashwin a dignified, wistful, beautiful, humorous lady of the old school; Mr Ashwin, like a Cavalier in breeches and gaiters, spent all his days in a separate office building on the edge of the shrubbery and stalked into the dining room for meals, graciously acknowledging the presence of us chil-dren. Their enormous limousine was all windows, like a greenhouse, driven by Robbins, the Plymouth Brethren chauffeur who considered it wicked to go to the pantomime. Shall never forget the unique smell of the hall, musty linseed oil on the black panelling mixed with Mansion polish. The empty drawing room where for long hours Thetis thumped on the piano and resented our interruptions. There was Bobbie, the good-looking, flagrantly pansy brother, whose friends were rotters; he died when he fell out of the back of a car in Piccadilly onto his head. Lamented by his adoring mother, whose first passion was her son Jim: he died of appendicitis at school in 1907, and might have continued the line had he lived. Harry a sort of castrato. We walked from the church through the garden, still so well kept up and tidy – the square dovecote, the barn, the old tennis court which echoed to our childish voices of gaiety, to the pealing church bells on Saturday evenings when the bell-pullers practised. The house so stuffy inside and un-beautiful, yet so continuous, so unchanging [a record] of this family, of whose 450 years I witnessed certainly seventy and probably more, for there are photographs of us in our perambulators at Bretforton, Harry an enormous baby in frills and a large linen hat, like an inflated balloon. Today I have seen the veil drawn. It is not only the Kedlestons, the Beltons, the Ugbrookes or the Powderhams which are vanishing, but the humbler manor houses of the small gentry. *Eheu!* I am inured to it all now, and hardly care, for the *dégringolade* has gone too far.

Friday, 17th June

The naked ballet dancer who spent a night in Holloway Prison said after her release, 'I wouldn't recommend it to anyone. They didn't like it when I asked for a napkin.'

Alec Clifton-Taylor and Eardley dined at Brooks's. For once an excellent meal, total bill £40. Alec very affable. Recognition has come to him in old age with his television series on old cities. Said he had realised his three ambitions, which were to get into *Who's Who*, appear on 'Desert Island Discs', and something equally fatuous which I forget. Said that, when asked which he thought to be the best modern building in Britain, he could not name one. Remarked that the retention of the able-seaman's uniform since the eighteenth century was the most sensible thing the navy had done, it having great sex-appeal for women. Not only women, I opine.

Went this morning to Clarence House, open to members of Georgian Group and SPAB,* of which the Queen Mother President. A great treat. Handsome house outside though so often altered since Nash's day. Charming inside, though architecture of rooms disappointing. Decoration acceptable, unexciting, not too pastellish. Lovely contents, all covetable. Royal portraits on walls along with contemporary artists. Good marks for Queen Elizabeth. Eclectic collection – Duncan Grant, Matthew Smith, Gunn, Monet, Augustus John (of Herself, and Bernard Shaw asleep), Ethel Walker, and of course de Laszlo and Seago. Not up-to-date; but why should she be, aged eighty-three? A whole room of John Pipers of Windsor Castle, well-framed. Splendid things. Much silver and gold plate and many bibelots, scattered on occasional tables. Innumerable clocks, French and English of first quality, all going and keeping time. A lady supervising said Yes, we have the clock man in twice a week. Footmen standing in passages and rooms (we were allowed upstairs) in scarlet tails, waistcoats with gold braid, white bow ties, somehow not chic.

Friday, 24th June

Two remarks made to me recently have made me ponder. When walking in the garden at Chatsworth with Debo and E. Winn, I said I could not think of any of our friends who had lived a life of unalloyed happiness. Debo said, 'I can think of one – yours.' I said, 'Yes, I have been very lucky.' Nevertheless, mine is not a happy disposition. I have always felt unfulfilled in love and work. And John Smith, when I met him in the Burlington Arcade, said, 'Do you still work in that

---

* Society for the Protection of Ancient Buildings.

beautiful Bath library, where you manufacture all those lies?' I laughed at the time, but the more I think about his remark, the more offensive I think it was. I wish I had made a retort which showed my displeasure.

Last weekend we had Selina Hastings to stay for two nights, and during this week Emma Tennant,* who accompanied A. on a [N.T.] Garden Panel expedition to Kingston Lacy. Both these girls are near perfection. Both extremely intelligent and attractive and entertaining. Both are approaching forty. I far prefer the company of this age group to my own. Eardley proposed himself for lunch on Wednesday and I was not a bit pleased to see him. People fail to realise that I need to be left alone to write; and when I am eating I am still thinking of what I am writing, and cannot concentrate on other things.

Thursday, 30th June

To London for the day. Met J.K.-B. at the V. & A. for snack luncheon at cafeteria. Good food but expensive. A young man playing sentimental music on a harp. J. very sweet and disarming, told me that if I died he would have no incentive to go on living. We looked at the Oliver Messel† exhibition, mostly of quick sketches for theatrical décor, not enough portraits, which he often did well. Too clichéd, too slick, too Twentyish-sophisticated, but undeniable talent. Standing before one exhibit and telling J. how Tilly Losch stuck pins into Diana Cooper to get her to move, I noticed a young god behind me attentively listening. As we proceeded we constantly ran into the young man, who smiled sweetly. As we parted, J. said, laughing, 'You have made a conquest.' Went to Museum shop and bought a postcard or two. There was the young god again. We both smiled. I said, 'You and I seem to have the same interests today,' and passed on. Then he came up to me and said, 'Excuse me, Sir' – the 'Sir' is upsetting – 'I could not help overhearing your conversation with your friend. Did you know Messel?' I told him I did. He said he was writing a thesis on Gertrude Lawrence and asked if I had known her. Alas, I hadn't. But I took his address, and promised that if any ideas came to me I would write. Tall, slim, wearing clean, tight jeans, pretty open shirt revealing gold chain,

---

* Lady Emma Cavendish (b. 1943), dau. of 11th Duke of Devonshire, m. 1963 Hon. Tobias Tennant, s. of 2nd Baron Glenconner.
† Theatrical producer, designer and artist (1904–78); brother of Anne, Countess of Rosse.

slender throat, fair complexion, head of Dionysus, thick, wavy, flaxen hair.

I was early for tea with Rosamond, so strolled around area near Hereford Square. Saw plaque on house where George Borrow* lived. Passed Bina Gardens, and house inhabited by General Allenby, to Wetherby Gardens, where my old friend Violet Gielgud, John's† aunt, lived, whom I used to visit for tea in the late 1920s when I first lived in London. An affected but kindly lady, who gave me small Everyman editions of *The Cloister and the Hearth*,‡ et cetera. Returned past Ashburnham Gardens, where dear George Chavchavadze§ had a room in his poor bachelor days and would play to me, I being transported both by the music and the romance of his being a Georgian prince. I passed some old people on the pavement and wondered if they too had frequented this backwater of London at the time, perhaps being even younger and handsomer than I. I found Ros very 'up', delighted with the filming of her novel¶ which is being done by a first-class team. Yet complained Selina would never finish her biography before she was dead. I told her one ought to be dead before one's biog. was published.

I dined with M., about to return to Iberian peninsula for a month. He was rather 'down', yet the more affectionate. Said Maître Blum had gone completely off her head, and was threatening to sue *Paris Match* for publishing some disobliging extract about the Duke of Windsor from the fake Hitler diaries.‖ M. remarked how curious it was that people accused others of failings they had themselves. He had seen X, who accused someone of being a fearful snob and toady. Now, these are two things for which dear X is pre-eminent. M. then saw

---

* Writer, traveller and linguist (1803–81).

† Sir John Gielgud, actor (1904–2000), with whom J.L.-M. had a six-week affair in 1931 (as revealed in *Deep Romantic Chasm*, 13 January and 7 March 1981).

‡ Historical romance by C. Reade (1861).

§ Chavchavadze's success as a concert pianist was said to owe more to his romantic looks and origins than his musical talents; he m. the Philadelphia heiress Elizabeth de Breteuil, *née* Ridgeway, who was killed with him in a car crash in the 1950s.

¶ *The Weather in the Streets* (1936).

‖ It had been sensationally announced in April 1983 that Hitler's diaries had been discovered by Gerd Heidemann, a reporter on the German magazine *Stern*. Extracts had begun appearing there and elsewhere, when the West German government, whose scientists had been examining the diaries, declared them to be 'grotesque and superficial forgeries'.

John Lehmann,* who was mightily indignant about the knighthood conferred upon his oldest friend and associate Stephen Spender, whom he accused of being an overrated poet and a crypto-Communist. But then John L. is a jealous and rather rancorous old man.

Monday, 4th July

Victoria Glendinning and her new husband, Terence de Vere White, stay the night. He is a charming man, speaking with perceptible Irish brogue, gentle like warm water bubbling over stones. Extremely clever, with retentive memory. Said that as Literary Editor of the *Irish Times* he had reviewed all my books. This seemed no exaggeration, for he quoted sentences I had written years ago and long forgotten. Victoria very sweet, very clever too. He, the husband, told me that he knew no one who was a more conscientious or professional writer. Weather this weekend perfect, hot in the sun and cool in the shade. The two Whites went for a walk by themselves in Swangrove woods, and came back ecstatic. He told me, as it were in confidence, that this walk had been the second high moment of their married life together, for during it they discussed their religious opinions. My regular attendance at Holy Communion impressed them, but they had decided they were Pantheists.

The previous night A. had taken me to a ghastly party given by a man called Francis Willey† at which were present Princess Antoinette of Monaco‡ and her husband-to-be John Gilpin, retired ballet dancer. She told A. they had loved one another for thirty years and only now were free to marry. At supper A. sat next to Gerald Lascelles§ and I to his wife, ex-model whom I did not much care for, though she has a deep love of animals. A. said that G. Lascelles by no means unintelligent. I looked across at this grandson of George V, very large and spread, with heavy jowls and gross features, not unlike Randolph Churchill became, and very Hanoverian. Am

---

* Author, publisher and critic (1907–87); brother of Rosamond.
† Of Ashlands Court, Tetbury, Gloucestershire.
‡ Sister (b. 1920) of Prince Rainier III of Monaco; she had been twice previously married.
§ Hon. Gerald Lascelles (b. 1924), yr s. of 6th Earl of Harewood and HRH The Princess Royal; m. (2nd) 1978 Elizabeth Collingwood; President of British Racing Drivers Club.

reading at this moment Kenneth Rose's biography of George V, readable and fair. I see why he thought it necessary to pick up threads which Harold had to leave untied [in his *King George V: His Life and Reign* (1952)].

Wednesday, 6th July

Motored to London to dine with John Betj. and Feeble. First of all to Brooks's where a young man called David Paton met me to talk about Robert [Byron]. Better than the last applicant, though has not finished his fourth term at Cambridge. At least he has read every book and article of Robert's. But has not yet seen Robert's sister Lucy, without whose consent and loan of papers it would be useless for him to proceed.* Then to Radnor Walk, arriving at eight. Feeble sweetly welcoming and prepared delicious roast chicken followed by strawberries and cream. John slumped in his armchair watching *Coronation Street* when I arrived, at an angle to the screen, two feet from it. Made signs of recognition. Spoke little. Mouth down at both sides. Difficult to elicit interest or response, yet I think he was fairly pleased to see me. Did not move to the table. Feeble put a board across arms of chair and gave him his helping, tied a bib, gave him a spoon. He toyed with his food like a baby. His trousers loose, not tied to his person by belt or braces. I talked to Feeble at the table. John heard what we said but did not join in beyond a grunt or two. Then his nurse came. 'Do you want to go to bed, darling?' Feeble asked at 8.45. 'Yes, I think so.' The nurse piloted him upstairs. I did not see him again. Talked to Feeble and left at 9.30. She said he was lucky, for he had no pain and was not lonely. Mind clear. Was read to by a young actor every afternoon. Is wheeled to his house each morning where his secretary opens letters and answers them for him. I asked about Bevis Hillier. F. groaned. Said she had not seen him. Did not see how he could write John's biography without mentioning her, yet did not want to be mentioned while she was alive. At least Jock Murray† has promised the book won't come out till John is dead.

---

* Paton was killed in a road accident soon afterwards. Byron's biography was eventually undertaken, with family approval, by James Knox, and is due to be published by John Murray Ltd in 2002.

† John Murray VI (1909–93); head of the publishing firm; Eton contemporary of J.L.-M.

Saturday, 9th July

Dined with Ian McCallum at American Museum to meet Princess Margaret of Hesse.* A delightful old bird, daughter of Lord Geddes and widow of a great-grandson of Queen Victoria. After dinner I sat with her and Robin Warrender. She entertained us by extracting from a wallet several crumpled old bits of paper from which she read apothegms which had tickled her fancy, such as

> With my peas I always eat honey.
> I have done this all through my life.
> I admit that the taste is quite funny,
> But at least the peas stick to the knife

and others of like nature. Then guffaws of laughter, her old teeth wobbling up and down and her head shaking the sparse strands of grey hair. She is very plain, plump, comfortable, genial and good-natured. Told us a long, involved story about a famous Holbein of a Madonna with spread cloak protecting two children, and a pair of donors (Swiss), which came to the Hesse family in the early nineteenth century. Says it is of great beauty and when K. Clark saw it he was moved to tears. At the outbreak of the last war, she and her husband removed it for safety to their castle in Silesia, thinking it would be safe there now the Russians were allies of Germany. They did this at some risk, as the Nazis had ordered all treasures to be kept where they were. Then Silesia was invaded by the Russians. They managed to smuggle picture to Dresden. All the people involved in the smuggle were killed in the Allies' raid, and the lorry carrying it destroyed. Picture remained intact. It returned to the castle in the West where the Hesses were incarcerated, where they kept it hidden under the bed. The castle was turned into a hostel for children. One night the lights failed, and stampeding children trampled over picture. Unharmed. Then Belgian authorities arrived and offered to buy it. The Hesses, deprived of food and every necessity, refused to sell. 'Just think what you could buy with the money we are offering,' said the Belgians. 'I would buy the

---

* Hon. Margaret Geddes (1913–99), dau. of 1st Baron Geddes; m. 1937 Prince Louis of Hesse (1908–68), who became head of the Grand Ducal House of Hesse (Darmstadt) when the aeroplane carrying his elder brother and children to his marriage in London crashed with no survivors.

Madonna,' replied the Prince. She calls it the Miraculous Madonna. She also told us there are to be centenary celebrations at Darmstadt next week in memory of the Tsarina's sister, who has been canonised by the Orthodox Church. She was buried alive for days in a cave. The Princess has just seen letters written by the Tsarina, her husband's aunt, from Ekaterinburg, describing ordeals so terrible that the mind boggles.

Monday, 18th July

Last week I went on two-day [N.T.] Arts Panel tour to Devon, visiting Knightshayes, Castle Drogo and Killerton. John Julius [Norwich] being away, I was chairman. The first house Victorian, second Edwardian, third Georgian and modern. I was looked after like a delicate parcel that might, unless cherished, come undone. The niceness of these N.T. boys is touching. And they are far cleverer than we lot were. The heat intense, ninety degrees. Stayed in Moretonhampstead Hotel in room like a furnace. Felt shy meeting the Aclands,* for I said some disobliging things about them in *Caves*.† Lady Acland said to me, 'I read *Ancestral Voices* and was rather relieved there was no mention of us.' This woman, whom I remember as aggressive and dogmatic, now charming.

Dined with Selina [Hastings] in London on Friday, only reaching her house at 9.45, worn out, as train late leaving Exeter. Selina sweet and not minding, giving me an excellent dinner to catch up on the others. A. brought dear Tony Scotland‡ who was at the Berkeleys'. The others Patrick Woodcock,§ who motored us all home after mid-

---

* Sir Richard Acland, 15th Bt (1906–90); radical campaigner, at various times MP for Liberal, Common Wealth and Labour Parties; m. 1936 Stella Alford; donated 19,000 ancestral acres in Devon and Somerset to N.T., 1944, including his houses at Killerton near Exeter and Holnicote near Porlock, on condition that stag hunting should be allowed to continue on the land.

† Of a visit which, accompanied by the Harold Nicolsons, he made to the Aclands at Killerton, J.L.-M. wrote on 9 August 1947: 'We all disliked this property, the garden, the ugly shrubs, the ménage, the dogmatic owners, and two plain little boys . . . In the house is established the Workers' Transport Company, people smelling of disinfectant . . . We saw no point in this property which is no more beautiful than the surrounding country.'

‡ Author, broadcaster and journalist (b. 1945); on staff of BBC Radio, 1970–91.

§ London GP and friend of the famous.

night, and Elizabeth Jane Howard,* who expects to be invited to bio-
graphise the Queen Mother. I could not remember who this
matronly and handsome woman was, until she reminded me I had
been an usher at her wedding to P. Scott. Maddening not to have
known.

Selina said that Diana Mosley was asked to lunch with Frank
Longford† in the House of Lords. She was ushered into a small
waiting-room. No Longford to greet her. Then in came a little,
down-at-heel, shoddy, shuffling man. Diana looked closely and said
in her gentle voice, 'Bryan!'‡ He gave a start, and said, 'Which one are
you?' He said to Selina later, 'Do you know, that was the first time I
have met Diana in fifty years that I have not wept.'

Tuesday, 19th July

Lunched deliciously with Francis Crowdy§ in his flat. He wants to
make a programme for the World Service about some N.T. properties. We settled which these were to be. He wants me to be one of the
speakers.

Attended what should have been my last Properties Committee,
but I have been asked to attend the October one at Marcus Worsley's
personal request. Am dreadfully afraid they may give me a present or
make a speech of appreciation. I shall not miss these meetings. They
give me no pleasure and I contribute little. Nowadays they consist
of discussing long, dreary reports, and seldom consider historic
houses.

Friday, 22nd July

A. and I motor to Chatsworth for weekend. It might have been one
of those house parties in a Disraeli novel: Andrew and Debo; Lady
Arran (Boofy's widow); Lady Margaret Tennant (called 'Maggots',

---

* Novelist and playwright (b. 1923); m. 1st 1942 Peter Scott, 3rd 1965 (as his 2nd wife)
Kingsley Amis.
† Francis Pakenham, 7th Earl of Longford (b. 1905); Labour Party politician, publisher
and humanitarian campaigner; m. 1931 Elizabeth Harman, writer.
‡ Diana Mosley's 1st husband Hon. Bryan Guinness (1905–92), whom she married aged
18 in 1928 and from whom she obtained a divorce, 1934; he s. his father as 2nd Baron
Moyne, 1944.
§ BBC World Service arts programme producer.

sister of Lord Airlie and Jean Lloyd); Kitty Mersey;* Heywood and
Anne Hill. To whom were added on Saturday St John Stevas (whom
I call Norman),† and Lord and Lady Gowrie.‡ The last is Minister for
the Arts and not well-equipped for the job, for he seems to know little
about music or painting. St John Stevas [his predecessor as Arts
Minister] was very bitchy about him before he arrived. In fact St J. S.
is a second-rate fellow, very pleased with himself, tactless, and as Anne
said, 'no oil painting'. He talks big, shoots a line. Rather bedint. Yet
friendly enough. Too much 'darling Debo' and name-dropping.
Loathes Mrs Thatcher and spoke with utmost contempt of Gowrie
for reducing spending on the arts, especially the Theatre Museum,
whereas the man was only following orders. Oh, one other guest was
Walter Lees.§ He and I walked round the pleasure grounds and talked
of M. and Charles Orwin, he besotted with the latter. Wonderful food
here. The Devonshires' French chef, who left for America where he
was offered enormous wages, has returned, saying no one appreciated
his cooking there and he preferred to be where he was appreciated.

Tuesday, 26th July

To London for the day. Took proofs of *Stuarts* to Chatto's, and spent
most of the day transferring two sets of proof corrections to my copy.
Unless they are Rupert [Hart-Davis], others do not correct properly.
The professional employed was hopeless. Fetched Joan Drogheda at
Albany and took her to lunch at Fortnum's. Felt very sad, for her mind
is far worse than at Christmas. She does not remember persons, places,
books or things. And she used to be so bright and clever. She said that

---

* Lady Katherine Petty-Fitzmaurice (1912–95), dau. of 6th Marquess of Lansdowne; m.
1933 Hon. Edward Bigham, later 3rd Viscount Mersey (d. 1979); succeeded brother to
Barony of Nairne, 1944.
† Norman St John-Stevas (b. 1929); Conservative politician, MP for Chelmsford,
1964–87; Leader of House of Commons, Chancellor of Duchy of Lancaster, and Minister
for the Arts, 1979–81; cr. life peer as Lord St John of Fawsley, 1987; Master, Emmanuel
College, Cambridge, from 1991.
‡ Alexander Hore-Ruthven, 2nd Earl of Gowrie (b. 1939); Minister for the Arts,
1983–5; Chairman of Sotheby's, 1985–93; m. (2nd) 1974 Adelheid, Gräfin von der
Schulenburg.
§ Major Walter Lees; sometime Head of Household at British Embassy in Paris; friend
of Duke and Duchess of Windsor; then personal assistant to French oil tycoon Pierre
Schlumberger.

when she is with Garrett, for fear of appearing foolish, she becomes even more forgetful than when she is on her own. I refrained from remarking that when on her own she has no need to remember anything. To dear Charlotte[Bonham-Carter]'s ninetieth birthday party at the Royal Academy. Heat so appalling that I broke into a sweat and bolted after ten minutes. I have never known such heat. Anyway, I made my *frais* with Charlotte and we have contributed an appreciation to her book as we were asked to do. Apparently so many did so that two books had to be bound to contain them all.

Sunday, 31st July

The Aids scare is alarming everyone. Last week an article in *The Times* described the symptoms six months after contraction – lethargy, temperature, then swelling of gland nodules, whatever they may be. Then a year's recovery when the patient believes all is well. Then recurrence of temperature, etc., and, from whatever complaint thereafter contracted, certain death, owing to immunity to all drugs and treatment. Terror reigns in the minds of all homosexuals.

Wednesday, 3rd August

Talked to 'Johnny' Faucigny-Lucinge* last night after dinner with Caroline [Somerset], who had trouble getting his name right in introducing him. He has taken the place of Charles de Noailles in that he stays annually at Sandringham with the Queen Mother and pilots her around France each summer. Told me the difficulty was finding suitable hosts who were rich enough and possessed large houses with rooms enough and servants enough to accommodate her retinue, consisting of himself, Lady Fermoy, the Graftons, two maids, two valets, two detectives. He had just come from Sandringham and said the Q.M. is the only member of the Royal Family one could call cultivated. She has humour, and is never overtly critical. Interested, reads her prep. before making visits. He was vastly amused by a little scene in the park. A lot of local old ladies were displaying their pet rabbits. One old lady, very eccentric and untidy, had an awful exhibit, an ancient, bald rabbit like a melon which she adorned with ribbons and

---

* Prince Jean-Louis de Faucingny-Lucinge (1904–92).

furbelows. The other old ladies did their utmost to shield this spectacle from the Queen. But the Q. made straight for her, talked to her only and stroked the animal. When urged by Fortune Grafton to walk on to some other stall she lingered, turning her head towards the proud owner as though most loth to leave. All the other respectable old lady competitors furious, of course. This an example of her compelling charm, he says.

At dinner, Caroline's mother brought a neighbour from Castle Combe, called Briggs.* Was a publisher, is now a writer, living in a cottage. Seemed like the don in *Brideshead Revisited*,† a smooth, pedantic, academic queen. How awful, I thought. But in talking to him I discovered how extremely intelligent and sympathetic he was. I was delighted when he said that he considered my *Harold* one of the best biographies of the twentieth century. Why on earth, I asked? Because you bring the character to life. Well, all I can say is that my doing so was a pure fluke.

Saturday, 6th August

In what does the perennial melancholy of August consist? The sniff of autumn; the lengthening sunbeams; the tiredness of grasses; the persistence of convolvulus in hedgerows; the disappearance from verges of blue geranium; few flowers, yet colour in the garden; bees bustling to accumulate whatever it is that they do accumulate before it is too late; and above all the quiet. This is the only windless month. Mornings and evenings are still. There is an echo in the firmament, for earth and sky become close, like the inside of a glass bell. And my birthday,‡ now recording the winter rather than the autumn of my life. It is mentioned in *The Times* now, a sign of mortality. Strangers send me birthday cards; bores pester me with sentimental, gushing letters. But I feel old; always tired; and for the past six weeks have suffered from arthritis in thumb joints and right shoulder. Shall I be alive next year? Or the next? Does it matter? One is aware of one's utter insignificance.

---

* Desmond Briggs (b. 1931); former partner of Blond & Briggs, publishers; novelist (as Rosamond Fitzroy); a JP for Wiltshire.
† Evelyn Waugh's smug and toadying Mr Samgrass was an obvious parody of Maurice Bowra of Wadham, whom J.L.-M. disliked.
‡ He was seventy-five that day.

Darling A., ever more precious to me with the passing years, gave a dinner party, having first asked Midi, whom I see too seldom, to stay the night. Party consisted of Audrey, Henry [Robinson] and his girl Susie, Bob Parsons. Not very exciting.

Sunday, 7th August

Motored to London, taking Midi with me. After lunching with M. at his flat, and leaving my car on Embankment, I joined an odd expedition. Had always wanted to see Field Place near Horsham where Shelley was born. Once tried and was repulsed by the then owner, Charrington. So I joined organised visit of Keats–Shelley Society, which set out from Embankment station in a bus. Party consisted of egregiously unattractive individuals of the arty-intellectual, raffia-hat and sandals variety. Didn't know a soul. Sat next to GP from Gloucester wearing a radiant chestnut wig. Bus arrived at Field Place at 3.45. We could have seen the house in half an hour, but were obliged to wait for hours. It is empty now, having been bought by a solicitor. Squire's house set in fields rather than park with lake at bottom. Main part late seventeenth-century. An 1840s colonnade connecting the two wings, which Shelley never knew, covers the spot where he sat on his last visit, denied entry by his father Timothy. Of Shelley's time a fine staircase, in well of which the Charringtons constructed a lift, destroying part of the balustrade. This staircase a good example of college-like joinery with thick handrail and stout turned balusters. The owner told me that the bailiff employed by Charrington remembered a quantity of papers fetched from attics, some of it in Shelley's handwriting, being carted away to put on bonfire. We stayed on for a ghastly entertainment, a concert by amateurs, Dowland on harpsichord, bearable, and endless recitations by an affected woman dressed like a Druid, agony. We were due to leave at eight but I persuaded two old ladies to take me to Horsham and drop me at the station. Finally after much delay reached Embankment at ten to see our bus drive off, having returned the rest of the party some time earlier.

Tuesday, 9th August

Am at Eton, having arrived on Monday morning for a week. Renting a guest flat in Hodgson's House opposite Upper Chapel graveyard.

Adequate, but uglily done up. Have now spent three days working in Royal Library at Windsor Castle, reading through Regy's letters to King Edward VII (mostly to Knollys,* the Secretary). Today I was informed that Sir Robin Mackworth-Young would see me at 12.40. Like being summoned to headmaster's study. Sir R., smaller than I remembered, sat at large writing-table with back to window, scanning me. I am always at my worst on these occasions and talk too much. I began talking of the Droghedas, assuming he would remember meeting us with them, but he evidently didn't. I said how splendid I found the Sovereigns' Private Secretaries to have been. He said that George III was not allowed to have one, for his ministers were supposed to be his Secretaries; so when he wrote a letter he copied it for filing in his own hand. George IV did have one, for he was lazy. Queen Victoria did not have one before and during her marriage. It was only after the Prince Consort's death that she engaged Grey. Mackworth-Young told me it would be appreciated if I gave a copy of my *Stuarts* to the Queen, inscribing it suitably and sending it to her Secretary. He said that, if she was interested – and she *was* interested in the Stuarts – she might read it herself before sending it to the Library at Windsor. Must remember to do this.

Yesterday evening I walked upstream, looking for Queen's Eyot where I used to tipple on cider on hot summer afternoons with Desmond [Parsons].† Couldn't find it. Wandered through Arches, a rather fine serpentine stretch carrying the railway, where I had unromantic trysts, with Tulloch *inter alia*. Still the river preserves its sinuous course – they can't take that away – and still it is bordered with willows, shimmering. Couldn't find Athens where we bathed. Now the bank crawling with trippers, much litter and noise. A train or two crossed Arches, an old-fashioned enough rumble as though a concession from the past to the present age. Not so the roar of the motorway, with tall lamps. Nor the aeroplanes, descending every two minutes for Heathrow. Sir Robin said the interval is sometimes only ninety seconds. Wonder how on earth the experts manage to control the entry. Judy's Passage unchanged, but the boys' houses are for the most part excessively ugly, untidy and scruffy, nothing to boast about for the world's most exclusive school.

---

* Francis, 1st Baron Knollys (1837–1924); Private Secretary to Edward VII as Prince of Wales and King, 1870–1910.
† Hon. Desmond Parsons (1910–37), brother of 6th Earl of Rosse.

Ghosts at every turn. Tom [Mitford]* emerging from Dobbs's, perhaps the prettiest of the boys' houses; Desmond skulking down the narrow passage entry (now removed) to m'tutor's; Rupert [Hart-Davis] with his ram's head; Hamish [St Clair Erskine]† and David Herbert; old Harry Ashwin at Brinton's; Teddie Underdown, so beautiful and the women's undoing, though Pop bitch in his day.‡ Yet it is all devoid of sentiment somehow. Too far removed in years. My schooldays in the 1920s were closer in time to my grandfather's in the 1860s than to today.

Thursday, 11th August

There is still a bookshop where Mrs Brown's bookshop once stood, but what a declension! Nothing I wanted, and seemed shrunken somehow. It was here that I bought a lovely nineteenth-century illustrated book of coloured prints of naked savages, ladies with full breasts and red scarves round their heads, gentlemen with spears. McNeile my tutor found it in my room, took it away and burnt it, informing my father of my unhealthy tastes. I have ever since regretted that book. What would Heywood Hill charge for it now? Mrs Brown looked like Queen Mary – utmost dignity, ramrod straight, busted, waisted, long skirt, grey hair in piles like a toy fortress, bland smile, gentle, yet one could not take liberties with her. Dear lady, where does she rest?

Saturday, 20th August

I have seen all Regy's letters to Kings Edward and George and their admirable Secretaries Knollys and Stamfordham, taking massive notes. Was taken to see the room which Esher is thought to have occupied; but it faces the North Terrace and Eton, not the Long Walk, as he described in his journal for 1901. The kindness, patience and help of Miss Langton and the other good ladies of the Royal Archives is beyond the conventional words of praise expressed in the

---

* Hon. Thomas Mitford (1909–45), only brother of the Mitford sisters.
† Hon. Hamish St Clair-Erskine, MC (1909–74), yr s. of 5th Earl of Rosslyn.
‡ An allusion to the era when the prettiest boy in the school was traditionally 'available' to the members of the Eton Society or 'Pop' – the privileged, self-electing club of senior boys, clad in fancy waistcoats, who act as school prefects.

introductions of books. We had coffee each morning, and discreet gossip about long-defunct royalties. I had two visitors, M. and J., on separate evenings, and walked with them around the playing fields and along the river. Both adorable and affectionate.

I went one evening to Cumberland Lodge in Windsor Great Park, escorted round by charming female colleague of Lord Vaizey.* She pumped me as to what the rooms were used for and looked like when I frequented the house more than forty years ago.† House very ugly outside and in, but the present incumbents care for it well and have decorated and furnished it in an unexceptionable manner. From there to dine with Garrett and Joan. G. made us look at television through-out dinner. Joan looking pretty, occasionally throwing an amused look when G's back turned, understanding little, memory worse than ever.

On my return to Badminton, I received polite letter from Sir Martin Gilliat‡ informing me that Queen Mother had no recollec-tions of Regy beyond remembering that he was always 'about', his advice being sought on all kinds of questions, particularly the 'art' ones. Also found A. in state of great excitement because Caroline had telephoned one morning at 10.30 saying she was bringing the Prince of Wales to see the garden. The Prince was charming and took a lively interest, being keen to improve his own garden at Highgrove. He asked where the whippets were. 'They are shut up, Sir, because I didn't want them to give you a nip.' 'I dare say they would prefer to give a nip to a fox, wouldn't they?' he retorted. So that old story has reached him.§ Then to her amazement she received a delightful letter of thanks from him in his own hand, referring to her 'magical' garden, and asking her for the names of old-fashioned roses. And 'When you write to me, put "To Himself" on the envelope.' For good manners he earns full marks.

---

* John Vaizey (1929–84); economist, cr. life peer, 1976; Principal of Foundation of St Catherine, Cumberland Lodge, 1982–4.

† In the 1930s and early 1940s, as he describes in his memoirs and diaries, J.L.-M. fre-quently visited Cumberland Lodge as the guest of the saintly retired Catholic statesman Lord FitzAlan (1855–1947).

‡ Lieut.-Col. Sir Martin Gilliat (1913–93); Private Secretary to HM Queen Elizabeth The Queen Mother, 1956–93.

§ On 21 May 1979 (as recorded in *Deep Romantic Chasm*), a stormy confrontation had taken place between the L.-Ms and the Duke of Beaufort after their dogs had chased a vixen.

Tuesday, 23rd August

On Saturday, A. and I dined at Nether Lypiatt with the Michaels of Kent. Can't make out why we were asked, having only met them once at the Hollands' annual concert four years ago.* I reluctant to accept; A. determined. So she put on her finery, necklaces and diamond earrings, I my dreary black tie. Bidden for eight, we thought for royalty we should be on time. We were, precisely, and the first guests, except for a couple staying in the house. Climbed the outside steps into the little hall. Greeted by nice lady in semi-maid's uniform. Made to sign gigantic visitors' book with thick nib in our most flowing Edwardian style. Old-fashioned family butler ushered us into long drawing-room. The Prince gave a kindly welcome. Dressed in white dinner jacket, with trim beard, the very image of his grandfather George V, he is a poor but very gentle and courteous little mouse. Other couple the Jonathan Aitkens,† he a Tory MP, very go-ahead, very clever, she Yugoslav-born, Swiss-bred, dull. 'Made' conversation over sherry and smoked oysters. With a rush as of Pentecostal wind, *She* appeared, like a gigantic Peter Pan fairy alighting on the stage at the end of a wire, large, handsome, Valkyrian, blonde hair over shoulders in straight Alice in Wonderland rays. Effusive, friendly, charming. Wearing white, spotted dress, *décolletée*, no jewelry at all. Then in came Micky Suffolk,‡ whom I did not recognise at first, along with female whom I took to be reigning wife. Not so; was Lady Bridport. I was introduced as author of 'Ancestral Prophecies'. Of course he had read it? Hadn't. Instead he cried out, 'You are the man to whom I owe the solution of my house, Charlton! I am eternally grateful.' The truth is that I did see him about this years ago, but don't believe I did anything. But did not disabuse him. Then later still the Duke and Duchess of Marlborough,§ he tall, handsome, pleased with himself, stuck-up. Very *gratin*, jet-settish.

---

* See *Deep Romantic Chasm*, 8 July 1979.

† Businessman and politician (b. 1942), grandson of 1st Baron Beaverbrook; MP (C) Thanet (1974–97); Chief Secretary to the Treasury, 1994–5, resigning to defend himself against allegations of impropriety; imprisoned on charges of perjury, 1998; m. 1979 Lolicia Azucki.

‡ Michael Howard, 21st Earl of Suffolk and 14th Earl of Berkshire (b. 1935); m. (3rd) 1983 Linda, *née* Paravicini, formerly wife of 4th Viscount Bridport.

§ John Spencer-Churchill, 11th Duke of Marlborough (b. 1926); m. (3rd) 1972 Rosita Douglas.

Much whispering between hostess and butler at door, she returning to say, 'It looks as though we shan't get anything to eat.' Finally, about 9.30, we went into dining room. We were ten. A. and I and the Aitkens, being 'rank-less', were put together in the middle, the Duke and Earl and their females on either side of Their Royal Highnesses. So odd this protocol business, nothing to do with distinction or age. I couldn't hear a word either of my women said. Struggled also to bite my way across a piece of beef swathed in grey sauce. Room too hot. This room undeniably pretty, white walls and lovely Dresden plates hanging in each panel, but spoiled by little search-lights put in ceiling. In fact this house is beautifully decorated, but like a town house in Mayfair. No longer the dark, brown oak little squire's gem it was when Violet Woodhouse* lived here.

When women left the room, conversation instantly turned to smut by Micky Suffolk, an attractive, jolly rascal. (I always maintain when questioned by women that men on these occasions talk politics and finance.) He had been at a slimming centre, starved and allowed only prunes to nibble. Said the treatment made him randier than he had ever felt in his life. Talked of a horse in his care – is he a trainer? – of incalculable value, millions. Belonged to the Queen or Aga Khan. He thought it had a cold and called in a vet. Vet produced a long thermometer like a parasol, pushed it up the mare's behind. They stood beside mare and talked. After talking looked down, mare still standing, but thermometer completely disappeared. Looked anxiously on ground. Not there. Horrors. Sent for a plumber with a pair of surgical gloves. Terrified lest glass thermometer had broken. Plumber by hideous operation fished the thing out and mare none the worse.

When we rejoined ladies in drawing room, Princess took me by the arm and hand and led me into a corner. Most intimate and cosy. Is flirtatious. I tried not to press her hand back, lest *lèse-majesté*. She told me how these last few years have taught her never to believe anything

---

* On 30 March 1944 J.L.-M. wrote (*Prophesying Peace*) that he 'drove without a break to Nether Lypiatt Manor, near Stroud, to lunch at this wonderful little house with Mrs Gordon Woodhouse . . . It is unspoilt late seventeenth century, and perfect in every way. In fact an ideal, if not *the* ideal small country house.' On 13 August 1947 he wrote (*Caves of Ice*): 'I think this is . . . the most covetable house in England. It combines the classical with the picturesque.' When the house came on the market in the late 1950s, the L.-Ms considered buying it, but were unable to afford it.

in the newspapers. Only one-ninth of press reports are accurate. Told me her mother was in prison when pregnant with her, just before end of war. Was released for birth of child. I said, 'Oh Ma'am, but how romantic it would have been for you to be born in prison.' Remark not favourably received. Her father was her mother's second husband, who died at ninety. She did not care for him. Was very saddened by the death of her favourite brown Persian cat. Knocked over by a car on road, it tried to walk home but died *en route*. She said with tears in her eyes that this cat's death meant more to her than the deaths of most of her friends and relations. She is writing life of Queen of Bohemia, but said she had too little time, and must resort to an assistant. At this I trembled, but said nothing. Said that hunting gave her most pleasure. Loved the danger. 'If your life consisted for the most part of cutting blue ribbons, wouldn't you want a change of some adventurous sort?' I asked if she had read Kenneth [Rose]'s *George V*. She is half-way through, and said what a *ghastly* man he was. I said he had his points. No, she said, stamp collecting and killing quantities of birds did not redeem him. I pointed out his kindness to Ramsay MacDonald. She shook her head. Said that when she had tiffs with her husband she would tell him he was no better than his grandfather.

It is impossible not to like this un-royal princess, with her beauty, vitality and friendliness. On parting she said how much she hoped to meet us again.

Saturday, 27th August

We lunched with Derry and Alexandra [Moore], and her parents the Nico Hendersons,[*] at Combe, a hamlet near Hungerford. A happy family. They share a converted schoolhouse in this tiny hamlet. The Hendersons have their own buildings, and the Moores a third, detached. We ate at a large round table on lawn, inlaid with mosaics by Vulliamy, a pupil of Boris Anrep.[†] The Moores' new baby, Benjamin, tumbling over the grass. A dear little boy aged six months. Henderson an easy man, very clever; Derry says a great enjoyer. She a bit whimsy, but gentle and attractive. While A. and Derry discussed

---

[*] Sir Nicholas Henderson, diplomatist (b. 1919); Ambassador to France (1975–9), to USA (1979–82); m. 1951 Mary Barber.
[†] Russian mosaicist (1883–1969), some of whose finest work may be seen at Westminster Cathedral and the National Gallery.

their [proposed] book,* Alexandra and I walked with the dogs to the
Manor. This is the house in which Rick Stewart-Jones† lived at the
end of his life, and adored. Then it was in desolate repair. But romantic, ghostly, remote. Indeed Combe is miles from anywhere in marvellous country, Downs all round. We could not enter house because
owners away. It is now in good order but not smartened up. Rick
would be pleased. We went into his little gazebo, dated 1666 on the
brick front. I thought of him, in this little room where he retired to
work. Today it smelt of cats. His spirit was about. Entered the church.
Some lovely handsome classical tombstones in churchyard. No
memorial to Rick, but then he did not live here long enough and was
but a tenant.

Sunday, 4th September

Poor Alex Moulton has had all his silver stolen. I telephoned to
condole. 'Yes,' he said, 'all my cutlery has been taken.' 'What! All your
cruets and serviette rings?' 'Yes, all,' he said.

Yesterday we lunched with Mary Dunn.‡ Fanny Partridge and
Francis Watson§ staying. Mary has a whimsical, penetrating, sharp
face, deep depths, no malice, affection, yet devil-may-care. Fanny
always disarming, with her sympathy, modesty, joyous nature, readi-
ness to discuss every subject. Francis not seen for years. Not much
changed. A bit queenly. Too pleased with himself, too jaunty, but spry
and entertaining. Kept referring to 'my two sons'. I said, 'One is
Chinese, isn't he?' 'Yes, adopted, and he can't make out which is the
more inferior race, the black or the white.'

Then we drove to tea with the Osbert Lancasters. Agreeably surprised, for Osbert not so bad as I had been led to believe. Rather deaf,
but if one talks loud and clear, he understands. Said he was only interested in the past and wanted to know whom I had lately seen.
Criticised John Betj. for 'laziness', saying that he enjoyed being

---

* See entry for 5 November 1983.
† Richard Stewart-Jones (1914–57), architectural conservationist; close friend of J.L.-M.,
who met him in 1938 and devoted a chapter of *Fourteen Friends* to him.
‡ Lady Mary St Clair-Erskine (b. 1912), dau. of 5th Earl of Rosslyn and brother of J.L.-
M's Eton friend Hamish; m. 1933–44 Philip Dunn (m. diss.).
§ Sir Francis Watson (b. 1907); Director, Wallace Collection, 1963–74 (Deputy Director,
1938–63); Surveyor of The Queen's Works of Art, 1963–72 (Deputy Surveyor, 1947–63).

waited on. I contradicted that assumption. Also spoke disparagingly
of K. Clark, saying he wrote books which were competent but not
memorable. I disagreed with this opinion. Talked of Randolph,
saying he was a shit like all Churchills – Duke John, Duke Sonnie,
Duke Bertie, present Duke, Lord Randolph, and present Young
Winston. Poor Anne has a terrible time, for Osbert can do nothing
for himself, not even dress. Sits asking for things, and smokes end-
lessly. But looks no older than he did when we were at Oxford. Said
he was persecuted by young people who came up to him in the street
and thrust their drawings into his unwilling hands, asking for his
opinion.

Tuesday, 8th September

Rather sad that John Gilpin has died suddenly, of heart. We met him
only in July before he married his Princess, and they came over to see
our garden. He was slight, neat and pretty, though over fifty. Must
have been as elegant as Dresden porcelain in his heyday, when indeed
I saw him dance.

Sunday, 25th September

A. and I returned last night from twelve days in Scotland. Motored
comfortably in her car from Edinburgh. At Halliburton,* my neighbour at dinner, Lady Somebody Napier,† told me that her father, the
late Lord Mansfield, who hated the English, declared that the niggers
began at Carlisle. When I asked Joan Lindsay who these Napiers
were, was shocked to learn that my cousin Joe Napier‡ is dead. Must
have happened when we were in South Africa. Must write letter of
apology and condolence to poor Isabel. Lunching at Rossie Priory
with the Kinnairds,§ I was shown a bust by Graham K. which I
instantly recognised as the Bartolini of Byron. Must have come to

---

* House in Perthshire formerly belonging to A.L.-M's mother's family, the Menzies; now
to Joan Lindsay.
† Lady Mariota Murray (b. 1945), dau. of 7th Earl of Mansfield and Mansfield (d. 1971),
m. 1969 Hon. Malcolm Napier, son of 13th Baron Napier.
‡ In fact Sir Joseph Napier, 4th Bt (b. 1895; m. 1931 Isabelle Surtees, cousin of J.L.-M.),
did not die until 1986.
§ Graham Kinnaird, 13th Lord Kinnaird (1912–97); m. (2nd) 1940, Diana Copeman.

him through Douglas K., Byron's friend and banker. Wonder whether it is the original version. Must find out from J.K.-B. Was shocked when Elizabeth Sutherland* at Tongue announced casually that she has sold a bust of Barry from Dunrobin Castle to a strange man who asked for it and offered £200. A. and I drove in the afternoon of a stormy day to Loch Erribol on the way to Cape Wrath. Cruel, deep purple, almost black curtains of rain and gold shafts of sunlight. This the most remote, unpopulated region of the British Isles, and immensely impressive. From Lairg to Tongue we seldom passed a but and ben. Wild tracts of country for miles, sort of lush, watered desert land. There are endless rainbows hereabouts, sometimes double, the ends quite close, within yards rather than miles from the spectator.

We stayed in several hotels. Very expensive, bills for the two of us, with breakfast and dinner, rarely coming to less than £70 a night. Edinburgh is one of the finest cities in Europe, with a character all its own. Only I missed the peculiar smell it had formerly, mixture of North Sea and railway engine smoke. The New Town is marvellous, those long Georgian crescents, circus and rows. Saw the house where I once stayed with dear Lady Kinross and Patrick,† where Stevenson formerly lived. Then there are some noble nineteenth-century buildings. A few ghastly contemps, including the King James Hotel, which is a scandal; and concrete lamp-posts galore. I spent a day and a half in the National Library reading Regy's letters to Rosebery, Haldane and Elibank – none very interesting – and a day at Dunrobin reading Millie Sutherland's‡ letters to Regy. At Halliburton, the portraits of A's grandfather and grandmother are by Rudolph Lehmann, who I think was Ros's grandfather. Strange and sad, seeing that A. refuses to relent and make it up with Ros. Elizabeth Sutherland a most sympathetic and intelligent woman.

---

* Countess of Sutherland, 24th in line (b. 1921), niece of 5th Duke of Sutherland and s. 1963 to his Earldom of Sutherland and Lordship of Strathnaver; kinswoman of A.L.-M's 1st husband, 3rd Viscount Chaplin.
† Patrick Balfour, 3rd Baron Kinross (1904–76), author and journalist; m. 1938 (as her 2nd husband, her first having been J.L.-M's friend John Churchill) Angela Culme-Seymour (m. diss., 1942); the subject of another essay in *Fourteen Friends*; his mother, 'dear Lady Kinross', was Caroline Johnstone-Douglas, a family connection of the Marquess of Queensberry.
‡ Lady Millicent St Clair-Erskine, dau. of 4th Earl of Rosslyn, m. 1884 the Marquess of Stafford, later 4th Duke of Sutherland.

Am always astonished at our whippets blackberrying. They nip the berries off the branches without ever getting prickles in their mouths and noses. If we hand them a blackberry they will not touch it.

Saturday, 1st October

Came back from Scotland to find a plague of daddy-long-legs. I took great pains to catch the first encountered, open the window and let it out. Then found the outside of doors and windows covered with them. Others in the sinks, which I had to swirl down the plug. Thus does one become indifferent and callous to the suffering of living creatures *en masse*. One's compassion is not inexhaustible, nor can it survive fragmentation.

Selina [Hastings] came to stay for two nights with her mother Margaret Lane, Lady Huntingdon, who was giving a lecture in Bath. Lady H. is seventy-six and still extremely pretty. There is something faintly bedint about her pronunciation of 'ows' for a woman of her generation, but her appearance and manner are *bien*. I liked her immensely. She was extremely funny. Told us that her husband (still alive) married his first wife, Cristina Casati, in face of great opposition from his parents, for she was a foreigner, a Communist and a Catholic.* The couple decided to make their married life in Australia and his mother, Australian by birth, gave him a large pile of letters addressed to friends there. On opening some of the letters, Jack Hastings discovered that they asked the addressees on no account to give any help or employment to him or his wife, so he pitched them all out of his port-hole. Lady H. was once invited by Vita to Sissinghurst. When she got there, V. seemed very abstracted, and while walking in the garden fell into a bed of roses. Gardeners appeared and carried her away. Lady H. expressed concern, but the gardeners assured her that this quite often happened. It did not occur to Lady H. that V. might have been drunk. She assumed it was heart trouble, and left.

I have just finished Victoria Glendinning's biography of Vita. It cannot be faulted. A. and I feature rather too much towards the end.†

---

* Cristina, dau. of the Marchese Casati; m. 1st Viscount Hastings 1925–43 (m. diss.), 2nd Hon. Wogan Philipps (later 2nd Baron Milford, who had m. 1st, 1928, Rosamond Lehmann); she d. 1953.
† See entry for 18 November 1982.

Tuesday, 11th October

Motored A. to Heathrow, she off to France to attend to Jagger's garden. Then to Eton (a quarter of an hour away) to look up names and careers of Regy's contemporaries. Strong, the archivist, friendly but a desiccated, academic bore. Not a very fruitful visit. Was shown Diana Berry's* room next to the Provost's secretary, Diana being commissioned to start an Eton Museum under the College Hall. Continued to London, dreading my last meeting of N.T. Properties Committee at which I feared I would be given a present and would have to respond suitably. But arrived at N.T. offices to discover I had got the date wrong and the meeting was next week. Tea with poor Eardley, suffering painfully from shingles. Ros dined with me at Brooks's. Ordered the most expensive item on menu, duck, which she could not finish. She is still distressed by her difference with A. I did my best and think she may write a letter to A. suggesting they meet and discuss this tiresome business.

Thursday, 13th October

Called on Diana Cooper† this morning, as I was staying with the Berkeleys next door. Was kept waiting while she prepared herself. Finally called upstairs. Diana lying propped up in large bed with everything within reach, doggie on sheets, telephone, books, pencils, paper, cigarettes. Wearing lace cap on back of head. Face white and strained, yet eyes as beautiful as ever, and bosom exposed, broadness thereof beautiful. Rather vague and deaf. Instantly began discussing words which are now out of date – rotter, ripping. Denied that her world ever said 'town' for London. But she is wrong, for it comes repeatedly into Regy's correspondence before 1914. On subject of [Cecil] Parkinson, she said Ministers of the Crown should uphold tenets of Christian faith which is foundation of Conservative

---

* Diana Keith Neal (b. 1948), dau. of W. Keith Neal, collector of antique firearms; m. 1977 Julian Berry; former staff member and future director of Sotheby's, then engaged by Lord Charteris, Provost of Eton, to create the Museum of Eton Life which opened in March 1985; first mentioned by J.L.-M. on 10 November 1975 (*Through Wood and Dale*) as a 'sweet girl' who 'confided her troubles' to him.
† Lady Diana Manners (1892–1986), officially dau. of 8th Duke of Rutland; m. 1919 Alfred Duff Cooper (1890–1954), cr. Viscount Norwich, 1953; mother of writer and broadcaster John Julius Norwich, 2nd Viscount.

Party.* Difficult to converse with her for she introduces a subject and is tenacious. But what a woman! How intelligent and easy! Said she was very unhappy and longed to die in her sleep. Obsessed by her last car accident, and can no longer drive. Chain-smoking in bed. She is still fun.

To Faber & Faber to discuss their paperbacking this autumn of *Another Self* and my three volumes of diaries. Very flattering, but they want me to read through and make corrections by end of this month, which will be a painful task. Told me that the N.T. definitely refused to have my diaries in their shops, considering them shocking and in bad taste. I have always suspected this.

Lunched with Sir Allan and Lady Adair† at 55 Green Street, old-fashioned and huge. Extremely welcoming and sweet old couple. Both giggle before and after making a remark. She is Regy's niece and had great regard for him. Told me little I did not already know, but lent me a little memoir of her life to take away.

Then hurried in pouring rain to K. Clark's memorial service at St James's, Piccadilly. Greeted by Alan Clark and wife standing at main door. Found self sitting at back with Janet Stone‡ and daughter, Janet looking distressed. Service lasted unprecedented hour and a half. Alan and John Sparrow§ read lessons; John Pope-Hennessy¶ over from USA read long address. Could hardly hear a word. An Irish Catholic priest gave another dissertation, claiming that before his death K. sent for him, received Communion according to the proper rites, and said, 'Thank you, Father, that is what I have been longing for'. Very surprising. Declined Alan's invitation to attend a party after service at John Murray's. Instead walked with J.K.-B. to Brooks's where we had tea. He reminded me that we met twenty-five years ago this month.

---

* Cecil Parkinson, despite taking the credit as Party Chairman for the recent Conservative election victory, had just resigned from the Cabinet following revelations by his former secretary that he had had an affair with and a child by her and broken a promise to marry her. Lady Diana's remark was presumably ironical, coming from the widow of a Conservative minister who had been a notorious philanderer.

† Major-General Sir Allan Adair, 6th Bt (1897–1986); m. Enid, dau. of Hon. Mrs Dudley Ward.

‡ Janet Woods; m. 1938 Reynolds Stone (1909–79), designer, graphic engraver and printer.

§ Warden of All Souls College, Oxford, 1952–77 (1906–92).

¶ Sir John Pope-Hennessy (1913–95); Chairman of Department of European Paintings, Metropolitan Museum, New York, 1977–86; brother of James P.-H.

Called at Radnor Walk to see Elizabeth and John Betj. J.B. sitting in his old armchair between window and fireplace looking different again since his latest heart attack. Totally bald, egg-shaped and dead white. A silent Buddha. Did not speak except to ask me, 'How's the Dame?' Eliz. says he rarely speaks now. Likes to be read to. Likely to be carried off by another attack, which could be tomorrow or in two years' time.

Saturday, 15th October

Simon Verity* and wife to luncheon. A nice couple. He an attractive, whimsical, slightly-built man, a leprechaun. Eager and appreciative. She solid, rock-like and dependable. I suppose he is not considered a good sculptor by the *avant-garde*. But his traditional designs for Michael Rosse's two memorials, a Kent-like one at Womersley [Park, Doncaster, Yorkshire] and a neo-Gothick one for Birr [Castle, Co. Offaly, Ireland], very pleasing. Has a high opinion of Anne, which is nice to hear. Says she is an inspiration, and has created the memorials herself, using him as an instrument.

Friday, 21st October

Interviewed on television, Harold Macmillan[†] was full of wisdom, humour and common sense. When accused of being frivolous, he replied that few things in life were worth taking too seriously, 'except what you might call morals, and I call civilised conduct and Christianity'. Said he could not have existed without his religion. He still reads six, sometimes eight hours a day. Still goes through agonies before making a speech. Loves young people, and finds a great improvement in them these past ten years. They are much cleaner, and you can now tell, without close inspection, to which sex they belong.

Sunday, 23rd October

A. and I motored to Cornwall for the night. Divine day, delicious sun and no wind. Lunched at Paignton. Looked at Oldway, the astonishing

---

* Memorial sculptor and letterer (b. 1945), who was commissioned, on J.L.-M's recommendation, to execute memorials to the 6th Earl of Rosse and 10th Duke of Beaufort (see entry for 27 November 1984); m. 1970 Judith Mills.
† Conservative politician (1894–1986); Prime Minister 1957–63; cr. Earl of Stockton, 1984.

house of the Singers, Princess Winnie's old home, built in the 1870s, like Versailles.* Now council offices. Could not get in. Tried but failed to find the Singer Mausoleum, where A. buried Winnie in 1943. She could not remember where it was. Stayed the night with Michael and Elizabeth Trinick at their house at Lanhydrock. We thought them a perfect family and their house a perfect house. Their youngest boy, William, aged eighteen, was staying. Beautiful manners. They motored us to Cothele, to attend a dinner given by Michael for Lady Hilaria Gibbs and her husband Colonel G.† in celebration of their golden wedding. We ate in the great hall, the first time Hilaria had ever eaten in it. Huge roaring wood fire. We assembled in the old kitchen. Fire there too, and candles and oil lamps. Michael made a short speech which I briefly endorsed, remarking that of all the N.T. donors I could not recall any couple kinder or more understanding than the old Mount Edgcumbes.

Michael Trinick, soon to retire, has made a great niche for himself in Cornwall. Is known and revered by all. A remarkable man who has done more than anyone I can think of for the N.T. Everything he does seems right. A pillar of the local church too. This morning I walked through the Ladies' Walk in the wood, along the edge of the park to Lanhydrock House. White sheep grazing in the valley. The grey granite stone of the house and gatehouse sparkling against the deep blue sky.

Left before midday and called at his request on Giles Clotworthy,‡ now public relations man for the N.T. I first met him when he was an editor at Country Life Publications when they were producing my Baroque Houses book.§ A very jolly boy then. Now forty and married with two children. Gave us great welcome, with champagne. Since his

---

* The German–American entrepreneur Isaac Singer (1811–75), having made a fortune out of his sewing machine, married a Frenchwoman and settled in Paris, but during the Franco-Prussian War moved to England, where he built his palace near Torquay. His daughter Winaretta (1865–1943), a lesbian who made a *marriage de convenance* with the elderly homosexual Prince Edmond de Polignac (d. 1901), became a noted patroness of the arts, especially music, her protégés including Fauré, Debussy, Satie and Stravinsky. Alvilde, then married to the aspiring composer Anthony Chaplin, became the close companion of her last years, and organised her funeral at Paignton in December 1943.

† Lady Hilaria Edgcumbe (b. 1908), e. dau. of 6th Earl of Mount Edgcumbe (donor of Cothele to N.T.); m. 1933 Lieut.-Col. Denis Gibbs, DSO (d. 1984).

‡ Joined Cornwall staff of N.T. 1983 (b. 1944); m. 1980 Jinny Rudorf.

§ *English Country Houses: Baroque, 1685–1714* (1969).

Country Life days he has done secret service work with Defence
Ministry. Told me that the four chief influences on his taste and interest were Pevsner,* Anthony Blunt, Michael Trinick and myself. He
began as a student at the Courtauld and venerated Blunt, while
finding him cold and suspicious. Then at the MoD he learnt the truth
about Blunt's spying, and thereafter felt obliged to cut him whenever
they met. I asked if Blunt had been paid by the Russians, and how far
he was responsible for ruining lives. Said he could not answer directly,
but that Blunt had never had need of money, being quite well off, and
that the result of his treachery was 'worse than murder'. Nice young
couple.

Mrs Julian, tenant of the Victorian wing of Cothele, asked me at
dinner, 'What are your hobbies?' I thought for a moment and
answered, 'None.' 'How dreadful!' she exclaimed, looking me hard
between the eyes. 'Yes, isn't it,' I replied.

Thursday, 27th October

For the past two days I have had a workman and mate to paint the
back yard stair railing and garden door. Cost £70, cheap I suppose.
He wanted it in cash, saying he was disabled and living on an inadequate pension. My car was in town being serviced so he had to drive
me to the bank. In the car, he mentioned he had worked for Tony
Snowdon. 'Now he's a real gentleman,' he said, 'and she's a perfect
lady.' Told me that snobbery is the preserve of the lower and middle
classes, the upper classes having no need of it as there is no one above
them. When he discovered I wrote books, he begged to see them. So
back in the flat I fished out several, which he held and stroked, reading
the blurbs on the jackets. Said he wanted to learn, and his children to
learn, but they could only do so 'from people like you, Sir'. I find this
sort of conversation embarrassing. And tried not to appear 'snobbish',
like the lower and middle classes.

Saturday, 5th November

We lunched with Zita and Teresa [the Jungman sisters] at their house
called The Eight-Gabled House, which describes what it is – a square

---

* Sir Nikolaus Pevsner (1902–83), Professor of Fine Art at Cambridge (1949–55) and
Oxford (1968–9); responsible for the *Buildings of England* series of guides.

manor-type house (though not a manor), next to the church and approached under a stone gateway, with half-timbered upper storey, very picturesque. Lovely position overlooking a valley towards Cheltenham, with a white expanse of water, a reservoir, visible in far distance. A Claude-like landscape. Other guests Desmond Guinness and Penny,* and Loelia Lindsay in strident form. I had bought Loelia's book yesterday in Bath, she having sent all her friends postcards urging them to do so. It is called *Cocktails and Laughter* and is a dreadful affair, sixty years of *Tatler*-like photographs, badly reproduced, captions all wrong, introduction by Hugo Vickers nothing to speak of. Funny to find these ladies, once so terrifying, now bland, dulcet and sweet, because no longer competing against each other. Much hilarity and excellent luncheon bought from Marks & Sparks and heated up. They have no servant and 'do' for themselves, yet the house clean and *gemütlich*.

Nick Robinson came to dinner to discuss A's proposed book with Derry Moore on the Englishwoman's house, which he wants to publish. Is losing his looks, which makes me sad.

Sunday, 6th November

Charlie and Jessica Douglas-Home lunched. I had not seen Charlie for two years and he is quite changed. Limps and walks with a stick. Bones crumbling. Yet cheerful. No longer good-looking, but sweet expression. He leaned across the table and asked what book I was working on. I could not resist saying, 'I am editing a volume of all the letters I have written to *The Times* down the years which they would not publish.' He said the newspaper had a box-file of the unpublished letters of his uncle William D.-H.† Said he was looking forward to reading my *Stuarts*. Like a fool I refrained from asking him to get *The Times* to review it.

Wednesday, 16th November

Met Audrey at Barnsley, probably for last time, to dine in pub. Horrible food, disgusting smell of fat and smoke. Found it very difficult to hear

---

* Hon. Desmond Guinness (b. 1931), son of Diana Mosley by her 1st marriage to Hon. Bryan Guinness (later 2nd Baron Moyne); founder and President of Irish Georgian Society; m. (2nd) 1985 Penelope (Penny) Cuthbertson, daughter of Teresa, *née* Jungman.
† Hon. William Douglas-Home (1912–93); playwright; m. 1959 Rachel Brand, later Baroness Dacre (27th in line).

her for she cannot or will not articulate. In consequence was once again rent in twain by intense irritation and deep compassion. Object of meeting to discuss her problem of moving house. She has half-moved to the cottage bought for her by Dale and James [Sutton], but so hates it that she has returned to Windrush Mill. Hopeless situation. Has dotty ideas about claiming large sums of compensation for being turned out. Or Richard [Robinson],* her grandson, may buy, so she can go there whenever she feels like it as caretakeress. Hopelessly unsatisfactory. Sad little farewell. I was overwhelmed with guilt when she said 'I don't want to bore you any longer.'

Saturday, 19th November

Dined with Somersets. About fifteen. Ali Forbes and Sebastian Walker, who loathe each other. Young William Waldegrave,† formerly of Mrs Thatcher's Think Tank, now Bristol MP. Charming, gentle and unassuming, unlike two previously named. He came up to me while Sebastian was proclaiming the joys of the modern world, and said, 'Anyone who supposes the world is improving must be raving mad.' Ali asked all the men to give their reply to the old-fashioned question which tailors used to ask, 'On what side do you dress, sir?' I said, 'On the left until I cross the Channel, and I have to reconsider the matter again when reaching the Austrian frontier.' Sebastian confided to me in a whisper his hopeless love for David Ford,‡ but also thought he might marry Anne Somerset,§ sitting opposite. Told him I thought this a non-starter. Shouting down the table, David asked me how it was possible for Harold [Nicolson] to have caught clap from a boy. Ali overcome by his naïveté.

---

* Youngest of J.L.-M's three Robinson great-nephews (b. 1957), who made a career in the City.
† Politician (b. 1946), yr s. of 12th Earl Waldegrave; Fellow of All Souls, 1971–86; MP (C) Bristol W. (1979–97); at this time Under Secretary for the Environment; cr. life peer, 1998.
‡ American publisher's assistant (b. 1946) who, then employed by Bamber Gascoigne, had done the picture research for J.L.-M's recent book on Bath (see *Deep Romantic Chasm*, entry for 31 January 1981), and now worked for Sebastian Walker.
§ Only daughter of David and Lady Caroline Somerset (b. 1955); m. 1988 Matthew Carr.

Sunday, 20th November

No Sunday review of *The Last Stuarts*. The book is a flop. I am very depressed, convinced that it is not a bad book, whereas plenty of trash gets recognition and sales. The fact that Kenneth Rose, next to whom I sat last week at a Foyle's luncheon, has received two (deserved) prizes for his *George V* does not make my plight any easier to endure. He was suitably self-deprecatory in receiving praise from all and sundry, yet I detected a smug sense of superiority.

Motor A. to Heathrow, she spending forthcoming week planting in Jagger's garden. I continued to London to lunch with Jack Rathbone at Oxford and Cambridge Club. Have little to say to him. Feel further and further removed from my old friends, those who survive.

Thursday, 24th November

Derek Hill rang me up yesterday in one of his usual states. Upset that I had not been in touch. Would I lunch with him on 13 December to meet the Queen Mother? She had particularly said she would like me to be there. I replied that I had just accepted an invitation to lunch that day with June Hutchinson to meet Pinkie Beckett.* 'But you must put that off.' No, I replied, I couldn't. Besides which I had no desire to meet the Q.M. I hated being with Royalty. They caused constraint. I also privately doubted that the Q.M. had expressed a wish to meet me. She doesn't know me and my name means nothing to her. Derek very cross and petulant. Said he would ring me up again today to find out if I had changed my mind. He did so as soon as I arrived in Bath, this time in dulcet mood. Took it well when I said I had not changed my mind, but was in despair as to when we should ever see each other again. The truth is that I like D. very much but don't particularly want to see him.

Tuesday, 29th November

To London for the day. Nightmare journey owing to train derailment last Sunday. Went straight to Como Lario in Chelsea to meet Anne [Rosse], sitting in her motor. Din appalling, as in all Italian restaurants. She said that, of her three sons, Tony was the least chivalrous. His

---

* Hon. Priscilla Brett (1921–2000), dau. of 3rd Viscount Esher; m. 1941 Sir Martyn Beckett, 2nd Bt.

recently published book included a photograph of Lady de Vesci which is the cruellest thing you ever saw. I told her that she ought to give her grandson Lord Linley a talking-to for replying, when asked what Christmas present he would least like to receive, 'a luncheon invitation from Princess Michael'. Anne said, 'I can never interfere in that quarter.' Then I dashed to the House of Lords, where my bag of London Library books was submitted to a thorough search. Met David Lloyd in peers' lobby. There are several life peers called Lloyd, but David is known to the staff as 'the' Lord Lloyd. Looks no worse. Face resembles old Lord Carson's.* Told me that John Charmley was going to visit him at Clouds Hill. Thank goodness I don't have to stage a luncheon. Asked my advice. I told him he must decide whether he is to write the biography himself, or ask Charmley to do it. He can't get Charmley to do the donkey work, he is too established. Suggested he let Charmley write the book, giving him every assistance.[†]

My poor father died thirty-four years ago today, God rest his precious soul.

Wednesday, 30th November

This morning I met David Somerset approaching on foot down the drive. Thought he was talking to me, and tried to reply to what he was saying. Then discovered that he was in fact talking to Michael Tree[‡] on some sort of portable telephone.

Thursday, 1st December

A very favourable review of *The Last Stuarts* in today's *Times*, by Woodrow Wyatt.[§] It has cheered me up, for I have had a paucity of

---

* Barrister and politician, champion of Ulster Unionism (1854–1935).

† After his earlier talk with Lord Lloyd about his father's biography (19 April 1983), J.L.-M. had approached Dr John Charmley of the University of East Anglia (b. 1955), a friend of Michael Bloch then working on Duff Cooper's biography. The introduction was a success (see entry for 28 January 1984), but Lord Lloyd died in 1985 and so did not live to see Charmley's book, *Lord Lloyd and the Decline of the British Empire*, published by Weidenfeld & Nicolson in 1987.

‡ Michael Lambert Tree, painter (b. 1921), son of Nancy Lancaster by her 2nd husband Ronald Tree; m. 1949 Lady Anne Cavendish, dau. of 10th Duke of Devonshire.

§ Sir Woodrow Wyatt (1918–98); former Labour MP, Chairman of Horserace Totalisator Board; cr. life peer, 1987.

notices. At least there is little risk of my committing a sin against the Holy Ghost by becoming too pleased with myself.

In Bath I went to buy a ball of string at Morley's little shop in George Street. To my great distress, the window was plastered with notices that their whole stock was on sale at reduced prices because the place was closing down. Asked the nice elderly ladies who have always served here, who gave usual reason – competition from super-markets and high rates etc. making it impossible to continue. Soon we shall be deprived of everything but these soulless, milling, vulgar emporia with piped music, absence of service, and shoddy goods.

Saturday, 3rd December

Saturday morning writing letters. Telephone rang. A. answered in the kitchen. Then came to my room to say, 'That was Junie [Hutchinson]. Diana Westmorland has died in her sleep.' They found her this morning in the exact position in which they had left her, only her eyes closed. Her heart must have given out. Previous evening she had eaten food and smoked a cigarette. June said to her, 'Mum, I really believe you are better. You will be able to see Jim tomorrow.' Yes, she replied, she would love to see Jim. Touching that these were the last words of this nonagarian darling, whom I so dearly loved. Felt extremely sad, yet glad she went out like this. Life held nothing more for her and she had been wretched these past six months. Ought to have gone after her ninetieth birthday party last May, which she greatly enjoyed.

Sunday, 4th December

After Communion at Little Badminton this morning, David Westmorland said, 'You will write something for *The Times*, won't you?' I have tried, but the result is not good. Difficult to steer between the Scylla of banality and the Charybdis of sentimentality when writing of someone to whom one was very devoted. I shall greatly miss her. She was far and away *my* greatest friend down here.

Beside her mother's bed, June found a little copy of *The Imitation of Christ* inscribed by Mr Gladstone for her Baptism in 1893, to which I have referred in my obit. Also, in emptying her mother's handbag, she found the love letter I had written to her on her ninetieth birth-day, which she carried around with her.

Monday, 5th December

M. telephoned this morning. He said, 'It has come.' I thought he was referring to the Duchess of Windsor's death. He meant the anticipated letter from Michael Colefax, reprimanding him for not yet having written Sibyl's biography, cancelling their agreement, asking for return of papers, and demanding an interview. I am distressed, having introduced him to the Colefaxes and being responsible for this commission.*

Thursday, 8th December

Darling Diana's funeral in the little Papist Church in Chipping Sodbury. A. unable to go, striken with bronchitis. Pouring with rain. I got there early to find a crowd of friends. Irish priest officiating in that maddening singsong voice, referring to 'our lost sister, Lady Diana', and lamenting the death of the church's best benefactor. Indeed, every year she raised funds by a sale and opened her garden for the church. Liturgy in English; no incense; the usual irritants. I thanked God all the while that I was no longer a Catholic. Some demon gets into me now in a Catholic church. Pathetic little coffin with sprays of half-budding lilies, very pretty and simple, yet so sad, like a child's coffin. I could not look at it when it was pushed past me down the narrow aisle. Had to go to tea at Lyegrove afterwards. Did not stay long, and motored Joanie Altrincham home afterwards. She was present as a girl of fourteen at Diana's first wedding to Percy Wyndham in 1913, which makes Joanie eighty-four.

Junie came over next day, bringing for me as a memento of D. the aforementioned *Imitation of Christ*. Greatly moved.

Tuesday, 13th December

Lunched with Junie in London to meet Pinkie Beckett, another of Regy's granddaughters. She hardly remembers her grandfather, but has read her father's 'secret book' about him† and calls him 'the awful

---

* Under an agreement which obliged him to share royalties with the family, Michael Bloch had been invited to write Sibyl Colefax's biography in 1980, but owing to other commitments (and a degree of indolence) had not got beyond the early stages of research. The task was taken up by Kirsty McLeod, whose book *A Passion for Friendship* was published eight years later.

† See entry for 12 July 1982.

old creature'. I liked her, because she is abrupt, to the point, no embellishments to her remarks. Told me little about Regy that I didn't know already, as usually the case with interviews, but spoke of her parents. When 'out', aged nineteen, she once went to supper with six friends, one of whom, a young man, escorted her home to Hill Street. Antoinette [Lady Esher] waiting on the threshold, purple with rage. Both Eshers always insistent that their children should be a social success and marry the right people. They did, except for the eldest girl who went into a semi-religious community, driven there.

June talked of Anthony Chaplin's cruelty. He was in love with her during the war and his possessiveness became obsessional. He tried to get her to leave nursing because he could not endure the thought of her touching the private parts of her male patients.

A. and I went to the N.T. dinner party given for me at Fenton House, Hampstead. I was dreading it but had no reason to be, for there were no speeches. Beautifully arranged. We were received in the drawing room upstairs where I used to have tea with Lady Binning, and ate in the large dining room. Was given a present before dinner. Saw it was a picture. Opened it upside-down. Had not my specs on. Saw it was the interior of some house. Martin Drury said, 'Don't you recognise it?' It was my library in Bath. A beautiful water-colour sketch by Mrs Gwynne-Jones, widow of the painter. A. of course in the know. Arranged for her to enter the library during weekends when I was not there. Delighted with the present. Now I have to thank countless friends who subscribed to it but did not attend the dinner, like the Graftons (who were not asked and, I later learned from Midi, were distressed). I sat between Dione Gibson, intelligent and sweet, and Francesca Wall. John Cornforth, Jack Rathbone, the [Tony] Mitchells. Both A. and I enjoyed ourselves. Stayed until after midnight. Discovered the house's current custodian was the son of my friend Mrs Jackson, the original custodian who died of cancer years ago. Much pre-historic chat.

Dudley Dodd* going round the rooms with me after dinner said, 'You were responsible for persuading Lady Binning not to leave her porcelain to the V. & A. with the rest of the Salting Bequest.' 'Was I?' 'Yes, it is all in the files.' I remarked on the charming alcoves, curved and glazed, which displayed the best china. 'You were responsible for

---

* Deputy Historic Buildings Secretary of N.T., 1981–2000 (b. 1947).

those. You designed them and got Geddes Hyslop* to carry them out.'
'Did I really?' I can't remember such details.

Saturday, 17th December

Called on poor old Mrs Gulwell at Lyegrove this afternoon. Found
her sitting before a coal fire in her downstairs room with little Singy,
Diana's beloved Peke. She is eighty-seven and absolutely lost.
Restrained her tears and then talked for an hour without once stop-
ping. Anyway, I wanted to hear what she had to say. She is Françoise
in Proust to the life, with the virtues and failings of the peasant.
(Garrulity counts as both.) Said she had started as parlourmaid to
Spooner at New College, Oxford. Yes, she remembered him making
spoonerisms. Then she worked for Sir Herbert Warren at the Provost's
Lodge, Magdalen, and at the Warrens' house after his retirement to
North Oxford. Now, I must have had the door opened to me several
times by her at both houses during the 1920s, an odd thought.† She
got engaged to a second horseman at Lyegrove, and has been there
ever since she married him, fifty years ago. Rose not yet born; Julian
a babe in arms. Lyegrove was a tip-top house, everything beautifully
done. Gardens with gardeners, a Rolls-Royce in the motor house.
The late Lord Westmorland was a drunkard, but lived like the lord he
was. Diana repeatedly put him to bed drunk. He was charming and
terrifying. Swore something awful. He and Diana would do everything separately. He would go to London by train, she by road. June
as a girl rode beautifully to hounds. One day she galloped ahead of the
Duchess [of Beaufort], in consequence of which The Lady (as she
terms Diana) was not invited to the big house again. (David Somerset
says rubbish.) Mr Julian‡ brought ladies down to be vetted by mother.
Mrs G. spied on them through the windows and told Diana after they
had gone whether they would 'do'.

Lady Gibson§ told me that the N.T. was going to rebuild the
garden house (destroyed by a bomb during the war) in which Henry
James wrote at Lamb House, Rye. I am delighted because I strenu-

---

* Architect in the classical tradition (1900–88); friend of Raymond Mortimer.
† J.L.-M. had been an undergraduate at Magdalen, 1928–31.
‡ Hon. Julian Fane (b. 1927), yr s. of 14th Earl of Westmorland; writer; m. 1976 Gillian
Swire.
§ Elisabeth Pearson, m. 1945 'Pat' Gibson (see entry for 5 March 1984).

ously advocated doing so thirty years ago, and the Committee then refused.

Friday, 23rd December

A. said at breakfast that, were it not for me, she would now emigrate to Australia without hesitation. A year ago I would certainly not have contemplated going; but today I would not particularly mind. I agree with A. that the nuclear cloud hanging over Europe is damnably depressing. Furthermore, I now feel I might just as well vegetate in a pleasant climate as here. For henceforth I shall merely read and listen to music and, I hope, walk. I shall not write any more books after this one; and I have no interests except M. to keep my affections in this country, to which I am absolutely indifferent. So shall we go off together?

1984

The past two nights I have been experimenting with a new sleeping pill for which Pat Trevor-Roper gave me a prescription. No use whatever. Just as nasty and ineffectual as the others which Dr King has given me in recent years. Half-sleep, restlessness, semi-headache, the mind floating like jetsam in whirlpools of horror, no shore, no outstretched arm, inability to sleep or wake, an in-between existence of non-reality. This past night during in-between periods of wakefulness I thought I was dying. Was sure that never would I be able to do anything again, never write, never think sanely; that I would be a hulk until death, which was not far off. Now, the strange thing is that while in bed, when relaxing, one feels one's worst, utterly feeble, done for. On the contrary one should be feeling recharged. Talked to Tony Powell about this at luncheon. He said he experienced exactly the same symptoms at night. Now I understand why most people die in their beds. This is the dangerous time when the body is most vulnerable, not when it is struggling to move itself about, is exerting every muscle and limb, on the move. It is stillness, relaxation that is the killer.

Janet Stone came to lunch too. Said she now felt the loss of Reynolds, who died over four years ago, more than ever. Said that although she had done all the physical work, running the house, looking after him who was incapable of coping, like Lennox, yet he supplied the moral power that kept her going. Without him she had no purpose. She told us that for thirty years K. Clark wrote to her once a week; that Reynolds understood K's great love for her. She didn't say, but I think implied, that he understood her great love for K.

M. came down by train to Bath to lunch with me. Very sweet of him and I enjoyed having him. Yet somehow I wondered how much pleasure it gave him, and if he does not regard me as a painless duty, but a duty all the same. He showed me an extract of his forthcoming book. Beautifully assimilated and most clearly enunciated. He is certainly a fine writer, and has yet to be proved.

Saturday, 7th January

Anne Tree whom I sat next to at Billy Henderson's* luncheon said that her uncle Harold Macmillan found Khrushchev the only Russian with whom it was possible to have a conversation man to man. He was at least a human being. Khrushchev told Macmillan that after Stalin's death a meeting of high-ranking officials was called in the Kremlin, K. being one of them. At this meeting the chairman announced that Beria must be sacked. Whereupon an armed attendant advanced from the back of the room and shot Beria dead. None of those present turned a hair.[†]

I find myself in curious sympathy with those awful women at Greenham Common.[‡] I can't bear them, of course – their methods and manners revolt me – yet I believe it is a great mistake our having American nuclear weapon sites on our soil. I think Britain should renounce nuclear weapons because they cost enormous sums of money and are absolutely useless. They cannot be used and their presence unused is a danger. On the other hand, I believe we should arm with conventional weapons to the hilt. If another world war breaks out it will not begin with nuclear weapons. The only hope for preventing war is for a united West to have a preponderance of conventional weapons.

Sunday, 8th January

We motored to Ewelme to lunch with Patricia Hambleden and David Herbert. David looking much older, his ginger toupee more obvious than ever, enormous rings on his fingers and a vast ring in his tie like a cartwheel. He was less exuberant and slightly depressed, not his dear usual self. Two guests staying, Barbara Moray,[§] whom I have not seen

---

* Painter (1903–93); ADC to Lord Linlithgow when Viceroy of India and stayed on as Comptroller to Lord Wavell until 1946.
† The lecherous secret police chief was in fact merely arrested at the Politburo meeting and later died under torture.
‡ A group of feminists were mounting a permanent protest against nuclear weapons outside the US Air Force base of that name.
§ Barbara Murray of New York; m. 1924 Francis Stuart (b. 1892), who s. 1930 as 18th Earl of Moray and d. 1943. J.L.-M. first met her on 31 December 1944 (*Prophesying Peace*) with Tom Mitford, who (she later claimed) would have married her had he not been killed in action soon afterwards (see *Midway on the Waves*, 1 February 1949). J.L.-M. saw her often in the late 1940s and was himself much seduced by her charms.

for years, and Sir Martin Gilliat, who talked of the luncheon Derek [Hill] gave last month at Buck's for the Queen Mother. Cost Derek more than £200. The Q.M. loved it. Gilliat told A. that the Q.M. had expressed a particular desire to meet me. So what Derek said was true.

Wednesday, 11th January

Burnet [Pavitt] and Derek [Hill] dined with me at Brooks's. Excellent food and claret for a change. Burnet said he was K. Clark's best man at his second wedding, in a Catholic church. At the altar the priest handed him a silver plate on which to put the ring. B. fumbled to get the ring out of its little leather case, and put it on the dish. Both priest and K. looked at it. Then K. could contain himself no longer. He said, 'Have you ever seen a more beautiful object? It is Coptic.' 'No, never,' replied the priest, 'and if you are interested in such things, what about the chasuble I am wearing? It is Puginesque.' K. duly admired. All the while the bride was waiting with outstretched finger.

Derek, who doesn't claim to be an art historian, nevertheless knows a good deal about pictures. He says that as a painter himself he is aware of other painters' tricks and details. We discussed the Kingston Lacy *Massacre of the Innocents*, attributed now to Sebastiano del Piombo but formerly to Giorgione. He is convinced it is indeed by the latter because of the peculiar fold of the clothing in the clasped hand of one of the subjects. It appears in other authenticated Giorgiones. John Pope-Hennessy agrees, though for other reasons. Concerning the Kingston Lacy painting, Mrs Hall, sister of the late Bankes owner, whom I met lunching today at Francis Crowdy's, told me she remembered Roger Fry[*] once staying the night at K.L. to look at the pictures. He said to her mother, 'That painting isn't by Giorgione, it's by Sebastiano del Piombo', of whom Mrs Bankes had never heard. She said not a word but walked to the fireplace, pulled the bell, and said to the appearing footman, 'Pack Mr Fry's bag. He is leaving by the next train.' Mrs Hall a perky old woman, bright and on the spot, a trifle facetious and pleased with her smart sallies, but sympathetic. She gave me a blown-up photograph of W. J. Bankes, 'the naughty one' as she calls him, and invited me to dine in February. Until her brother's death in 1982 she had not been inside Kingston Lacy since she was a

---

[*] Painter and critic (1866–1934).

girl in the 1920s. Said he was a most difficult man. I think she married someone he considered *indigne*.*

A dinner was given at Brooks's last night by the Duke of St Albans†
to celebrate the tercentenary of his dukedom. All the guests had to be descendants of Nell Gwynne, a charming and romantic notion. I see that David Somerset was not present, but Mrs Dom Mintoff,‡ wife of the awful Prime Minister of Malta, was, which is surprising. Pottiness characterises the Beauclerk family, but I would rather be one of Nell Gwynne's descendants than Barbara Villiers's,§ with their Roundhead flavour of vice wrapped up in do-goodness.

Sunday, 22nd January

Reading Norman Angell's¶ autobiography I was reminded that he had rooms at 4 King's Bench Walk, above Harold [Nicolson]'s. I used to see his name on the board at the foot of the staircase every time I went in and out, and used to think 'that ghastly man', simply because George Lloyd regarded all pacifists as traitors. He was of course nothing of the kind, but one of the wisest and most far-sighted men of his generation. Absolutely right in his support of non-belligerency in 1914 and belligerency in 1939. He rightly argued that war brought nought to the victors, and reparations were pointless as well as wicked.

Saturday, 28th January

Spent last evening with John Harris.‖ He disclosed that he had a vast library of books about the First World War, having been close to an

---

* Under her maiden name, Viola Bankes, Mrs Hall (b. 1900) later published reminiscences ('collected by Pamela Watkin') describing how she was disowned by her family after her betrothal to the Australian doctor Norman Hall in 1927 (*A Kingston Lacy childhood*, Dovecote Press, 1986).

† Charles Beauclerk, 13th Duke of St Albans (1915–88).

‡ She was Moyra de Vere Bentinck; m. 1947.

§ The senior living descendant of Charles II and his mistress Barbara Villiers, Countess of Castlemaine and Duchess of Cleveland, was J.L.-M's friend Hugh, Duke of Grafton.

¶ Sir Norman Angell (1873–1967); economist and pacifist; author of *The Great Illusion* (1910) and winner of the Nobel Peace Prize in 1933.

‖ Writer on architectural subjects (b. 1931) and curator, 1960–86, of the RIBA Library and Drawings Collection and Heinz Gallery. Lived at one time in the flat below J.L.-M's in Thurloe Square; in the Prologue to his *No Voice from the Hall* (John Murray, 1998) attributed his RIBA appointment to J.L.-M's recommendation.

uncle who came through it, a sawyer by profession who became a
shepherd on the Wiltshire Downs. John comes from Uxbridge, and
returns there every year to give a lecture on architecture. Says there
are still unspoilt villages on the edge of Heathrow Airport whose
inhabitants' lives are made intolerable by planes passing every minute
over their ancient roofs. John is tracing his ancestry in parish registers
and has got back to 1830. Descended from a line of craftsmen, book-
binders, upholsterers, joiners; yet he himself is no craftsman, except
in words. Some of his forebears came from Henley. Is intrigued by the
portrait of Lord Malmesbury in one of Reynolds's Dilettante Society
groups now at Brooks's. This Lord M. exactly resembles himself, and
John thinks there may be a connection *de la main gauche*, for the
Malmesburys went to live at Park Place, Henley after the death of
Marshal Conway, Horace Walpole's friend. Curious how every his-
torically-minded man wants to investigate his lineage and connect up
with a figure or family that played a part in history, the more patrician
the better. I like John and am glad to have had him alone again. His
interests are wide. Sees no hope for the country house. Asked me what
I thought. I said I had given up long ago. There was absolutely no
future.

Received a letter from John Charmley that he is already installed at
Clouds Hill and is to write the biography of George Lloyd. Most satisfactory. Seldom do plans work out like this. M. introduced me to
him; I introduced him to David Lloyd.

Wednesday, 1st February

The Times being on strike again one misses the deaths. Poor old Hansel
Pless died suddenly last week. I wanted to write to him after reading
the book of his mother Daisy with much enjoyment. From this I learnt
to my surprise that he fought in the First World War, winning the Iron
Cross. He married a Hohenlohe during that war, being only about
nineteen. When he returned to Poland after the Second World War he
could find no trace of her. Daisy Pless gives a fascinating account of
Germany under the Kaiser, who was always friendly to her, she having
been close to his mother, the Empress Frederick. Describes him as *au
fond* a good man, carried away by fantasies and resentments and envy.
'Of course, Hansel never liked women,' Sally [Westminster] says.

To London for the night, staying with Eardley. Spent the day in
British Museum archives reading Esher papers. Not very exciting. In

evening went to see John Betj. at Radnor Walk. Worse than ever. Very tragic. Sitting in his chair like a sack, his head lolling to one side. Feeble went up, kissed him and said she would set him straight. Promptly the head fell to the other side. Did not recognise me. I left feeling very sad.

Thursday, 2nd February

London Library all morning. Walked to Eaton Square and lunched with dear Ralph Dutton.* He asked me to read out a letter he had just received from Geoffrey Houghton-Brown.† Can't see to read the newspaper headlines, let alone letters. But in excellent form and absolutely *compos*. Said he had taken his seat in the House of Lords, being led up to the woolsack and prompted when to bow to Hailsham. Then led out of the chamber. Had tea at Oxford and Cambridge Club with M. Said his book was getting on at a spanking rate, and he had just signed a contract with Weidenfeld to edit the love letters of the Duke and Duchess of Windsor. His father has bought him a flat off Hyde Park Square, by which he is delighted.

Sunday, 5th February

On return from lunching at Claverton, and walking the dogs in Park Piece, I was hailed by a shabby old man in a shabby car. It was Bill Llewellyn.‡ I asked what he was doing here. He said, 'I have been talking to Tom Gibson at the Vicarage. You know Master died today at twelve o'clock?' Sally told A. last night that she had had to bring him back from following hounds in the afternoon as he felt giddy. He had a very bad heart attack, suffering much pain until given morphia or equivalent. Bill had tried four times to convey to Mary that Master was dead. All she said the fourth time was, 'Do tell my father [who has been dead these fifty years], I am sure he will be most interested.' Last Sunday Master told the Vicar that when walking his dogs at dawn that morning he saw three foxes sitting on the graves of his father and

---

* Architectural historian and writer (1898–1985); s. cousin as 8th Baron Sherborne, 1982.
† Dilettante and painter (1903–93) in whose house in Thurloe Square, South Kensington J.L.-M. kept a flat from 1946 to 1961.
‡ Rt Revd William Llewellyn (b. 1907); Vicar of Badminton, 1937–49; Bishop of Lynn, 1961–72; Assistant Curate of Tetbury since 1977; Eton contemporary of J.L.-M.

grandfather. He had never seen any foxes so close to the church before. He has left directions that he is to be buried beside these two graves. The Dukes are always buried in this patch by the church, but I believe the Duchesses are buried separately at Little Badminton. So in death are the exalted divided.

Tuesday, 7th February

Curious what an effect *the* death has caused in this village. A muted silence in the streets these two days past. Much publicity in the local papers and on television. Cottage tenants expressing loyal appreciation – great gentleman, etc. They could hardly do otherwise. Yet one did say there were occasions when His Grace could be extremely angry, and they were fearsome. Vicar told A. that on Monday he arranged for the coffin to be taken into the church at a time when Mary was walking in the park with her dogs, accompanied by her nice old friend Tuppie, who is thought to have more influence over her than anyone else. On their return Mary must have sensed that something was happening, for she made for the church and walked in, Tuppie trying to stop her in vain. She went straight up to the coffin and demanded that the lid be opened. This was done. She bent over the face and gently kissed it. Turned away and walked straight out of the church without a word. But went into the kitchen and said to the cook, 'I shall only want luncheon for Miss Tuppie and myself today. His Grace will be out.' So no one yet knows whether she understands or not. Poor Caroline has been sent for. Discovered in Bangkok, half-way through her tour of Burma and Siam. She had a presentiment, and insisted on being called back if Master died. The Queen is coming to the service, which is very unusual. The Royals looked upon the old man as an uncle figure, like Mountbatten.

Wednesday, 8th February

Second very stormy night. Did not sleep well. Honey was restless at the bottom of my bed because, I think, the hounds kept baying all night, and our dogs hate the hounds. Normally they never keep up continuous 'singing' (as it is called here) but sing for five minutes or so and then stop. Sally says that when she left Master on Saturday she walked her dog in Swangrove, and heard an owl hoot three times. Owls never hoot in the daytime. Another omen.

A. returned from London in time for luncheon. By two o'clock so many cars and people on foot were passing our gate for the church that we set out, although service not due to begin before three. Even so there was no room for us in the church. Were ushered into a large marquee on the lawn with an amplifier connected to the church. Marquee likewise jammed with people; everyone from the estate, the Hunt, the county had turned up. The old Hornbys* grumbling that they had not been let into the church. Nicole sent messages to the ushers that she was a close relation, and she and Michael (*aet* 87) were given a pew. Charlie [Hornby] left behind told us that his mother was no relation at all, but always got her way. The service, hymns, prayers relayed to us in the marquee. Then, when the Committal about to begin, someone undid the flaps of the marquee, so we, sitting in the front row, had a good view of the cortège. Huge coffin trundled on wheels from the church door, draped with the Beaufort standard, fleur de lys, etc., very Plantagenet and medieval. Poor David, looking miserable, stood alone with Mary, tiny and bewildered in black. Did she realise what was happening? When coffin lowered into the grave they advanced, looked down, and he piloted her away. Followed by the Queen; Queen Mother, splendid in mink tippet down to the ground; Prince and Princess of Wales, he in black morning coat; Princess Anne and Phillips, Prince and Princess Michael, Princess Alexandra. The bearers of the coffin from its wheeled contraption to the graveside included our Peggy's husband, Gerald, the chauffeur, gardeners. Leslie the butler carrying huge sheaf of irises, flunkeys and dailys following him. The three huntsmen in white breeches, blue and buff liveries, long, brightly polished riding boots, velvet caps, very impressive and handsome. Last Post played by bugler of the Gloucestershire Hussars. Caroline had difficulty keeping her floppy brown hat from blowing off. Icy cold wind. Flag over the house hanging at half-mast. Robust-looking coffin – when family flag removed – of grey oak, cut from a tree on the estate sixty years ago for this very purpose, and kept in an attic of the house all these years. What makes people do this sort of thing? It will never be seen again and must rot and be eaten by worms.

Received very funny bad-taste postcard through the letter-box from Selina Hastings this afternoon: 'I couldn't help thinking of

---

* Michael and Nicole Hornby of Pusey House, Faringdon, Oxfordshire.

Honey and Folly when I read the paper yesterday. They must be very happy little dogs. Will they be having a party to celebrate? And will pheasant pâté or fox pie feature on the menu?"* And Derry [Moore] who is staying two nights says the late Duke's mistresses ought to have been parked, like nuns behind a grille, in the gallery of the church during the funeral – the Dowager Duchess of Norfolk,† Sally Duchess of Westminster, Lady Glanusk,‡ *et al.*, in order of precedence. How they would have hated each other.

Friday, 10th February

Daphne Moore§ jumped off her old bicycle in the village street to say, 'Have you heard? The public have stolen all the wreath cards of the Royal Family, written in their own hands.' Pretty ghoulish, I admit.

Went this evening to Dr King about my prostate. He examined and said it was swollen but he could not tell if worse than when he last examined. At all events I am to take a 'specimen' to the Royal United on Monday and have an X-ray. I have so many symptoms that I know it is worse than formerly. E. is having similar trouble, and if he is operated on may not be able to come with me to Ravello. Now it is possible I may not be able to go myself.

Wednesday, 15th February

Staying with Eardley in London. After breakfast we went to three exhibitions. First Walter Greaves in Motcomb Street. Then drawings of country houses, including one by Lugar of Glanusk Park, *circa* 1822. I thought I must buy this early illustration of my great-grandfather's house, but it was not for sale. Then twentieth-century celebrities at National Portrait Gallery. E. rather put out that neither Raymond [Mortimer] nor Desmond [Shawe-Taylor] was represented.

---

* See note for 20 August 1983.

† Hon. Lavinia Strutt (1916–95), o. dau. of 3rd Baron Belper; m. 1937 16th Duke of Norfolk (1908–1975).

‡ Lorna Andrews; m. 1941 David Bailey (1919–97), who s. 1948 as 4th Baron Glanusk (he being a cousin of J.L.-M., whose grandfather had been an uncle of 1st Baron); she d. 1997.

§ Eccentric resident of Badminton, protégée of Mary, Duchess of Beaufort.

M. and I had a delicious lunch at a Malaysian restaurant near
Paddington and then went to look at his new flat in Strathearn Place.
Very nice it could be made, though rather dark, for facing north. He
showed me what I had never seen, a small metal object like a chipo-
lata within the jamb of the sitting room. Painted over when flat last
redecorated. M. explained that it contains a fragment of Holy Writ,
and means that Jews once occupied the apartment.

Thursday, 23rd February

At breakfast the telephone rang. It was Diana Cooper, wishing to
know whether A. had received her contribution to *The Englishwoman's
House*, and whether she liked it. A. had gone to London for the day,
but I assured her we both did. I asked how she was. 'I must and do get
worse every day at my age,' she said, being ninety-one. She had been
to Harold Macmillan's ninetieth birthday luncheon at which were a
hundred guests, and was seated next to her host. Everyone was waiting
and watching for Mrs Thatcher, who left before she arrived.

Friday, 24th February

Eardley's operation went well. Small growth in early stages removed.
Prospects are bright, so Mattei says.

Saturday, 25th February

Motored to tea with Eliza Wansbrough at Broughton Poggs. A darling
woman. Was touched at how pleased she was to see me. When alone
with her I can get her to hear perfectly well. And in spite of this dis-
ability, she is very quick on the uptake. We talked of the Eshers mostly.
She said that old Nellie Esher was both ugly and horrid.

Wednesday, 29th February

To London for the day. In the morning to Quality Court off Chancery
Lane to consult National Register of Archives. Looked up Regy, and
found listed all known papers relating to him and their whereabouts.
Discovered, for instance, that all the Harcourt papers are in the
Bodleian, so need not have bothered Mrs Gascoigne, Bill Harcourt's
daughter and their owner. Lunched with Derek at Boodle's. He asked

me to go to Mount Athos with him again in September, to stay three weeks at Chilandari Monastery while he painted and wrote. Not on your life. The very idea of being in that depressing place, sharing a dormitory, eating congealed beans and not washing more than hands or face. London Library in afternoon, and then at 3.45 dear M. came to Brooks's. He is flying to Ischia tomorrow to stay with an ex-Nazi ambassadress in search of Windsor material.* Called on Eardley in Edward VII Hospital. He lying supine, looking white and frail in a white hospital smock. Today allowed to drink for first time, hitherto fed and given liquid by drips through the arms. Tomorrow he will begin eating. Does not realise quite how ill he has been. Pleased to see me. I stayed but ten minutes. I think he is going to be all right, but wonder if he will ever be quite the same again.

A man, whom I know well but can't put a name to, met me on the staircase at Boodle's and said, 'You have left a large hole behind you'. Derek asked what he meant. I think he was referring to the N.T. Properties Committee. Many people have commented on my letter in *The Times* last week replying to a vicious article by Roger Scruton† on the N.T. Am glad I wrote it.‡

Sunday, 4th March

Having motored A. to Heathrow to fly to France – Jagger's garden again – I called for Ros and took her to luncheon at the Garrick Club. Indifferent expensive meal, almost £20 for the two of us without wine. Ros says she is pleased with the film of *The Weather in the Streets*, which is generally considered not to do her novel justice. Then, having taken her home, went again to Eardley in hospital. Was very shocked by his appearance. He was out of bed, in a chair, back to the window. A very old man, hollow-eyed, waxen white face, become small overnight, his teeth correspondingly too big for him, skeleton-thin, not having eaten for a week, large hands tightly gripping the chair arms. Barely a smile

---

* This was Maria-Ursula von Stohrer, whose husband had been German Ambassador to Spain when Ribbentrop tried to apprehend the Duke of Windsor there in the summer of 1940 – the episode forming the subject of M.B's forthcoming book *Operation Willi*; she still lived in a villa in Ischia given her by Count Ciano, her sometime lover.
† Cambridge-educated philosopher (b. 1944); Reader (later Professor), Birkbeck College, London; editor, *Salisbury Review*.
‡ For the text and context of this letter (published 24 February 1984), see Appendix II.

elicited, and no interest in anything I had to impart. I felt most inadequate and believe my visit gave no pleasure, and possibly displeasure. Felt very sad in consequence. Went to have a cup of tea with J.K.-B. Very sweet. But thinks he will not complete Terence Davis's book on Paxton, which has been put to him.

Monday, 5th March

Kenneth Hudson, my neighbour from 18 Lansdown Crescent, called this morning with an assistant to record me for a programme called *Heritage* on Radio Four. He asked two questions. Did I feel the presence of Beckford in my library, and if so, did it inspire or hinder my work? And did I think that N.T. houses had a beneficial effect on the masses who visited them? I was not at a loss for answers, but afterwards thought of better ways of expressing what I had said. This interview has arisen from the correspondence in *The Times* resulting from my reply to Roger Scruton (whom *Private Eye* calls 'Dr Scrotum'), for which I have had letters of thanks from both Pat Gibson[*] and Angus Stirling.[†]

Wednesday, 7th March

Had a bit of a shock this afternoon. Was rung up yesterday by surgery telling me to see a specialist named Charlton in Bath. When I called on Dr King last night for the X-ray photographs of my bladder, etc., he murmured what I took to be, 'The prostate is normal.' I wondered what Charlton could tell me. A nice man, talking sensibly and candidly, or what seemed to be candidly. Examined prostate, then said dress and let us have a talk. Then said, 'Your prostate is abnormal', which I suppose is what Dr King said to me last night. Charlton told me I must have an operation soon. I told him that I was booked to go to Ravello on 5 April, having on the strength of the report that my urine was negative bought an air ticket and booked a room at lovely Palumbo Hotel. He said it would be unwise to go, especially alone, as the prostate might blow up and the bladder refuse to pee, which would be awful. As I left I said casually, 'I presume there is no growth, since you speak of an

---

[*] Richard Patrick Tallentyre Gibson (b. 1916); director of companies; cr. life peer, 1975; Chairman of N.T., 1977–86.
[†] Director-General of N.T., 1983–95 (Deputy Director, 1979–83); (b. 1933; kt, 1994).

obstruction.' He replied, 'I don't know. We shall have to see when we examine the tissues.' Not a very nice piece of intelligence. My father died of cancer of the bladder at the age of sixty-nine. And, if all goes well, I shall not be able to work for four weeks at least. Damn!

What are my feelings? Of course dreading the worst. But not so shaken as I would have been twenty years ago, for I am approaching the natural term of my life. I don't want poor darling A. to be worried and unhappy. I don't want to leave her. But apart from abandoning her to wrestle alone, without very intimate friends and with that irresponsible and demanding Luke family, there is no one else but M. I regret leaving. And he being so young cannot miss me for long. One thing I dread, and that is recovering from this operation to be told I have got cancer, and dragging on, operation after operation, drug after drug, being a perfect nuisance to others and an abject misery to myself. In that event I would prefer to die under the anaesthetic. But I would like to finish Regy, my novel, and tidying up my remaining diaries. I have no other ambitions.

Thursday, 8th March

Felt very low all day until after dinner my specialist Charlton telephoned to inform me of the date of my operation, which is Monday week. He also wants more blood tests. I suppose they suspect malignancy, and yet I suffer no pain and am feeling unusually well. Yet poor Eardley never felt ill and was gardening and cooking dinner for friends on the eve of his op. And look at him now. That is the dread. Being reduced to impotency and advanced old age merely by undergoing two hours under an anaesthetic.

Saturday, 10th March

For some reason I am now feeling cheerful and resigned. Is it because my operation has been deferred for a week? And will the dread return? One's reactions under a cloud are strange. Now, if I were under a cloud of imminent disgrace, say about to appear in court for some discreditable misdemeanour which would bring distress to A., it would be far worse. After all, I am not disgraced by having a prostate operation. Am not telling friends because I don't want sympathy or attention. Even so, I have told Eardley, because we are in the same boat, so to speak; Alex Moulton, as he has been clamouring for me to go motoring with him, and I could find no other excuse; and M., who telephoned from Paris yesterday asking the result of my X-rays. I have no secrets from him. But I don't want even him to visit me in hospital; and I want no attentions except from A.

Sunday, 11th March

A. and I lunched with Tony and Violet [Powell]. I do like them both so much. The taciturn, melancholic son John there as always. Other guests were Lord and Lady Quinton,* he a life peer and President of Trinity College, Oxford. Typical don, very genial, talks long and loud, very clever indeed, a bit of a show-off in the Maurice Bowra tradition, which I never find congenial. Poor A. stuck with him during and after luncheon and found it difficult to live up to his smart repartees. The Lady semi-Bohemian, Post Office red hair, teeth all over the place, likewise bright. I talked to Tony on the sofa after. Always enjoy his emphatic enunciation, though low and gentle. Told me that in his opinion the most moving passage in English literature is when Lord Scamperdale in *Mr Sponge's Sporting Tour*† realises that his stooge – forget the name – is dead. The man he has for years mocked, slave-driven, yet loved without realising it until he was no more. Tony said a novelist must write what he 'hears' rather than 'sees' of environments of which he is an outsider. Had Dickens written what he heard the upper classes say rather than what he imagined they might say, his portraits of the Dedlocks‡ might have been more convincing. We talked about *Daniel Deronda*, which led to a discussion of whether Gentiles were circumcised in the 1830s and 40s. We thought not, because Apollo and other naked gods were not depicted thus by late neo-classical sculptors such as Baillie and John Gibson. Tony thinks it only became *de rigueur* among the upper and upper-middle classes in the 1890s. Pointing to his late seventeenth- and eighteenth-century ancestors on the wall above the books, Tony said they were all probably painted by itinerant portrait painters. They went the rounds of the lesser gentry, laden with canvases on which clothes and even ladies' busts already painted, and merely added the head. I remarked that even

---

* Anthony Meredith Quinton (b. 1925), philosopher; President of Trinity College, Oxford, 1978–87; m. 1952 Marcelle Wegier; cr. life peer, 1983.
† By R. S. Surtees (1853).
‡ In *Bleak House*.

the heads looked much the same in those times, bags under the eyes, cheeks swollen from gumboils.

Lady de Vesci has died aged a hundred and one. Anne [Rosse] rushes up for the funeral and, although she can never have loved her mother-in-law, is sad. I recall Lady de V. in Eton days when she came to see Michael [Rosse] and Desmond [Parsons], often with the old Duke of Newcastle, for Clumber was her home. Very upright she was and hand-some, with those dark, sunken, eagle-like eyes. Proud too, and exclu-sive. Then I stayed with her at Abbey Leix and Monk Hopton, Lord de V., Ivo, a dark figure in the background. She was always nice to me, but never a warm, forthcoming person. On the contrary was cold and withdrawn. Nevertheless fascinating, because so beautiful and patrician. She clipped her *g*'s. Introduced me to her cousin Prince Doria and his wife Gesine, with whom I became close friends in those Roman days. So long as I was not married to A., they received us both in the Palazzo Doria; as soon as I married they dropped me like a stone.* Also her cousin, dear, wicked Orietta Borromeo, with her dark, flashing eyes and black underlids, her infectious laugh and enthusiasms, her hatred of her niece's husband Pogson. She was as warm as Lady de V. was cold. What links, what associations does Lady de V's death not bring back.

Friday, 16th March

A. and I motored to London for the day. Met Max Egremont on the pavement who enquired how Regy progressing. Said he gave him the creeps. Having plenty of time I walked slowly to Eaton Place. To my horror I realised I had come without Mrs Hall's letter inviting me to lunch and I had no idea which her number was. Panic set in. Searched for the names of flat owners on doors, but many had no names. Rang one bell for caretaker, who was a foreigner and understood little. Rushed to public call box. Operator miraculously able to find tele-phone number, and hence give me number of house, where I arrived ten minutes late. Mrs Hall is eighty-four and the widow of Norman Hall, OBE, whoever that may have been. She told me that, when she

---

* As A.L.-M. had been unable to obtain a papal annulment of her previous marriage to Lord Chaplin, her union with J.L.-M. remained illicit in the eyes of the Church. Lady de Vesci's mother was a daughter of the 6th Duke of Newcastle, and another daughter m. Prince Alfonso Doria Pamphili (1882); Orietta Borromeo was a dau. of that marriage, while a granddaughter m. (1958) an English naval officer, Frank Pogson.

married sixty years ago, her brother told her he never wished to see her again. She has only once returned to her family home at Kingston Lacy, when her brother opened it to the public. The guides were astonished by her knowledge of the contents and asked her who she was. When she told them, they said, 'Mr Bankes will want to see you.' She replied, 'No, he won't, and what's more I don't the least want to see him.' Said that her Bankes nephew, who was cut out of Kingston Lacy, is very well off but lives like a tramp in a large, empty house. Bearded down to the waist, shoes so down-at-heel that bare feet touch the pavement. Wears worn-out 1930s Homburg hat which, on meeting her, he doffs as politely as Disraeli might on meeting Lady Bradford, but he will never ask her to the house. The caprices of the English gentry surpass anything in fiction.

I went with M. to his new flat to see what he was getting his build-ers to do. Then to the Berkeleys', Lennox wandering round like a lost sheep. A. and I then drove to Gloucester Walk to dine with Susie Faulkner who is to marry Henry Robinson. Nice dinner party. My nephews looked so handsome and smart I felt proud of them.

Sunday, 18th March

It is Sunday. I have taken the dogs for two long walks. I have lunched with the Loewensteins alone, because poor A. feeling unwell. I feel as well as I have felt for ages, better in fact, and yet this time tomorrow I shall be in the operating theatre preparing to meet my fate or Maker. I shall be ill for a month even if the operation goes as it should, without complications. I have written several loving letters to friends without mentioning impending op. Meanwhile I am very worried about [brother] Dick's illness. Simon told me last night that they are waiting for him to recover from the move to hospital [in Cyprus] before scan-ning his liver to ascertain how deteriorated it is. I don't like it.

Sunday, 25th March

Well, here I am, home again, being looked after angelically by A., and feeling fine. Strange experience. Woke up in intensive care, ministered to by succession of sweet nurses. Indeed, I have never met with such an agglomeration of sheer goodness and kindness. Every nurse and sister was an angel to me, and I grew to love my surgeon Mr Charlton, a most sympathetic, intelligent and humane man. We had long talks when he visited me in my room. He wants to write the History of the Catheter. I advised him not to make it too surgical, and to search through diaries, such as Parson Woodforde's, for references. He told me that a hundred years ago country doctors carried catheters in their hats and inserted them into their patients with a minimum of cleaning. In fact, excessive sterilisation has lowered our resistance to diseases. He says bacteria take their revenge by being more cunning and persistent than formerly. That is why so many patients develop urinary infections after operations. The bacteria rush in hordes upon the victim, seeking the most unguarded approaches to the bastions from which the sterilisers have sought to exclude them. Charlton told me he did at least thirty operations per week and sometimes forty. Amazing. He cuts out the prostate with an inserted instrument which has a torch and microscope attached, so he can see what he is doing.

On Thursday morning, three days after operation, had my catheter removed. This was agony. Slept very little the previous night, because of anxiety. At six the nurse did the work. I screamed. She sent for the sister who comforted me like a mother. When it was over I burst into tears. At eight o'clock a clergyman in full canonicals entered the room. I had forgotten that the previous evening I had said I would like to take Communion. Was convinced he had come to give me extreme unction, and was highly alarmed. I said to this soulless stick of a man, 'I have just been disembowelled and flayed. Will you read the lesson for St Barnabas Day?' He looked astonished and said, 'You can't have been disembowelled. Just hold this prayer book and follow me. I won't be long.' Indeed he wasn't, but I wept throughout, incapable of answering the responses. I thanked him and he asked if I was prepared to offer something. 'Take £5 from my trouser pocket and be gone!' I managed to say through my tears.

Wednesday, 28th March

Simon telephoned with grave news of poor Dick's condition in Nicosia Hospital. The tests reveal that he has cancer secondaries on liver, and primaries on chest and throat. His case is hopeless, and one must trust that his future is as short and painless as possible. I feel sad, sad. Have tried to write poem about Dick, but cannot make progress. Poetry is evanescent and fugitive, will not be cajoled.

Billy Henderson and his old friend William lunched today. Caroline joined us, and afterwards took us to the big house. On the way up the stairs Caroline pointed out the door of Mary's bedroom. As we tiptoed past, there issued from it a scream, more like Mrs Rochester in *Jane Eyre* than any earthly scream, though probably just a yell of anger directed at one of the dogs. William visibly wilted.

Friday, 30th March

Dined with the Somersets* at the Cottage. Caroline told us that old Hilda Murrell, A's friend the old rose grower from Shrewsbury, had been murdered. Apparently she witnessed some young people burgling a neighbour's house, so they grabbed her, stabbed her and dumped her in a ditch. There she was found two days later, having, so the doctors affirmed, died just a few hours before. So this old lady of seventy-nine lay bleeding to death in a ditch for forty-eight hours. There is no limit to the enormities committed today. I believe civil war is not far distant, what with hooligans in London uniting to smash up the City and the miners inciting violence all over the country.†

David spoke to me about the library at Badminton. Asked if I considered it would be wrong to take away a length of morocco-bound books to allow them to put their modern library on the shelves. I said I thought it would be a sad mistake to scrap what is a complete and very beautiful library of calf-bound books. Advised that they should be treated like wallpaper. Rich portraits could be hung on silken cords and tassels over the books. The room needed deep, warm colours. Could not a modern library be made in a similar room upstairs? I think D. is worried about the responsibilities that have fallen on his shoulders. He has noticeably aged recently, though as handsome as ever. I shall do what I should have done long ago – read up and familiarise myself with the history of the Beaufort family and the architectural development of the house.

Wednesday, 4th April

Pam [Jackson]‡ and Debo [Devonshire] called on me at Lansdown Crescent. Debo said their French chef applied for post of chef at the

---

* Now Duke and Duchess of Beaufort.
† The year-long strike of the National Union of Mineworkers had begun on 12 March.
‡ Pamela Mitford (1907–94), second of the Mitford sisters, known to intimates as 'Woman'; m. 1936 (as 2nd of his 6 wives) Professor Derek Jackson (d. 1982).

new Royal Crescent Hotel in Bath. He had no intention of accepting the post, but applied out of curiosity. The wage offered was £18,000. Pam asked Debo what the Devonshires paid him. Answer, £10,000.

M. is worried that a letter he wrote to me at Badminton last week has not been delivered. In it he described a visit he paid to the Prince of Wales's butler at Kensington Palace, who happens to be a former footman of the Duchess of Windsor and friend of her butler, Georges. The butler – a jolly old queen who is as fat as Mr Smith the Liberal MP* – told M. some indiscreet things about the Prince, such as that he is extremely vain of his person, etc. I have advised M. that it is extremely unwise of him to consort with these servants of persons in high places. M. is concerned that his letter may have been 'intercepted' and the man may get into trouble or even lose his job. He also believes that his telephone line is bugged.

Tuesday, 10th April

Elaine telephoned from Cyprus just as we were going to look at a film on the telly. Poor thing, she was probably a little drunk and repeated herself. Said that Dick is no longer in pain, and talking cheerfully. He never refers to his condition. This so often the case with the dying, who do not care to face up to the inevitable, and believe that by some miracle they may recover. Towards the end of the talk she let fall that the doctors give him about ten days. I felt extremely sad and wrote him a difficult letter. What can one say? One cannot express a hope that he will be better soon, yet must not alarm. And jokes seem inopportune.

Sunday, 15th April

Simon Blow,† spending two nights with us for awful Three-Day Event, talked to me over breakfast of his grandfather, Detmar Blow.

---

* Cyril Smith (b. 1928; kt 1988); MP for Rochdale, 1972–87.
† Author, former racing jockey (b. 1945); yr s. of Purcell Blow (e. s. of Detmar Blow [1867–1939], architect and sometime adviser to 2nd Duke of Westminster) and Diana Bethell (dau. of Hon. Clare Tennant by her 1st marriage); his publications include works of family history and autobiography such as *Broken Blood* (1987) and *No Time to Grow* (1999).

Maintains that his treatment by the Grosvenor estate was outrageous, although Loelia, reigning Duchess at the time, instigated his dismissal. From ducal architect he became confidential adviser, and Bendor would do nothing without consulting him. They travelled everywhere together, walking arm-in-arm down the streets. Loelia was jealous. Finally Duke accused him of double-dealing and demanded back all the presents he had poured upon him. Detmar, much hurt, agreed to give them back, even though it would ruin him. Then he reflected that the ducal demand was grossly unfair, and demurred, thus forfeiting the sympathy of mutual friends. He was left with nothing but his own house and a few acres which surrounded it, and died a few years later of a broken heart. I told Simon he ought to write his grandfather's story rather than semi-coffee table books like his recent hunting miscellany, and the sort of society trash which his friends Christopher Sykes[*] and Sophie Cavendish[†] produce *ad nauseam*.

This morning Sybil Cholmondeley[‡] telephoned me from Houghton to say she had found all Regy's letters to her brother Philip Sassoon.[§] Says there are so many she cannot read through them, and is posting them all to me. I may do what I like with them, and she will trust me not to publish anything that contains indiscretions. Wondering what she meant by this, I asked her to be more particular. She said Esher was an incorrigible gossip and encouraged her brother to be another. After all, she said, Philip was private secretary to Douglas Haig and Lloyd George, and she would not like to have published any criticisms he may have put on paper about these chiefs, or Winston Churchill or Kitchener. I tried to convey to her that these people are now historical figures. She, being over ninety, sees them as friends of hers who have recently died. I begged her to tell me frankly what it was about Esher she disliked, thinking she might imply, if not state categorically, that it was his homosexual tendencies and manner. Not at all. 'He was such a busybody, such a gossip, such an intriguer. These things made him a sinister man.' It is splendid of her to send me these papers.

---

[*] Christopher Simon Sykes (b. 1948), writer and photographer, nephew of J.L.-M's old friend Christopher Sykes (1907–86).

[†] Lady Sophia Cavendish (b. 1957), yst dau. of Duke and Duchess of Devonshire; author of books on Devonshire and Mitford families.

[‡] Sybil Sassoon (1894–89); m. 1913 Earl of Rocksavage, later 5th Marquess of Cholmondeley (d. 1968); châtelaine of Houghton Hall, Norfolk.

[§] Sir Philip Sassoon, 3rd Bt (1888–1939), politician and aesthete.

Tuesday, 17th April

To London yesterday, working in London Library. This morning I went to Colindale to consult old newspapers, rushing back to give Kenneth Rose luncheon at Brooks's. Emerging from Piccadilly Circus station found St James's Square cordoned off. At Brooks's was told that the so-called diplomats in the Libyan People's Bureau had opened fire on a harmless anti-Gaddafi demonstration, killing a poor little policewoman and injuring about ten others. All streets in area cleared of traffic and armed police on watch. Kenneth three-quarters of an hour late, having come on foot from Fleet Street. He talked too loudly and boastfully of his social and literary success. Was spiky about Rupert Hart-Davis, whose last volume of Lyttelton letters I was carrying, because Rupert had written to say it would be absurd for him and his fellow judges to award the W. H. Smith Prize to Kenneth for his *George V*, which had already been awarded three other prizes. Kenneth looking over my shoulder at more interesting eaters. While I was paying the bill, he ganged up with Nico Henderson, and Lords Jellicoe[*] and Shackleton,[†] and brought them to drink coffee. I didn't mind, beyond disappointment at having little opportunity to talk to K. He and Henderson and I walked towards London Library, I meaning to collect sack of books I left there yesterday. Police told us no one could enter St James's Square. Tiresome because I need these books. It is horrifying that these savages should rake the streets with bullets from their embassy window, in our London. Bloody people. When they come out, I hope the assassins will be caught and tried, and the rest packed off. But Gaddafi has the effrontery to announce to the world that England has insulted his embassy officials and that our police did the shooting. Is it likely? The *fiancé* of the little policewoman killed is one of them.

Saturday, 21st April

Today is my poor father's birthday. He would be a hundred and four, were he still alive. As it was he died of excruciating cancer of the bladder in 1949. I cannot forget the suffering he endured.

---

[*] 2nd Earl Jellicoe (b. 1918); Conservative Party politician; Lord Privy Seal and Leader of the House of Lords, 1970–3 (resigned over the 'call girl affair' provoked by the private life of Lord Lambton, MP: see *Ancient as the Hills*, 26 May 1973).
[†] Edward Shackleton (1911–94), mountaineer and Labour Party politician; cr. life peer, 1958; Leader of the House of Lords, 1968–70.

This morning I went by appointment to see Mr Charlton, my specialist. I told him that my trouble was little better than before my operation; in one respect worse, in that there were times when I was
suddenly taken short. He then said, 'I am going to do another small
operation on you. I am going to remove your testicles, because they
are so nearly connected with your prostate. Your prostate was diseased,
you know.' So I, who have always averred that I never wanted to know,
said without hesitation, 'By which you mean that I had cancer of the
prostate?' 'Yes,' he said. To be told this, which I have always dreaded,
was not the tremendous shock I expected. Charlton was wonderfully
soothing and encouraging, assuring me that there was an 80 per cent
chance of my living another five years or even more.* The removal of
my balls was precautionary, an alternative to treatment with female
hormones. So brother Dick and I have both got cancer. How odd it
seems. This draws me closer to Dick than ever. Unfortunately I
cannot get in touch with them by telephone, and they have not rung
me for a week.

When I got home, darling A. greeted me. 'Well, how did you get
on?' 'He told me everything,' I said. 'I now know what I suppose you
were told all along.' 'Yes,' she said, 'I knew after your operation. I rang
Charlton up this morning and he told me you were to have another
operation. So I asked him what he would say if you asked him outright. He replied that he would tell you the truth.' My one overpow-
ering desire now is to be with A.

Charlton said to me, 'If you want me to, I will take charge throughout.' 'I do, I do,' I said. Then I told him that beyond this operation I
was determined not to undergo any more operations. Also I refused
to be given radium treatment or have my life prolonged in agonies.
He indicated, though without saying so, that he would agree to this.
A splendid man. I like him so much.

Monday, 23rd April

Two nights ago in bed, it being Good Friday, I read the last few chapters of St John's Gospel. Was amazed by the number of references to
himself as 'the disciple whom Jesus loved', who during the Last
Supper 'lay with his head on Jesus's breast'. And by his depreciation of

---

* He was to survive for another fourteen years and publish ten more books.

St Peter, whose exploits on the water he seems to deride and whose slowness in running to the sepulchre is remarked upon. Should Jesus have had a favourite, if indeed he did and St John was not romancing? And do these chapters give credence to the Gay Brigade's assertion that Jesus was homosexual?

Then I read the ultimate chapters of St Luke. Was deeply moved by the story of the two malefactors crucified on either side of Christ, one abusing him, the other rebuking the first one, saying they were both wicked men while Christ was a good man, and turning to Jesus and asking him to remember him, and Christ saying, 'You will be with me this time next day in Paradise.' Such compassion and humanity are rare in the Testaments. And as for St Peter and the denial of Christ before the cock crowed thrice, ending with the words 'He wept', well, this always makes me weep.

Then read St Matthew's account. Not so vivid as St Luke and St John. Much emphasis on events taking place 'according to the prophets', almost as if the Evangelists were determined to shape events to suit those maddening Old Testament prophecies. Jesus himself emphasises these coincidences. How conservative the Jews were.

Tuesday, 24th April

Tricia rang from Cyprus. Dick is sinking fast. She said he was not unconscious and was struggling to live. A strange circumstance is that Dick asked to see an Anglican priest; has done so twice, and derived much comfort from him. Dick, who never went to church and was, I imagined, thoroughly agnostic. How often this happens to the dying. K. Clark, whom his agnostic friends scoffed at for being received by a Roman priest at the end. I believe it is the teaching of extreme youth, implanted into the infant mind, resurging in second childhood. Dick must have been thinking of the church services at Wickhamford, at which he always fainted, we never knew whether genuinely or merely in order to be removed by the nurse. He was able to take in my last letter to him, and laughed at my description of walking round the corridors of the Bath Clinic with my tube and bottle concealed in a shopping bag. I find myself thinking of him most of the day, and feel part of me is draining away with him, as though we were twins. Yet we drifted apart in life, without a jot of mutual dislike, just through sheer difference of environment and interests, coupled with the fact that Elaine never let us have a moment together.

Thursday, 26th April

Last weekend was, apart from our worries, one of the nicest I can remember. Burnet [Pavitt] and Selina Hastings to stay. Selina enchanting. Went for a long walk with her talking about her book and the Mitfords. She is quick, amusing, a brilliant conversationalist, understanding, with all the virtues I so loved in Vita. Yet she, like me, feels ill-at-ease among the highbrows, whose every sentence has a cerebral import, and who, she feels, are weighing every word one utters.

Because I had on Saturday morning learnt about my cancer, I confided in Burnet, who is such an old friend and such a sympathetic one. He counselled me not to confide in anyone else. If I do, he or she will confide in his or her best friend, and so it will circulate. Besides, he says, compassionate though people may seem, the idea of a friend losing his balls is a subject for hilarity.

The weather is ideal. I have always noticed that divine weather often coincides with disaster, such as the outbreak of the last war, and the fall of France.

Spoke to Simon today on the telephone. He has said goodbye to Dick, who is not expected to live through the night.

Friday, 27th April

After dining alone with Sally [Westminster] I reached home last night at 10.30. The telephone was ringing as I unlocked the door. Rebuffing the dogs who were giving me their usual ecstatic welcome I picked up the receiver. Tricia from Cyprus to announce that Dick had died at ten o'clock their time, just as I was going in to dinner with Sally. For a time I was more concerned with the loss of the latchkeys to my Bath flat. During my bath and in bed the true sadness dawned.

Saturday, 28th April

Motoring into town yesterday I found myself behind a small car in the back window of which was a printed label, 'Flash your lights if you find me sexy.' I could only see the driver's head. It did not make a sensational appeal. Now, ten years ago I would have flashed for the fun of the adventure. Alas, I thought, I have a mere three days left in which I remain a man, and even so, the experience is out of the question.

I telephoned Elaine. She was wonderfully controlled and dignified. Told me that today's funeral was of the simplest kind. The 'darling' clergyman conducted it. His visit to Dick when he was in a bad mental state brought him the greatest comfort. She held his hand all the time he was dying. He was perfectly happy, and suffered no physical pain. She says she is all right provided no one sympathises with her. Thanked God he died first, for he could never have survived without her. 'You know, Jim, how much I loved him.'

M. came down at midday and spent the night with me here. A great joy to have him. A marvellous guest, and wanted to go for walks. We ambled, sat in the garden, and talked. Perfect spring weather. M. gave me admirable advice – to leave Regy for six months, once I have finished researches at the end of June. For remaining six months of year to concentrate on editing my diaries,* by which writings I am now best known. He could never edit them; I alone can and must do this. It is just possible that within the six-month period I may be able to continue my novel. All this if I am spared.

Monday, 30th April

At one o'clock went to the Bath Clinic again, exactly six weeks since my last operation. I was more fearful on this occasion. By the time I was given the pre-med prick in the behind, was in a silly state of nerves. Humiliating little ceremony in bathroom with sister shaving my pudenda. Experience of waking up in intensive care not agreeable. Brightly lit, bustling with people in white, much laughter and jokes, and other patients calling out. When one comes to, one wants calm and peace. This was hellish. 'Nurse, nurse!' I found myself calling, just for recognition, reassurance that I was alive, wanting a drink badly. Wanting to be away, wanting calm. Soon wheeled to my own room. Thank God.

Saturday, 5th May

My life is a catalogue of deaths and funerals. Rosemary [Verey] rang up on Thursday morning to announce that David had died in the night. A shock to me, who thought he had recovered from his cancer. Today A. and I went to his funeral at Barnsley church. Touching little prelude was a little granddaughter of ten playing Handel on the flute,

---

* That is, the last of his diaries for the 1940s, published the following year as *Midway on the Waves*.

before the chief mourners arrived. Over by 11.45. We waited, standing and chatting, until one o'clock when we were given a stand-up luncheon. I had to sit, for wound still aches. It is curious to be emasculated.

Am reading a new life of Randolph Churchill. Very good, well composed, by Brian Roberts who called on me a couple of years ago to see letters written to me by Randolph at Eton.* Really, Randolph was an inexcusably awful person. Bombastic, lecherous, insensitive, wrong-headed, and rude, rude such as can never have been evinced before in a civilised society.

Sunday, 13th May

My bleeding persists. Tomorrow I am to have more stitches put into scrotum under local anaesthetic, my third operation in eight weeks. Yesterday we lunched with Billy Henderson and Frank Tait.† The latter called me out into the garden and asked me about my condition. He was very reassuring and agreed that my nice specialist Charlton was quite right to have done what he did rather than give me female hormones. Frank said they were given to Cecil Beaton, who in consequence developed breasts of enormous size and was extremely unhappy. Cecil refused to have his testicles removed, telling Frank he might want to have children one day, a desire his friends had never noticed before. In fact he had a horror of mutilation, of being physically incomplete. Don't we all? I think the psychological pain is worse than the physical in this particular matter. Frank is a heavenly human being – superb cook, splendid doctor with reassuring manner, excellent raconteur, and abounding in understanding and sympathy.

Cathy Sutherland was staying. Maddening. She puts on an absurd act when she is to meet people, her society nonsense. Looks grotesque and terrifying, like an evil Queen of the Night. What these women do to their eyes – pencil lines where they ought not to be, eyelashes caked in mascara. She said to me on greeting, 'I dreamt last night that I was talking to Graham about you. He said, "Jim is a genius".' Oh, I said, that's going a bit far. 'Yes,' she replied, 'in his lifetime I only remember him saying that about Michaelangelo.' Frank, who knows every aspect of her affairs, says she lives in a hideous suite in the

---

* See *Deep Romantic Chasm*, 26 September 1981.
† Australian child psychiatrist (b. 1923).

Connaught Hotel costing her £60,000 a year. She doesn't have a single object of her own, not even a drawing of Graham's. Says she doesn't want any reminders of her happy past, yet dreams of him and lives with his memory. Leads a selfish, vacant life. When a Jesuit from Farm Street told her she ought to join Graham on high, she asked if he meant she ought to commit suicide. Of course he meant that she ought to do something for others during her remaining years and thus attain a nearness to God, in the vicinity of whom she supposes Graham to be.

On leaving I kissed Cathy and said how nice it was to see her again. She was kind enough to agree, and added, 'We did have fun those evenings we four dined in Monte and Mentone, until you scolded me.' So she remembers the row which ended our friendship. I said, 'Someone' – I did not remind her that it had been she – 'made terrible mischief between us and the K. Clarks.'*

A. and I walked with the dogs along the verge of the Fonthill lake.† Most beautiful sunny afternoon, although bitter wind still. Two pairs of swans, lifting themselves out of the water, flying a few yards, beating the quiet surface with harsh strokes. Moorhens cackling. Ancient beeches with their feet in the water. Beckford may have planted them. Then out through the Palladian arch and past the giant ferns. What a beautiful, haunted place.

Wednesday, 16th May

On Monday A. drove me to the Bath Clinic. I was mightily depressed all morning, dreading the operation and 'coming round' process. Put on white smock shroud and lay on bier-bed, the lamb for slaughter. Charlton came with anaesthetist. Examined my poor person. He said there is no discharge, the whole thing is healing, and decided after all not to operate. I felt like the young Isaac snatched from the knife of Abraham. Fortunately no poor lamb took my sacrificial place.

None the less, my bleeding still persists. Can it be that the wound just hasn't healed after more than a fortnight, as Charlton maintains? Or is it haemorrhage which is associated with cancer? Am I being deceived? I cannot trust anyone, and don't know that I want to be

---

* See entry for 25 July 1982.
† Between Fonthill Gifford and Bishop's Fonthill, Wiltshire, in the grounds of William Beckford's Fonthill Abbey.

undeceived. At moments I have awful forebodings that my life expectation is a matter of months, and I ought to drop Regy entirely to concentrate on tidying diaries.

Wednesday, 23rd May

John Betj. died in his sleep at the end of last week. Funeral Tuesday at midday. I telephoned Feeble in Cornwall, where J. died, and she said she would like me to attend. So I went by train on Monday and stayed with the dear Trinicks at Lanhydrock. Marvellous day of early summer, the spring freshness just gone. The stretch of riviera coast after Exeter and Powderham is exceptionally beautiful. Train chugs through short tunnels. On the right, high honeycombed cliffs of soft sandstone, weird lunar shapes, but warm, apricot colour. Wild flowers powdering the slopes of the grassy intervals, the moving train making the focus muzzy.

But the funeral yesterday was in driving rain. Hired a taxi to Trebetherick. Arrived about 11.20, meaning to call on Elizabeth and leave my suitcase at the cottage, but we met them on the road. I offered to give them a lift. But E. said you can't drive, only walk. So I dismissed taxi, got out and carried suitcase. Mercifully had put on galoshes in the car, and had my flimsy plastic mac. Even so, after three-quarter mile walk across open field to little St Enodoch Church, with low spire, got soaked. Had to shut umbrella, which threatened to blow inside out. Plunged into tiny church, dark as pitch save for a few oil lamps and candles. Was put into a two-seater pew next to Jock Murray, who whispered throughout. In front of us Penelope [Betjeman] and Billa [Harrod]. Church by no means full. Reserved for family, a few intimate friends and some neighbours. The battery of wind and rain somewhat distracted concentration, yet added to the drama. Paul Betjeman read the lesson. He could barely see and had to take the Bible to the only non-stained window pane for light. We stood in the porch while John's coffin was carried by bearers across the field and lowered into grave beside the lych-gate. Struggled back across field with Anne Tree to Elizabeth's and John's cottage where a fire burning. Given toast with cottage cheese and a glass of whisky. The others went to a neighbouring house for luncheon with Penelope, whom I did not see to talk to, only embraced silently after the cortège had followed the coffin to the graveyard, to Nunc Dimittis.

Horrid journey back in uncomfortable old-fashioned carriage, changing at Bristol. Darling A. arrived back from the Chelsea Flower

Show and gave me dinner. Anyway, I paid my respects to the best man who ever lived and the most loveable. Have written to the two widows – difficult. The poignancy of sitting on John's little death-bed with Archie the teddy bear and Jumbo the elephant propped against the pillow.

Saturday, 26th May

On Wednesday Alex Moulton called for me in his beautiful brown Rolls-Royce and whisked me off to Liverpool. I was tired by my excursion to Cornwall, and this expedition has also tired me. We stayed at the Adelphi, great hotel of Edwardian era, splendour and riches of Liverpool, White Star and Cunard glories. Liverpool now terribly down-at-heel. Rubbish litters the streets, old Georgian terraces being pulled or just falling down, walls disfigured by subversive words. We dined with Larry Rathbone* and wife, nice, tall, straight, grey-haired lady whom he snubs aggressively. Largish uneven house with many good pictures bought for Larry by Eardley, taste non-existent otherwise. Alex very successful, talking to Larry about Liverpool conditions, which are hopeless at present, the city being bankrupt. They warned us that no one ever walked the streets after dark. Indeed, Larry summoned a taxi which, we later learned, had arrived and driven away because the driver had not dared leave the cab to look for and pull the bell.

I spent next morning at the University Library looking through some 160 letters to Regy. Found nothing much of interest except several photographs of correspondents attached to letters. Visited the R.C. Cathedral which I think little of. Gimmicky. Of concrete, which has of course weathered atrociously, iron rust streaks. The prominent lantern with too-flimsy skimpy finials. Inside cheerless in spite of large circular nave and high lantern and splodges of ugly glass. On the other hand, the Anglican Cathedral by Giles Gilbert Scott really is a masterpiece. Quite traditional of course, foundation stone laid in 1904 by Edward VII, fifty years or more construction, but all of a piece. Alex much moved, as was I.

Stayed that night at Southport, charming Edwardian resort for the proletariat, in Prince of Wales Hotel, cosy and old-fashioned. Next day we visited Walker Art Gallery and Lady Lever Gallery, filled with

---

* Lawrence Rathbone (b. 1913); senior partner of Rathbone Bros & Co. (J.L.-M's investment managers); brother of Jack Rathbone.

first-rate furniture and many pictures known since childhood, such as
The Scapegoat by Holman Hunt. Greatly impressed by Port Sunlight
village layout. Houses carefully grouped round grass lawns. Cottages
of half-timber, with parget-work dated 1892, pebbledash, oriels, bow
windows, Arts and Craftsy wood carving and barge-boards, tile-
hanging, casement windows – a museum of pre-1914 style and quality.
We continued to Hawarden* where, in spite of non-receipt of letter
from Gladstones, we walked into the park and viewed the Castle from
the front. Extremely rude of Gladstones to ignore my polite letter
with stamped addressed envelope.

Sunday, 27th May

The Nicholas Ridleys† lunched. She, the second wife (the first, Clayre,
is a pearl but was driven away by N's infidelities) is a chirpy little trout,
very agreeable. Nicholas was, when he first joined the Executive
Committee of the N.T., the most beautiful young man imaginable. I
remember how on his entry to the board room for the first time all
heads swivelled in his direction, and Gerry Wellington nearly fainted.
Now he is a middle-aged parliamentarian and Minister of Transport.
(We should have known, but had to ask.) He has little charm. I had a
short abortive conversation with him after luncheon on the sofa. I asked
if he was worried by the Gulf troubles. He said in that airy stiff-upper-
lip manner, 'Not at all. We have our own North Sea Oil.' But, I said,
we are told that is our chief export, that we keep none for ourselves.
He said we get enough to supply our needs. On the subject of conservation he deprecated the scare-mongers, meaning me. I remarked that
these days there were no frogs, no butterflies. He said he had many in
his garden. Yes, I laughed ironically, but you are too young to remember that fifty years ago the country swarmed with them. Besides, butterflies come in the late summer and are all poisoned by pesticides, like

---

* Sixteenth-century castle in Flintshire, country residence of W. E. Gladstone and still
inhabited by his descendants.
† Hon. Nicholas Ridley (1929–93), yr s. of 3rd Viscount Ridley; MP (C) Cirencester and
Tewkesbury; became Sec. of State for Environment (1986–89) and Trade and Industry
(1989–90) but resigned from Government in July 1990 after an unguarded interview
during which he expressed himself in colourful language on the subject of Germany and
the Germans; m. 1st 1950 Hon. Clayre Campbell, dau. of 4th Baron Stratheden and
Campbell (m. diss. 1974), 2nd 1979 Judy Kendall.

birds. He retorted that many birds throve on pesticides. The falcon has increased in numbers. Yes, said I, but this year no one in these parts has heard a single cuckoo. But there are more buntings, he said. I gave up.

I have been sent my copy of Roger Hinks's* diaries which that splendid fellow Michael Russell has published.† I was one of the sponsors. Dozens of publishers refused to take it. It is chock-a-block with wisdom and intellectual speculation about art and life, a wonderful book. I wish the whole diary could have been published instead of snippets. What a reflection on publishers and the reading public that this extremely serious work could only be printed twenty years after the author's death after a handful of his friends had guaranteed it.

Thursday, 31st May

Went to London yesterday evening in time to dine with M. at the Oxford and Cambridge Club. He kindly got me a room for the night there, since Brooks's would not oblige. He has finished his new book on the abortive abduction of the Duke of Windsor, which will come out in the autumn. Is now editing the Windsor letters, but is having trouble with his Master,‡ aged eighty-five, whom he loves dearly. She objects even to the few well-merited criticisms of the D. of W. in his present book. I told him that he must on no account give in to her or he will be false to himself. M. very sweet and rang me when he got home to find out if I was all right in my room, and again at breakfast just to give me his love.

Worked in London Library. Just because I am financially ruined by doctors' and hospital bills, I bought myself two expensive shirts today and two pairs of French socks at Harvic & Hudson. They told me I was their oldest customer. Then to John Harris's house to look up references to Regy in his enormous collection of books on the First

---

* Roger Packman Hinks (1903–63); Assistant Keeper of Greek and Roman Antiquities at British Museum, 1926–39 (resigning over a scandal concerning the cleaning of the Elgin Marbles: see entry for 30 June 1984); British Council Representative in Rome (1945–49), Amsterdam (1949–55), Athens (1955–7), Paris (1959–63).
† *Gymnasium of the Mind: The Journals of Roger Hinks, 1933–1963*, ed. John Goldsmith, with a Foreword by Kenneth Clark and a Portrait Memoir by Patrick Leigh Fermor (Michael Russell, 1984). Russell was the 'charming' publisher who had commissioned J.L.-M. to write a biography of William Beckford nine years earlier (*Through Wood and Dale*, 10 January 1975).
‡ Maître Blum.

World War. John abroad but his wife Eileen, a sweet character, let me browse. She says this is his mania. It comes before architecture, and he reads nothing but these books. He had an uncle of whom he was fonder than of his parents, who came right through the war and told John stories of his adventures. He became hooked. Also the war poets of that generation are his favourite poetry reading.

A. has got the job of resurrecting and running the garden at Lyegrove, which has been bought by a millionaire tycoon. She is asking an enormous sum for the job. Added to Mick Jagger's garden and her new book, *The Englishwoman's House*, she, in her mid seventies, is earning enormous sums, far larger than I have ever earned. She has become a household name in the gardening world.

Monday, 4th June

I went to see Guy Charlton about my bleeding. He just smiled and said I was doing well and it would shortly stop. It has been going on for five weeks, so I am not encouraged.

Thursday, 7th June

Roger Hinks's dissertations on art are comparable with Proust's, and he tells that Proust is a great influence, the only novelist he reads. Much of his philosophical speculation is above my head. This proud, prissy, snubbing man reveals himself to be vulnerable. Did not like parties or people. Loved a few friends, notably the American Robertses.* Hated his sojourn in Athens and seldom left his flat. Hated the city, the great heat, and the landscape devoid of architecture. Debunked the Parthenon which, comparing it to photographs taken in the 1850s and earlier engravings and drawings, he pronounced a fake from top to toe, rebuilt or restored.

Monday, 11th June

A. took me to Prokoviev's *Romeo and Juliet* in the Bristol Hippodrome. Covent Garden cast: Wayne Eagling as Romeo and Lesley Collier as

---

* Laurence and Isabel Roberts. He had been director of the American Academy in Rome; as a couple, they travelled widely, in the manner of characters from the novels of Henry James.

Juliet. Sets and clothes by Nicholas Georgiadis, choreography by Kenneth MacMillan. We last saw this ballet in 1965 with Nureyev and Margot Fonteyn. This performance was every bit as good. Wonderful drill in the fighting scenes. Heavenly dreamy music. That Russian astringency, like Stravinsky, but more melodious, and soaring and transporting.

Thursday, 14th June

A. and I drive to London. Appalling traffic jams, London awash with tourists and congestion. To buffet luncheon given by Faber & Faber for this autumn's paperback authors of which I am one, my three diary volumes and *Another Self* being published in August. I take minimum interest in such an event, but am pleased with the jacket designs. I think Faber's a charming old-fashioned publisher, as Chatto's used to be and Murray's still is. Rosemary Goad, spinster director, very sweet, like Jane Langton [of Royal Archives]. Talked to another, Richard de la Mare, grandson of poet. Anthony Wedgwood Benn* among the authors present. A., asked if she would like to be introduced to him, said; 'Not on your life.' Sat next to an ancient man of eighty-two called 'Gip' Wells,† legitimate son of H.G. A round old bundle, with white hair and expansive smile, but taciturn.

Joined M. at his new flat in Strathearn Place. He has done it charmingly, with beautifully made double bookcases of mahogany, looking glasses under central pediments, completely covering facing walls of sitting room. He has bought from junk auctioneers a splendid writing table of immense size *c.*1900. Sumptuous little bathroom in mahogany and brass. All very cosy and autumnal. I am very impressed that M. who has little visual sense is making such an attractive bachelor nest. He gave me a painting on hardboard dated 1913 of a whippet sitting in a wicker chair. Enchanting. Said it reminded him of Folly, which it does. We dined happily. All is well with him, his second book finished, thank God.

I stayed the night at Brooks's. All very comfortable and old-fashioned, though my bedroom smelled disagreeably of cats. Breakfast well served by attentive waitresses. Reparked car in forecourt of

---

* Rt. Hon. Anthony Wedgwood Benn, formerly 2nd Viscount Stansgate (disclaimed, 1963); Secretary of State for Energy 1975–9, subsequently the leading radical in the Parliamentary Labour Party.
† Professor G.P. Wells (1901–85), er s. of H.G. Wells; zoologist.

Society of Antiquaries. Fetching my ticket from the library, thought how beautiful that room was for working. If it were not for expense, this is how I should always like to stay in London.

Monday, 18th June

A. and I went to supper with Penelope [Betjeman]* at Blacklands [Wiltshire], Candida and Rupert Lycett Green† being away. Lovely midsummer eve. Plunged off horrid main road on the edge of Calne into drive. A tunnel of lush trees, opening into a park of long corn and hay in process of mowing, with vast, spreading chestnut trees like tea cosies. Smell of amber hay strong and sweet. Long shadows. The large Georgian block serene in evening light, front door open with view onto garden side beyond. Wide river softly flowing just below house to a cascade. Garden a dream. Penelope is a stalwart character. Less nonsense about her than anyone I have known in a long life. Cares nothing about clothes or appearances. Like a wizened old apple. Only thing that worried me was her sunken eyes. She talked much about John and their life together in the old days. Said that I was the first person to mention John's existence to her, when I told her that I had met a real poet. She later met him through sending an article for publication to the *Architectural Review*. Strange that he should have a memorial service in Westminster Abbey, when one thought of her parents' disapproval of her marriage to 'that middle-class Dutchman'. She has made a *démarche* to Elizabeth [Cavendish], who has replied that she cannot bring herself to meet P. for at least a year. Sounds so unlike dear Feeble. We ate in a summer-house, one granddaughter present. P. recalled her 'wedding' to Johnnie Churchill in the Wytham Woods.‡ I was to be the priest, but they could not find me. P. believes that, had I been found and 'married' them – I was with Desmond [Parsons] and John Sutro§ – it would have been valid, for the sacrament of marriage

---

* Hon. Penelope Chetwode (1910–86), m. 1933 John Betjeman.
† Candida (b. 1942), o. dau. of Sir John and Lady Betjeman; m. 1963 Rupert Lycett Green, founder of Blades, fashionable tailors; writer on architectural and horticultural subjects and editor of her father's letters in two volumes.
‡ This episode took place in the autumn of 1930, Wytham Abbey near Oxford then belonging to John Churchill's grandmother Lady Abingdon: Penelope's parents disapproved of Churchill's suit and took her to spend the next year in India.
§ Aesthete, *bon vivant*, and film-maker; founder of Oxford Railway Club (1904–85).

is sealed by the consent of the parties. Said that John had been a Quaker before going to Oxford, and became an Anglo-Catholic with Billy Clonmore.* Would never reconcile himself to the Romans, which was the principal undoing of their marriage.† A. and I sipped white wine, P. water, while the shadows lengthened, the swans roused themselves on the water and the blackbirds raised their voices. Across the water the Downs and the White Horse. Two steel pylons on the summit actually enhance the view. A nice untidy house full of children. P. told us that she plans to retire to a hotel at Llandrindod Wells, run by nuns.

Saturday, 23rd June

A. and I motored to Sussex. Lunched with Camilla Fairbairn and John‡ at Cuckfield where we at four attended Henry Robinson's wedding in the large church. It was full of unknown folk. Bride and dear Henry both looked handsome. He acquitted himself well. Nick an usher, very sweet with bridesmaids and pages. I have not attended a wedding for twenty-five years and wore an ordinary dark suit, the only male so accoutred. All the others, old and young, in well-fitted tail coats. Motored half an hour to the bride's father's house, unexceptional stockbroker good taste. Met Simon Glenarthur,§ who came up to me unrecognising. He is a Minister of State, a Lord in Waiting, and I don't know what else. Since one may discount old Uncle Matt, the first Baron, who robbed the till at Arthur & Co., this charming and good-looking young man is the first of the dynasty to distinguish himself.

We did not stay for the dance but slipped away to dine and stay two nights with Betty Hussey.¶ Much enjoyed this. She is a darling, and

---

* William Howard, Lord Clonmore (1902–78); social and literary figure of 1930s, who converted to Roman Catholicism shortly before J.L.-M. did so in 1934; s. father as 8th Earl of Wicklow, 1946.
† Penelope had become a Roman Catholic in 1948.
‡ John Sydney Fairbairn (b. 1934), m. 1968 Camilla Fry (formerly wife of the L.-Ms' friend Jeremy Fry, inventor and resident of Bath); director of companies and charities, and a Deputy-Lieutenant for West Sussex.
§ Simon Arthur, 4th Baron Glenarthur (b. 1944), son of 3rd Baron by his 2nd wife (1st wife having been J.L.-M's sister Audrey); Conservative politician; Parliamentary Under Secretary at DHSS, 1983–5, later Minister of State at Foreign Office; m. 1969 Susan Barry.
¶ Widow of Christopher Hussey, architectural historian and sometime editor of *Country Life*, and owner of Scotney Castle, Kent (whose gardens she had donated to N.T.).

such fun, always laughing and joking, though suffering from an arthritic knee. An example of how the rich don't know what they possess: she showed us a downstairs room which is part of a flat she is letting, which turned out to be crammed with furniture, rugs and wine which she said she had never seen before, but are presumably hers.

Saturday, 30th June

I had a bad scare staying at Brooks's on the 26th. Thought I was having a haemorrhage. Was up four or five times in the night, and nearly chucked N.T. Arts Panel tour next day. It passed. Two days at Belton and Calke Abbey. Too many staff present, about thirty to six of Panel. Stayed one night in hotel in Southwell, and visited the Minster. Very large, purest Romanesque, impressive. Roof modern, and impression that Minster may have been a ruin and restored at turn of the century. Touching wall tablet to sergeant-major put up by his fellow NCOs; another to an oologist (*sic*) who brought the first waxbill's eggs to Britain. Myles Hildyard[*] showed me the house on the edge of the town where Byron lived before he inherited, the little lame boy with his mother. Nice, unspoilt late Georgian house. Chrissy Gibbs[†] very intelligent and no-nonsense, full of good ideas. Johnny Walker[‡] good-natured with sense of humour, inclined to be a bore. Talking of Hinks's diaries, he told me that in the 1930s, before the scandal at the British Museum over the Elgin Marbles, he was taken by Duveen[§] into the gallery he had built for them. To his amazement Duveen ordered an attendant to fetch him a bucket of hot water and a brush and proceeded to scrub a Parthenon Metope, saying, 'There, that looks better.'

Attended John Betjeman's memorial service in Westminster Abbey. We were given best possible seats, two stalls in choir, though A. alas unable to come owing to sprained wrist. I sat next to Michael Tree. I

---

[*] Squire of Flintham Hall, Nottinghamshire (b. 1914); war hero, local historian, and sometime honorary representative of N.T.

[†] Art dealer (b. 1938).

[‡] Former Director of National Gallery in Washington, DC.

[§] Joseph, Baron Duveen (1869–1939), London art dealer who made a fortune selling European masterpieces (some of them wrongly attributed) to American collections; ennobled in 1933 on account of his charitable bequests, including a gallery at the British Museum to house the Elgin Marbles.

think he wept, and I certainly did at times. Before service opened we listened to John's favourite tunes, *In a Monastery Garden*, other Elgar, and school songs he loved. Immensely long procession of twenty-five to thirty clergymen I would guess, dear old Gerard Irvine* prancing among them, followed by Archbishop of Canterbury in white mitre. Feeble to whom I blew a kiss was lunching with him afterwards. Billa shocked that he should entertain, as she put it, 'not the widow but the concubine'. The Prince of Wales read the first lesson beautifully, strong, good voice, slowly, pausing in the right places. Jock Murray read the second, equally well until the last sentence when he was so moved that he could barely get out the words. Apposite somehow, and touching. I congratulated him when we left, and he said, 'By Jove, I barely made it.' I thought how amazed J.B. would have been, when I first knew him fifty years ago, at this national hero's apotheosis. Harry Williams's† tribute was excellent and paid oblique tribute to Feeble's thirty years of friendship and nursing. The Abbey packed with close friends and unknown admirers. Special prayers written for John. Much emphasis on the love he inspired. Moving and magnificent ceremony.

When I got to Badminton, there was Rupert Loewenstein with Mick Jagger. A nice little man, unassuming. He had been looking at schools for his daughter. Dressed very soberly, as a parent should. He is tiny. Fresh, youthful face. Figure not good. Too thin and chest hollow. Proffers the fingers to shake hand. No firm grip.

Thursday, 5th July

A miracle has happened. My discharge has ended. I really seem to be better, and feel renewed in strength. I wrote to M. in Paris, where he is editing the Duchess of Windsor's letters, that I feel I am walking on the edge of a precipice, but intend to look inland rather than out to sea and hope for the best. I have put Regy temporarily aside, having finished the research and returned the papers to Churchill College. In

---

* Anglo-Catholic priest (b. 1921), Rector of St Matthew's, Westminster, friend of Sir John Betjeman, whom J.L.-M. found 'nice, slightly absurd, cultivated, popular' (*Ancient as the Hills*, 11 May 1973).
† Close friend and spiritual mentor of J.B. and Lady Elizabeth Cavendish; resigned as Dean of Trinity College, Cambridge, 1969, to join Community of the Resurrection, Mirfield, Yorkshire as a monk.

the fear that I had not long to live, I started editing my diaries for 1948–9 in the last week of June. They are a mess, but I can make something of them. The fact that the thoughts and events of those days are recorded at all is what matters. I have already got to July 1949. To type them up will take several weeks. And I still want to finish my 'German' novel. Meanwhile I have agreed to write two reviews, each of three books, for *Country Life*. Foolish in view of the amount of work I have in hand, but good practice which will keep the hand and eye in tune.

Sunday, 8th July

We are enjoying a heat wave, tempered with usual anxieties about shortage of water. A's garden *embaumé* with roses and honeysuckle, arbutus, clematis, lilies. Never so full and luscious as now. There is a wild convolvulus out at the moment, with a snow white trumpet as virginal and almost as large as that of the arum lily, and yet we take it for granted and scarcely observe it. Yellow stonecrop makes a wonderful curry cushion along the tops of the remaining stone walls. The lime tree flowers smelling more strongly than usual, due to this exceptionally sunny summer. My divine blue *Geranium pratense* along the verges, which the brutes have scythed before they have seeded. Will there be any next year?

To Communion this morning at the big church. Eight women and three men, all middle class. Never the proletariat, who presumably know a thing or two and are not going to be bothered with all this nonsense. And do the middle classes go to church for prestigious reasons? I don't think so. It is because they speculate, wonder, want something beyond the mundane. Also because they are patriotic, traditionalist, law abiding, decent.

We have Elizabeth Winn staying. A nice woman but tiring, for she talks and mimics incessantly. Two nights ago A. and I dined with Woman [Pamela Jackson] at Caudle Green. Debo [Devonshire] and Diana [Mosley] staying, the latter looking rather haggard. I had long talks with her about days of yore. She told me how, in the end, Aunt Maud liked her and depended on her visits. Both she and Tom loved Aunt Dorothy.* Debo frolicsome.

---

* Maud Mosley (*née* Heathcote-Edwards) was Diana Mosley's mother-in-law; her sister Dorothy had married J.L.-M's paternal uncle Alec Milne Lees-Milne, who died in 1931.

Received a sad letter from Archie Aberdeen,[*] telling that he had his prostate punctured two years ago and it has now gone bad on him. When I telephoned him I noticed his voice sounded softer, and more halting.

Monday, 9th July

At the Hollands' annual concert I was made aware of my increasing inability to recognise friends. An absurd lady, who knows me, said, 'I simply love your books. I always keep *Whispering Galleries* beside my bed.' I thanked her, and hoped it was enjoyable. Was introduced to Lord Gowrie and hadn't a clue who this distinguished man with a bad complexion could be, though we met a year ago at Chatsworth.[†] He said he felt he knew me intimately through my books. He made a speech before the pianist played, very good and without a single note. I envied him this facility.

Today I motored to Wellington College to see the Master, David Newsome.[‡] Such a nice man. We were at once on Christian name terms. Even so, I find it shy-making to be with a headmaster, although he must be twenty years my junior. He generously gave me extracts from A. C. Benson's journals referring to Esher. Benson clearly did not much like Esher, but his comments are interesting, coming from a contemporary. We lunched at a pub near the College, for it was the end of term. Talked about romantic friendships between Victorian boys. He told me that the 'mores' of the boys changed with each generation. Whereas twenty-five years ago Wellington boys thought it chic to be queer, and boasted of their prowess, true or untrue, today it was an unmentionable subject. Any boy suspected of being so was the victim of taunts. We agreed that we both disliked Oscar Browning who was lecherous, and liked William Cory who was romantic.

[*] Lord Archibald Gordon (1913–84), s. brother 1974 as 5th Marquess of Aberdeen; befriended J.L.-M. in 1930s when he worked for Council for the Protection of Rural England; on staff of BBC Radio, 1946–72.
[†] See entry for 22 July 1983.
[‡] Dr David Newsome (b. 1929); Master of Wellington College, 1980–89; author (whose book *On the Edge of Paradise* [John Murray, 1980], based on the diaries of A. C. Benson and dealing with platonic romances between dons and undergraduates, had interested J.L-M. [see *Deep Romantic Chasm*, 12 October 1980]).

Thursday, 12th July

The Droghedas stay the night. A painful experience. Joan is quite out of reach now. We took them to dine with the Beauforts at the Cottage. She did not know who they were, nor their immensely rich American guest Mrs Wrightsman, who embraced her as an old friend. Was always losing something, her bag, her handkerchief, turning aimlessly in circles, searching. She cannot bear Garrett to be out of her sight, feels nervous without him. He is extremely patient with her, but admitted to me that it was all very wearing, and that he himself is not at all well. When I think of these two forty years ago, he so spry and handsome, she so quick, amused, gay and beautiful, I feel sad.

Mrs Wrightsman came by hired helicopter. The next day she asked Caroline where she would like to be taken to. C. said Burghley. So between luncheon and tea they went, taking A. with them. A. said it was wonderful skimming the earth at a thousand feet, looking at country houses below.

At dinner David said that the Rothschilds were so inter-bred that Jacob* only had two great-grandfathers instead of the usual four. This must be an exaggeration. And Victor Rothschild [Jacob's father] had told him of his lifelong fear of madness.

Friday, 13th July

Walking my dogs on Bath golf course I came upon a man with six whippets on leads. He told me he was retired and determined not to become a crock. He said, 'I have two doctors, my left leg and my right. I walk every day for miles.'

Sunday, 15th July

We lunched with Michael and Anne Tree. No country is more beautiful than theirs at Donhead St Mary. Michael showed me Cecil Beaton's appalling caricatures of Anne Rosse. The cruellest funniest drawings. I laughed so hard I thought my teeth would fall out. Felt most disloyal.[†]

---

[*] Hon. N. C. J. Rothschild (b. 1936), banker; s. father as 4th Baron Rothschild, 1990.

[†] *Autre temps, autre mœurs*: ten years earlier, J.L.-M. had found them just as cruel, but 'infused with vitriol and devilish hate' (*Ancient as the Hills*, 20 June 1974) rather than funny.

Penelope Mortimer,* who is writing yet another biography of the Queen Mother, came to tea. I warned her that I did not know the Q.M. But she persisted, and brought a tape recorder, which always alarms me when the owners are unscrupulous women. This weather-beaten lady is not dislikeable, but not clever either. So long as the machine was whizzing I remained discreet.

Caroline says we would be amazed how many of her friends are 'nicer' to her now she is a duchess. She is also inundated with requests to open things in Bristol and the neighbourhood. She loves it. I cannot believe she does it very well, but doubtless her naturalness appeals.

Wednesday, 18th July

John Cornforth came to see me in Bath to discuss his new book on the development of taste in country house conservation. We talked for four solid hours. He wondered what caused the peculiar philistinism among the British upper classes in the nineteenth century. We agreed that it must have been Dr Arnold.† I said I thought the 'upper' upper classes, Lords Curzon, Rosebery, etc., did not deprecate learning. On the contrary, they combined love of sport (as opposed to games) with book-collecting, et cetera. It was the small squires like my father who inherited a sort of Squire Weston contempt for learning, raising both sport and games to preposterous heights. Even so, the Roseberys and Derbys thought it unbecoming in a gentleman to admire fine furniture and pictures, as the young Lord Crawford‡ discovered at Knowsley.

Sunday, 22nd July

Staying at Chatsworth. An enjoyable weekend, as nearly always here. At one of our meals, A. said to Andrew, 'It must be a huge satisfaction to know what you have done for Chatsworth and see the huge numbers of visitors to whom you have given pleasure', pointing to the

---

* Writer (1918–99); m. 2nd 1949–72 John Mortimer, QC, playwright and author (b. 1923).
† Dr Thomas Arnold (1795–1842), headmaster of Rugby School and exponent of 'muscular Christianity'.
‡ Presumably David Lindsay, 28th Earl of Crawford and 11th Earl of Balcarres (1900–75), Chairman of N.T., 1945–65, whose father had been a friend of Edward Stanley, 17th Earl of Derby (1865–1948), owner of Knowsley, Lancashire.

public outside the window. 'Yes,' he replied with a sigh, 'I love to see them here, but wish it could be for free.' At any rate he is not ashamed to express his delight in getting £20 million for a few drawings at Christie's. At church this morning the vicar gave an admirable sermon. His argument was that it is not merely through words that we reach God, but also through the senses, touch, feeling, smell, taste. In the graveyard Debo took us to look at the Cavendish tombs. She said in her most casual manner, 'Here are two gravestones of my babies. There ought to be a third, I wonder where it can be.' No one else would refer to such things in this way, even if she realised her guests had already noticed them.

Tuesday, 24th July

Much enjoy staying at Brooks's now. The rooms are old-fashioned and comfortable. Worn out by five o'clock after tearing around London, the Rococo exhibition, the Tate in a vain attempt to solve mystery of my Turner watercolour of Dartmouth Castle. Had nice cup of Indian tea and lay on my bed until eight. Kenneth Rose then called for me and gave me a delicious meal at Overton's. Alone he is charming, clever, amusing and gossipy. His greatest friends he told me are Matthew Ridley, brother of Nick (whom he dislikes, says everyone does) and the Duke of Kent, with whom he goes abroad on sightseeing trips. Says he is the nicest man in the world and not stupid, filled with curiosity and a voracious reader. But the Duchess is pious and puritanical. Told me he voted for me to be made a Companion of Literature. I laughed at the idea. On the strength of his *George V*, which won every conceivable prize, Weidenfeld has offered him an advance of £19,000 to write a biographical dictionary of twentieth-century royalty and courtiers.* Not very interesting for him, but he can do it standing on his head, and needs the money. K. a generous host; always takes one to the most succulent and expensive restaurants.

Thursday, 2nd August

Real gardeners, like A., don't need to see plants and flowers in bloom in order to appreciate the quality of a strange garden. They

---

* *Kings, Queens and Courtiers* (Weidenfeld & Nicolson, 1985).

are like real musicians, who don't need to hear a symphony, but can judge it by the score. I don't mean that a gardener does not prefer to see a garden in bloom, or a musical person to hear a symphony performed; but they can do without. Now to me, such a thing is inconceivable.

Saturday, 4th August

A. and I drove to Northamptonshire to stay one night with Gervase Jackson-Stops. Met Gervase with Sachie [Sitwell] at Weston at midday. Sachie surprisingly well and cheerful. Only his memory is bad. Full of chaff and enjoyed being told stories and telling his own. The same adorable chortle and screwing up of his dear face. Francis* and his charming wife now live in part of the house, an admirable arrangement. We three went on to Canons Ashby to see what the N.T. and Gervase in particular have done. It is a miracle of restoration. Three years ago the house was nearly ruinous and empty of furniture. Of course the garden is still bare and new, but the romantic house I knew in the 1930s is there to emerge with the years. A wonderful achievement.

The other great achievement is G's Menagerie at Horton, which I first saw with Robert Byron who would have bought and restored it had he survived the war. But poor Robert would not have done such a splendid job as G., whose knowledge and taste are without parallel. The great room a marvel, re-stuccoed out of nothing, for more than half had been destroyed by vandals and cattle.

Sunday, 5th August

We lunched at Deene. The Brudenells too absurd for words. He remarked of somebody, 'She is quite nice considering how she is not well born.' He notices everything, A's pearl-and-diamond bracelet, and my links which belonged to my father, crystal containing a fox's mask, of which he has an identical pair. Before Deene we called at Boughton. Saw David Scott, greatly reduced and very deaf. I fear he will not last long. Then to Mollie [Buccleuch], much

---

* Francis Sitwell (b. 1935), yr s. of Sir Sacheverell, due to inherit Weston Hall from his father (his elder brother Reresby, heir to the baronetcy, having assumed responsibility for Renishaw Hall near Sheffield on the death of his uncle, Sir Osbert).

aged too but very affectionate. Horrid little apartment carved out of the great house which belonged to her. The English primogeniture system does bring the mighty low. To think of Mollie, once the mistress of Boughton, Drumlanrig, Dalkeith, now an old woman living in a tiny flat, worried to death about her couple leaving. But no complaints.

Monday, 6th August

My birthday in *The Times* today. Rather chic to be plain Mr. Like Daisy Fellowes* wearing a cork necklace at the ball at the Royal Palace in Monaco.

Tuesday, 7th August

London for the day. Coutts & Co. in the Strand so opulent and the attendants so polite that I become reckless and am driven to cash cheques for enormous sums. J.K.-B. lunched at the In & Out.† He was sweet, and interesting about his book on Paxton. We went to the Samuel Johnson exhibition at Arts Council. The Doctor was indeed a very ugly man. Five of six portraits by Reynolds and a death mask, frightening, with mouth drawn to one side. Very blind he was, too. One portrait shows him clutching at thin air. Also went to the exhibition of the Vorticist William Roberts, RA. Forceful, but I do not like this school which ignores shadows and shading. Harsh terminal lines of hair, like wigs. A cup of tea with M. before returning to Paddington. His flat could be so nice, but is chaotic still, like the last. Although he has little sense of decorative style, he likes quality, and is buying old furniture at auctions. This makes the flat unpretentious and individual. M. is off to Sweden, happy to have got rid of second Windsor book. I still dote on him. He gave me A. N. Wilson's biography of Hilaire Belloc for my birthday.

---

* Marguerite, daughter of 4th duc Decazes by his American wife Isabelle Singer (sister of A.L.-M's close friend Winaretta, Princesse Edmond de Polignac); Anglo-French society figure, notorious for her malice; m. 1st Prince Jean de Broglie (d. 1918), 2nd Hon. Reginald Fellowes.

† The Naval and Military Club, so called because of the directions posted at the entrance and exit of the carriage drive of the fine clubhouse in Piccadilly (formerly Palmerston's house) which it occupied until 1998.

Saturday, 11th August

Folly is a clever dog. For several days now she has made a detour when walking from the kitchen door up the garden path, looking suspiciously at a certain point as if she had seen a ghost. I looked and discovered there was a wasps' nest in the low wall under the border. She had discovered it without being stung.

As there was a breeze, I took both dogs for the four-mile Cherry Orchard walk. Watched one brimstone butterfly being mobbed by a covey of little meadow browns, first butterflies seen this year. Between the barn and the Cherry Orchard I met the funny old farmer sitting in car gazing into the field, where I have passed him many a weekend. He wears a pork-pie hat jammed over his forehead, his neck subsided into his body, his body a sack. I asked why he always stopped at this particular gate. He said, 'I always does. It is difficult to get out of the habit of fifty years.' He told me this year was the centenary of his family being tenants of one of the Beaufort farms. Then disclosed that he was eleven years younger than me.

Wednesday, 22nd August

This evening we came back from East Germany, or rather West Berlin, where we spent the last two nights of our tour, about which I jotted some disconnected notes of no great interest in a marbled notebook.

This has not been found; but before leaving Berlin, J.L.-M. had summarised his experiences in a letter to the editor from the Hotel Metropol.

. . . After East Germany and East Berlin this West side strikes a horribly vulgar and decadent note. I suppose living in a pocket surrounded by the enemy with a thin umbilical cord between them and civilisation gives the inhabitants a reckless feeling of unease. The contrast between the two parts of the city is so marked (as well as incongruous) that it is impossible surely to last. The greyness and sombreness and puritanism of the East lowers the tempo and induces sadness. No colour in any city bar one – Weimar. Very little traffic in Leipzig and Dresden. One walks across wide boulevards without waiting for the lights to go green.

All the party of thirty very nice, some dull, but only one bore whom we shunned. Didn't know a soul when we started. We had a most intelligent, human, humorous and kindly guide called Susanna. And she told me a lot about conditions without directly criticising her country. When we parted from her, standing with her cheap little plastic suit-case waving us goodbye, tears were in all eyes as well as her own . . .

Dresden more terribly bombed that I had imagined and only the Zwinger and the Dom have been rebuilt. Beautiful Rococo they are too. But pictures galore in all galleries. The lack of private enterprise, lack of extremes, would drive us mad. I didn't dislike the people. Indeed, all were charming, but pitiable. One did not want to scold but to pat them.

Oh, Weimar is so *gemütlich*. A dear little university town over which the spirits of the Grand Duke Charles Augustus, Goethe and Schiller preside. Unfortunately we went there for the day only, a Sunday too. Goethe's house was jammed with rather smelly workers; we were so packed like sardines that I could not breathe, and hardly saw a thing. Disappointing, for Weimar was what I particularly wished to see. A pretty park, river and little houses with gardens of sunflowers, petunias and tall trees. I won't bore you with a catalogue of the paintings seen in gallery and palace. Sans Souci is divine . . .

The diaries resume.

Friday, 24th August

Dining at the Loewensteins', Josephine's mother, Miss, very funny in her outdated manner, who had remained silent at the table for some time, announced, 'The lower classes always steal plugs. The moment you find the chain of your plug loose, watch out.' Rupert laughed till he cried.

Saturday, 25th August

Billa [Harrod] came to stay for three nights. With such an old friend no extra effort is required. It was lovely having her. She had come from staying with poor Christopher Sykes in Tunbridge Wells, immobile, unable to rise from chair unaided, but *compos*. While here Billa was telephoned from Glenarm by Hector McDonnell that his mother Angela Antrim was dying.[*] Billa went for a walk with me in Park Piece. We came across a cow with a newly born calf at her feet, that

---

[*] Angela Sykes (1911–84), sister of Christopher; m. 1934 Randall McDonnell, 13th Earl of Antrim (1911–77), Chairman of N.T. 1965–77.

horrid caul dangling from the standing cow's posterior. Billa did not know what it was. Then she spied the old bull and fled, shrieking. I have known this dear old bull for years. He is quite harmless. For a countrywoman Billa is a disgrace.

Great excitement when I went down to the village this morn. A crowd collected outside the cottage of old Mr Potter, who always rises at 5 a.m. but had not yet appeared. He has diabetes. No one liked to break open the door. They rang for the police, who did so. Mr P. was indeed on his bed, alive, but in a coma. An ambulance soon fetched him away. '*He* won't come back,' they all say resignedly.

Wednesday, 29th August

Today being my mother's hundredth birthday, were she alive, I decided to do something to celebrate the occasion. So I wrote to the Vicar of Badsey and Wickhamford asking if he would give me Communion in the church. He replied charmingly that he would be delighted to do so. This was arranged a month ago. So I duly motored over and arrived before 11.30. Walked down the familiar steps into the dear church. The Vicar already there. As charming as his letter had been. He said, 'I expect you would prefer the 1661 version.' 'I would indeed.' 'Where would you feel most at home?' Pointing to our old pew, I said, 'I would feel most at home here, but as the congregation consists of me only, perhaps I had better be in the chancel.' Indeed, from the box pew I could not have seen him. Very uncomfortably I perched on a tall upright oak chair in the chancel, and kneeling on a hassock had nothing to lean against. Got very hot and exhausted from the effort. But it was a lovely experience kneeling before those divine Sandys tombs. I brought with me Mama's silver and tortoiseshell prayer book, which belonged to her grandmother, the print of which was so small and the wording of the liturgy, in spite of it being 1661, different in many respects. It must be over fifty years since I last took Communion at these rails, an extraordinary thought.* Mama would have smiled, did she know that I was doing this in remembrance of her.† After the little

---

* J.L.-M. was a practising Roman Catholic from 1934 until the late 1960s.
† In *Another Self*, J.L.-M. described his mother's attitude towards religion as 'at first indifferent, and in her middle and old age positively hostile. God, she would declare before the last war, was no better than a nuisance; and during the war indistinguishable from Hitler.'

service the charming Vicar told me that a great discovery had been made. The Charles II arms under the Doom turn out not to be Charles II in spite of the date, added later, but James II. In view of that monarch's short reign and being a papist, this is very rare. There are only five others known in the whole country. The whole thing is to be restored and, I suspect, touched up. I gave Vicar a cheque for £100 for the church, my favourite church in this wide world.

Then the Vicar took me to the Manor, for he had forewarned the present owners, a pleasant young couple called Ryan-Bell. House well cared-for and less gloomy than when I last visited. Garden much deteriorated. Pond choked.

Sunday, 2nd September

Lunching at Anne Cowdray's* I met Tim Walker,† who is chairman of the English branch of the World Wildlife Fund. He told me this is the organisation closest to the heart of the Duke of Edinburgh, who takes his role as President of the International Committee extremely seriously. Says the Duke is a clever man who, had he not been Prince Consort, would nevertheless have distinguished himself. He does not suffer fools gladly but when he gets to know and approve of you, is a staunch friend. I asked Walker if the wildlife cause was a lost one. Not quite, he replied. European nations are taking heed and there is a strong Green Party in Germany. But in South America there is no urgency to save the rain forests and they resent what they consider European interference. The Muslim world is pretty hopeless, too.

We motored on to Audrey's cottage at Penselwood where I had an interesting talk with [her son-in-law] James Sutton. He is an engineer–inventor, employed by Ministry of Defence, having formerly worked for Lister's, a private firm. Then he was given a job with a deadline, whereas the Ministry imposes no time limit. No one cares when it is done, or is motivated by pride in work. No wonder Mrs Thatcher is trying to 'privatise' as many nationalised industries as she can.

---

* Lady Anne Bridgeman, dau. of 5th Earl of Bradford, m. 1939–50 3rd Viscount Cowdray.
† Businessman and philanthropist who established a wildlife park at Midway Manor, Bradford-on-Avon, Wiltshire.

Saturday, 8th September

Have just finished Wilson's biography of Belloc. A good and competent biog. – not that I like him, or liked him when I met him at Pixton,
where he was such a trouble to Mary Herbert. He was the most preju-
diced of men, his Catholicism calculated to antagonise all non-
Catholics, and his anti-Semitism most unattractive. Yet his *Cautionary
Verses* are works of genius as much as Lewis Carroll.

On Wednesday to London for the day. Pat Trevor-Roper inspected
my left eye which has deteriorated badly of late. He concluded that
no good would be done by giving me a new lens. The left eye is still
as good for reading as it was two years ago, and for long distance my
right eye can do the work necessary. In other words, there is nothing
to be done unless the cataract gets much worse. I left Pat joyfully, I
can't think why for he had done little to reassure me.

Dear nephew Nick lunched at Brooks's. On arrival I saw the two
hall porters together in their box and said to them, 'You look like the
heavenly twins.' There was a pause, and one replied, 'I have had a nice
holiday, thank you, Mr L.-M.' That was a *non sequitur* all right. I said
to Nick that one should not make poor jokes with people of that sort.
Nick is an angel and I can talk to him about anything; he is as easy as
any of my friends. Had tea and a scrambled egg with M. He has just
realised something he ought to have mentioned in his book – that
Hitler delayed giving the final order to launch the air war against
England until the day the Duke of Windsor sailed from Portugal for
the Bahamas.* This suggests that H. hoped the ex-King might
somehow prevent this necessity, and that the failed Nazi plot to detain
him may perversely have saved England. M. just in time to add a foot-
note to this effect.

This morning *The Times* announced Archie Aberdeen's death. I am
saddened, for he was another to whom I could say anything. A good
old soul, and great fun. Dear Archie. He was the ugliest man I knew,
with his sparse red hair, great goggly eyes, blind as a bat, thickest
lenses, and pasty, puffy face. Keen sense of humour, great love of the
country, a true aesthete. He survived his prostate operation by just two
years, as did David Verey. *The Times* also carried a longish review of
my paperback books. It says I portray my father as a brutish man,
which he was not. This is a fault for which I shall have to pay dearly

---

* 1 August 1940.

in the next world. It also expresses amazement at the unpleasant things a person of my taste thought fit to be printed.

Monday, 10th September

On Saturday at luncheon I got up from my chair to hand round a large and heavy jug of cider cup A. had made. I fell flat, dropping the jug which smashed to smithereens and spilt the sticky liquid all over the kitchen floor. The young Messels who were lunching showed much concern. I merely bruised the left leg below the knee, but felt shaken. Wonder if I suffered a small stroke. I have had a headache ever since.

Yesterday I finished typing and correcting my 1948–9 diary. It has taken me about two months. A. is reading 1949.* It will depend on her verdict whether I can now submit it for publication. If she vetoes, it can be published after our deaths. I am glad I have polished this little matter off. I can now destroy the original manuscript, which I never wished anyone to see. It is the last of the day-to-day diaries I kept. There is a blank for ten years. Then scrappy jottings ensue.†

Thursday, 13th September

Publication today of A's book [*The Englishwoman's House*], which has in fact been illicitly on sale by bookshops for weeks, one more sign of general anarchy. Ghastly launch party in Philip Ziegler's‡ maisonette in Cottesmore Gardens, low ceiling, too hot, din such that I could hear nothing. Attended by contributors and their husbands. When I took Gladwyn [Jebb] to task on his assertion in today's *Times* that Eastern European countries should thank their stars for having fallen under Russian rather than German hegemony, he gave me what I'm sure was a most informative lecture of twenty minutes, not one word of which did I hear. The Michaels of Kent arrived late and were the last to leave. She is extremely friendly, if a trifle common. I asked her how her book on the Winter Queen was progressing. She said the Queen

---

* The year in which he fell in love with and proposed marriage to her.

† J.L.-M. did in fact keep a diary for much of 1953 and 1954, later included in *A Mingled Measure*. Most of the 'scrappy jottings' for the late 1950s and 1960s he later destroyed. He resumed a regular journal in July 1971 and kept it until a few weeks before his death in December 1997.

‡ Author (b. 1929); editorial director, William Collins & Co.

was reposing because she had been offered an enormous sum by Weidenfeld to write a book on nineteenth-century princesses from various lands who married crowned heads, and the misery and home-sickness they endured.* A good subject for her. She has beautiful eyes and complexion but clumsy legs and hands. He very well-dressed and smart with well-trimmed beard. Just like the Czar, and like him charming but dumb. He asked me about John Julius, saying he liked him on television because he was one of those clever people who made him feel cleverer than he knew himself to be.

We dined afterwards at an Italian restaurant with the Moores and Ziegler. Latter a nice man who went through terrible experience when his first wife was murdered in front of his eyes by desperadoes when he was in South America with the Foreign Office. He expressed amazement when I told him how dependent I was on advice and encouragement from publishers, thinking that, having what he called such a confident and polished style, I was so assured that I would spurn advice. He spoke of Mountbatten whose biography he has just fin-ished, describing him as a man without original thoughts or ideas, whose character he found deplorable. He kept a notice in front of him on his desk while he was writing saying, 'Remember that he was a Great Man'. Enjoyed the dinner.

Friday, 14th September

M. breakfasted with me at Brooks's. He gave me his typescript of the Duchess of Windsor's letters to read† and I gave him typescript of my 1948–9 diaries. Then to the National Trust to talk to half a dozen charming young people who are acting in play for teenagers on the acquisition of Blickling by the N.T. in 1941. I am apparently the only person left who remembers Lord Lothian,‡ Matheson§ and the place

---

* *Crowned in a Far Country: Portraits of 8 Royal Brides* (Weidenfeld & Nicolson, 1986).
† Published on her death in 1986 as *Wallis & Edward: Letters 1931–1937* (Weidenfeld & Nicolson).
‡ Philip Kerr, 11th Marquess of Lothian (1882–1940), Liberal statesman, whose speech to the Annual Meeting of the N.T. in 1934 inspired the setting-up of the Country House Scheme of which J.L.-M. became Secretary, and who bequeathed Blickling, his Jacobean house in Norfolk, to the N.T. on his premature death (at which time he was serving as British Ambassador to the United States).
§ Donald MacLeod Matheson (1896–1979), the dedicated but eccentric Secretary of N.T., 1932–45.

in pre-war days. I was struck by their profound naïvety and ignorance. But they were charming and thanked me profusely when I left them to lunch at the Travellers' with Hugh Montgomery-Massingberd. I like Hugh very much. Such a nice, gentle, harrassed, hesitant man. Has two wives and two children to support, and little money. Adores Gunby,* longs to live there in retirement if he can afford it. Hugh's lack of self-assertiveness may explain the occasional aggressiveness in his writing. We agreed that in writing the devil gets into one at times.

In pouring rain to National Gallery to small exhibition of Danish painting from late eighteenth to mid nineteenth centuries. Delightful, for the most part small conversation piece pictures, village landscapes, and portraits of an intimate, naturalistic kind. Also scenes of Rome and Greece. Just my cup of tea. C. W. Eckersberg the progenitor of this school, Constantin Hanser and Christen Købke the main followers.

Hurried off to Rosamond Lehmann. In the tube a good-looking, well-dressed, sophisticated young man of thirty called Derek Jennings† introduced himself to me on the platform and reminded me that we had met lunching with Anna-Maria Cicogna‡ in Venice two years ago. Leaves for Rome tomorrow to begin six years training for the priesthood. He said he had just come from Sandoe's shop where he had ordered a set of my new paperbacks to be sent to him in Rome. I remarked that I did not suppose they would stand him in good stead with the Fathers of God.

Ros much older. Large, yet frail and hand shaking. I stayed two and a half hours, during which she mostly talked of clairvoyancy. She assured me that she knew more than most about the subject, having read all the authorities. Exhorted me to read William James.§ She is absolutely convinced of the after-life and was critical of John Betjeman for closing his mind to contemporary studies of religious experiences.

---

* House and estate in Lincolnshire donated to N.T. during Second World War by Hugh Montgomery-Massingberd's great-uncle and great-aunt, Field Marshal Sir Archibald and Lady M.-M. – an episode of which J.L.-M., who loved both the house and its owners, wrote nostalgically in *People and Places* (John Murray, 1992). Towards the end of his life, J.L.-M. endowed a library there.

† Derek Jennings (1946–95), Anglican convert to Roman Catholicism, formerly on staff of English Heritage.

‡ Contessa Cicogna, long-standing resident of Venice, with whom the L.-Ms had become acquainted through Nancy Mitford (see entry for 2 November, 1984).

§ American philosopher (brother of the novelist Henry), regarded as a founder of the science of psychology (1842–1910).

Sunday, 16th–Tuesday, 18th September

I accompanied A. to France for two nights in a motel outside Amboise. She had to see Jagger's garden which she is creating at the Château de Fourchette before the summer is over, while flowers and shrubs are still in bloom. It is a charming little 'manoir' in the village of Docé-sur-Cisse. Situation delightful. One drives through an avenue of walnuts and chestnuts, mentioned by the duchesse de Choiseul in a letter to Madame du Deffand. House is backed by a high ridge covered with trees. Behind and on both sides of the house are deep caves cut in the rocks for storing wine. In front the ground slopes towards a *douve* or fosse of rather stagnant water. A. has cleverly made divisions. The first terrace comprises formal parterre. She has planted two flanking avenues of hornbeam, to be trimmed or trained. Also will plant two arbours of yellow laburnum. I was deeply impressed by the way she dealt with agents, gardeners, seedsmen, plantsmen, masons in her faultless French, her confidence in her own knowledge unshakeable. All evening she made notes of what she wished the gardener to do before her next visit in November. A. has extraordinary energy, intelligence and organising ability and ought to have been Prime Minister. In a sense hers has been a wasted life.

We walked from our motel to the deliciously-named Pagode de Chanteloup. We have a painting of it by Paul Methuen, and I had never seen it before. Enchanting, and open to visitors day and night. Nothing to stop one walking in except ferocious *gardienne* who pops out of adjacent cottage demanding six francs. The pagoda is of six or seven diminishing stages, the ground one of Classical doric order. In fact it is not in the Chinese style but the Classical. I climbed to the very top and, although it was a wet evening, marvelled at the views over the moon-shaped lake and down the straight, radiating avenues. A plaque inside records that the building was erected by the duc de Choiseul in thanksgiving for his return from exile, at the 1814 Restoration I imagine.*
Lately I have claimed that architecture no longer interests me, but this evening's visit made me realise that it can still ignite a fire within me.

---

* J.L.-M. was evidently somewhat vague about the details of the life of Etienne François, duc de Choiseul (1719–85), Louis XV's adventurist foreign minister, who was dismissed by his sovereign in December 1770 and 'exiled' from Versailles to Chanteloup for four years, later erecting his Pagoda as a tribute to the loyal friends who had stood by him during this period of disgrace.

Last Saturday I went with A. to see the improvements she has effected at Lyegrove. She left me in the garden with the dogs to walk home. But I first wandered down the raised walk which overlooks the open fields. As I returned in the early dusk of a drizzling evening, the house looked gaunt, almost haunted, empty, deserted and infinitely sad. The rooks cawed in a melancholy manner. I was reminded of a scene by Atkinson Grimshaw. Only one dim light from an upstair window was lacking. Was filled with loving memories of darling Diana W.

Wednesday, 26th September

To London for the day. A lovely day of golden sun. I walked to M's flat and drank coffee with him. We discussed whether to remove certain passages in my diaries which may embarrass my friends. His view is that I have already caused so much offence in the first three volumes that I might as well continue in the fourth. Walked to Heraldry Today in Beauchamp Place to collect *Ruvigny's European Peerage*, which costs £40 and weighs a ton. Then to Brooks's where Eardley was waiting for me. We lunched upstairs and although we both expressed pleasure at seeing one another our meeting was not a success. I suppose old friends get bored with one another if they do not meet often. Then I walked to Westminster Hospital to see Norah Smallwood in her ward. Very distressing. She lay with her eyes closed, mind wandering, holding my hand throughout visit. Is maddened by the noise of the ward, lies awake at night in great torment and misery. I left her feeling wretched.

Monday, 1st–Sunday, 7th October

In Austria, staying at Salzburg with George Dix. Kept daily diary in separate marbled notebook.*

Thursday, 11th October

Freda [Berkeley] rang me this morning to say that Norah [Smallwood] died at 5 a.m. I knew from reports that this was to be. Dear Norah, a most gallant and clever and loveable friend. I owe much to her, for she

---

* Not found.

was a candid critic of my writing, and an encourager, who published some of my better books.

Tuesday, 16th October

Stayed last night with J.K.-B. in Hollywood Road. We dined agreeably alone at Brooks's. He is a faithful, affectionate friend. This morning to Archie Aberdeen's memorial service at St Margaret's, Westminster. A beautiful service. Church quite full. Service of Thanksgiving is a new term which I don't much like. It is a euphemism, a cowardly term, a not-facing-up to grief. We must all be cheery instead. I don't feel cheerful when my old friends like Archie are dead. Indeed, in an excellent address given, somewhat to my surprise, by Lord Hailsham, he said one should never be ashamed of shedding tears. And he quoted the shortest sentence in the Gospels: 'Jesus wept.' He said he was some sort of relation and remembered Archie as a child some seven years younger than himself, for Archie was younger than me. Archie's brother, the new Marquess, read one of the lessons, and his sister, Lady Jessamine Harmsworth, sang a most moving anthem to the words of S. S. Wesley, 'Lead me Lord in thy righteousness. Make thy ways plain.' She has a fine contralto voice and did it well. Both she and the brother are plain and resemble Archie. The brother's voice exactly like Archie's, without the affectation. Walked back across St James's Park to Brooks's where M. lunched with me.

Monday, 22nd October

Mary Downer* stayed the weekend. First time I had seen her since we stayed at Martinsell in South Australia. She talked of her great friend and neighbour, Byron MacLachlan. I said, 'He is one of the largest landowners in Australia, isn't he?' 'Oh yes,' she said, 'his acreage is larger than the whole of the British Isles.'

Wednesday, 24th October

We went to London for Christina Foyle's dinner to celebrate eightieth anniversary of the firm's foundation by her father. I changed into black

---

* Widow of Sir Alexander Downer (1910–81), Australian politician and High Commissioner in London, 1964–72.

tie at the Berkeleys' where A. was staying. Although she had ordered a
car it did not turn up. In panic we hailed a cab and drove to the
Dorchester. Pelting rain and Mitterrand's* visit combined to cause terrible traffic jams. We arrived half an hour late. Found Miss Foyle
waiting by herself in ante-room, the hundred or so guests already seated
at tables in the Orchid Room. I was dishevelled and fussed, the sort of
anxiety that takes years off my life. We were both seated at Table 1, and
to my intense surprise I found myself placed on Christina's right. Felt
honoured but perplexed, for at our table were Lord Balogh,[†] Sir Arthur
Bryant,[‡] wife of Harold Wilson. Witty speech by broadcasting man,
forget name. Christina Foyle replied fearlessly in a rather sweet little
baby voice, but running her words into each other. No punctuation.
She is very sweet to talk to. Can't converse, but talks agreeably. She has
that milky royal complexion and very good teeth. A nice woman. I like
her. At the conclusion she gave everyone a present of her commonplace book, which I see is for sale at £10. A. loved Sir Arthur. I spoke
to him for a minute after dinner and he remembers Regy. Told me he
was a man whom one could not much like. But he had humility, and
great wisdom. His influence upon Edward VII immense and beneficial.
He said we must pay him a visit, which we propose to do. The rever-
berating noise of voices made hearing impossible.

Thursday, 25th October

The French visit has made London very jittery. Police cars with scream-
ing klaxons force their way through traffic. Papers full of idiotic beha-
viour of Mitterrand's French bodyguard planting unfused explosives in
the French Embassy to test English security precautions. Our sniffer
dogs of course detected them and we are furious at the impertinence
of the French. The press considers it insulting after the Brighton incident, the horror waves of which have not yet died down.[§]

---

* François Mitterrand, President of France 1981–95.
[†] Thomas Balogh (1905–85), Hungarian-born economist; Fellow of Balliol, 1945–73;
Economic Adviser to Cabinet, 1964–7; cr. life peer, 1968; Minister of State at Dept of
Energy, 1974–9.
[‡] Sir Arthur Bryant (1899–85), author; m. 1st 1924–39 Sylvia (1900–50), dau. of Sir
Walter Shakerley, 3rd Bt; 2nd 1941–76 Anne Brooke of Sarawak.
[§] The IRA had detonated a bomb at the Grand Hotel at Brighton during the
Conservative Party Conference the previous month, several politicians and their wives
sustaining injuries and Mrs Thatcher narrowly escaping death.

Margaret Willes [of Sidgwick & Jackson] lunched with me at a
wine bar. The bill for one course and one glass of wine each came to
over £20. I wanted to talk to her about the Esher book, not having
spoken to Sidgwick & Jackson for two years. She said they are still
keen to do it, and got me to sign the contract of two years ago there
and then. I suppose this was unbusinesslike, for an agent would have
raised the advance. I did ask if I might first consult Bruce Hunter,* but
she said, since we have eased him out, don't let's ease him back in. I
can see that agents are a nuisance to publishers. M. Willes told me
that Diana Mosley was being difficult over proofs of her new book,
which comes out in February. Writes strident letters to Margaret,
asking her to tell her Nigerian teenager not to fiddle with her punctuation, etc. Of course these editorial girls are a frightful nuisance to
authors.

Stayed the night at Brooks's, by far the nicest way of staying in
London. In the afternoon I was able to lie on my bed and read. At five
went to Bruce Hunter and told him I had finished both novel and
1948–9 diary. Asked him to take over for I prefer to go to Faber and
leave Chatto, for now dear Norah is dead I don't think Chatto is either
very enthusiastic or publicity-minded, whereas Faber shows signs of
being both. Bruce fears I am obliged to offer to Chatto. Refers me to
contract for *Caves of Ice*. Have done so, and find this is the case. But
Bruce thinks there may be ways out if Faber offer more.

Back to bed again for half an hour, then changed for French
Embassy after-banquet party. Berkeleys gave us dinner before we went
to Embassy in their car driven by the dotty French chauffeur George.
Ghastly party as I feared. A wooden aircraft hangar erected in garden
approached by fabricated passages dotted with Calor gas stoves. We
did not even enter Embassy building. From 10.10 to 11.45 we stood
in this stark hut, hung with two tapestries it is true, but no seats.
Champagne which I hate, served with *petits fours*. First on one leg,
then the other. Noise excruciating like waves of the sea or continuous clapping of hands. Hardly a soul we knew. Lost A. at one time and
set off on a tour round the room. Decided this was a foretaste of hell,
looking for Alvilde and never finding her. Then on leaving we could

---

* Australian-born literary agent (b. 1941); joined London firm of David Higham in 1962
and became J.L.-M's agent following death of D.H. in 1979 (although Norah
Smallwood, J.L.-M's principal publisher at that time, refused to deal with her authors
through agents).

not find George or the Berkeleys' car. Wandered in the cold (mercifully no rain) up Millionaires' Row, lined with police and detectives.

Today Mitterrand visited the office where Clarissa [Luke] works which was once the headquarters of General de Gaulle. One of his French bodyguard hearing her speak French offered her an invitation to tonight's party. C. did not use it but might have been a terrorist. I told A. she ought to write to the Margeries* about this extraordinary incident.

Queen came down the steps of the Embassy into the garden hangar, wearing the most beautiful tiara ever seen. At night she looks her splendid best. Was wearing orange sash, some Frog decoration I suppose. She said to A., 'You live in Badminton, don't you?'

Arthur Bryant said to A. that, in his writing, his rule was to cut out every unnecessary word ruthlessly, and go over and over what he has written. An octogenarian, he says he writes today for the semi-educated young. I don't. I write for people like myself, middlebrows and literates.

Friday, 26th October

M. breakfasts with me at Brooks's. I love this. He came late, having gone to buy the newspapers to look for reviews of his *Operation Willi*. He is thrilled by a rave in the *Telegraph* by D. Cameron Watt, eminent history professor, describing it as 'the sort of book historians dream of'. So pleased.

To the Vermeer and de Hooch exhibitions at Burlington House. It was so crowded with visitors I could not see the culminating room, so returned early next morning when was impeded by a thousand school children with drawing boards and notebooks, crawling between my feet. The early seventeenth-century Dutch paintings inclined to the coarseness of peasant life and the puritanism of the middle classes. But when one reaches Vermeer and de Hooch one enters another world – magical, poetical. I suppose no school of genre painting is so revealing of a way of life. Always a map on the wall in the living room. Great importance attached to glass of wine, drunk by women as well as men. Letter-writing plays a large part. Dubiety as to the story and moral painted. Is she a loose woman about to be paid

---

* Emmanuel de Margerie (b. 1924), French Ambassador in London 1981–4; m. 1953 Hélène Hottinguer.

for her services, or is she collecting for the poor? Was lute playing more than a fashion, like Regency women with harps, or 1920s women with mandolins?

Wednesday, 31st October

At the end of June I returned to Churchill College the papers they lent me, kept in the back room at Bath. I put aside Reginald, Viscount Esher, intending the break to last until the end of the year. Whereupon I edited for publication, either by me or by M. after my demise, my diaries for 1948–9, and also wrote the third part of my novel begun over two years ago and left unfinished. Whether either book will be published remains to be seen, but I am taking them to Bruce Hunter in London on 7 November. I have also written an article of 1,200 words for the American *Architectural Digest* for which I am being paid a fee of $1,500. So I am two months in advance, and shall begin writing my biography of Regy tomorrow, All Saints' Day. May it be a propitious festival. The task daunts me, and I wonder if I shall remain well enough for long enough to complete it, and *compos mentis*.

Thursday, 1 November

Making the beds with Peggy, A. being in Londinio, I love hearing the village gossip. How the doctor would not come when Miss Davis, the *malade imaginaire* of Badminton, summoned him by telephone to say she thought she might be suffering from paralysis of the spine. Peggy said, 'It might have been true and then the doctor would have had her death on his conscience.' I said he might on the contrary be mightily relieved. Then Mrs Hamnet, a great reader, went to bed late and left the light on in her downstairs room. Woke at 3 a.m., saw light on, assumed it was burglars and called the police, who were not pleased.

At 7.30 I went to Holy Communion in Badminton Church. The Vicar told me after the service that for ten years a stranger has come every All Saints' Day asking for the key of the church. He leaves a contribution in the box and departs. This year the Vicar asked him where he came from and why he did this. He is from Wantage, and explained that twenty years ago his son went climbing in the Alps and never returned, his body being discovered a year later at the foot of a precipice. Soon after the tragedy the father happened to pass through Badminton, with which he had no previous connection, and so liked the church that he makes an annual pilgrimage in the son's memory. I suggested that it may have been more like an Italian or Classical church than any he had seen in this country.

All Souls' Day, Friday, 2nd November

A wasted day. At 12.30, Ian McCallum came to see my Bath library with two guests, Anna-Maria Cicogna and Lady Thorneycroft.* A. joined us and we all went to lunch at Claverton. Luncheon did not begin until 2.15 and I left at 3.45 before the coffee. Sat next to Anna-Maria who looked bad colour following operation. To my surprise, she told me she would never meet Diana Mosley when she made her annual visit to Venice, even when these visits coincided with Nancy's to A.-M. She says she will never speak to anyone who was an avowed Fascist in the last war. And yet her father Count Volpi was Mussolini's finance minister and made a fortune out of his support for the Fascist Party, presumably the source of A.-M's great wealth. Strange. I did not like to press her on the subject of her father's association with Musso, but she mumbled that it had been in the Twenties.

Sunday, 11th November

In the afternoon, A. and I drove to Salisbury to have tea with Sir Arthur Bryant. This delightful old man lives in Myles Place, the large early Georgian house in the Close which we looked at years ago. Beautiful but too large; yet ideal otherwise, for one front has outstanding view of Cathedral, and the other a long, narrow garden leading to the river. Fine steep staircase. Lovely library of tunnel shape, like mine, but more beautiful being *circa* 1720. Lovely furniture and pictures. Delicious tea provided by housekeeper, with chocolate cake, scones, etc. We talked of links with the past. He pointed to a portrait of a young man in Oxford mortarboard, as it might be by Reynolds, name Shakerley, date of birth on label 1767. Sir Arthur

---

* Countess Carla Roberti; m. 1949 Peter Thorneycroft, MP (1909–94; cr. life peer 1967).

told us this was an ancestor of his [first] wife and that, when he first married, he met an old man on the Shakerley estate who actually remembered this man.*

Sir A. has a profound belief in the ultimate recovery of the British people. Indolence is their besetting sin. I said that I doubted if the sterling British virtues could survive given the percentage of people who were of recent immigrant stock. He said the only way to preserve these virtues was by encouraging miscegenation. They were not inherited but transmitted. The do-gooders were doing much evil in not making coloured people integrate but providing them instead with their own schools, housing estates, et cetera. They should not be kept in ghettos.

He asked us pointedly if we read his books. A. admitted that she hadn't, and naughtily turned to me to ask if I had. I said hesitantly, I fear not convincingly, that I had read his trilogy on Pepys, which I have in fact only skimmed. He gave us a copy of *Set in a Silver Sea*. Agreeable interlude. Charming and wise old man. He spoke again of Regy Esher, but said he had never met him personally.† Asked if he had been homosexual, but did not pursue the matter.

When we left, the Cathedral was floodlit, and seen sideways was the most beautiful spectacle ever beheld.

Tuesday, 13th November

M. telephoned this morning that Charles Orwin has been offered a job in Singapore, which he (Charles) regards as a hell-on-earth but where he wants to join his Chinese friend. When dining with me last Wednesday, Charles spoke to me of this friend. I cautioned him that passion generally endures for seven years, and thereafter attachment is dependent on mutual interests. He quite rightly paid no attention. I am sorry for M. and indeed for myself, for Charles is a delightful young man. I wish him well, but wonder if I shall live to see him returned home, desperately seeking another job in his late thirties.

---

* This is not impossible: Sir Arthur m. Sylvia Shakerley in 1924; Charles Shakerley, b. 1767, d. 1834.
† Esher's daughter Sylvia had married into the family of Bryant's 2nd wife, the Brookes of Sarawak.

Thursday, 22nd November

Hugh Massingberd has written such a vitriolic review of Peter Coats's*
admittedly rather ghastly new book that I am wondering whether I
ought to stop Bruce Hunter submitting my diaries to a publisher. It
would kill me to receive such a review.

Yesterday in London I lunched with Alec Clifton-Taylor. He is as
good as gold, one of life's crest-of-the-wavers; yet he bores me. He
told me that people accost him in the street, in the tube, in shops, to
congratulate him on his TV series, *Six Towns*. Some say, 'Mr Clifton-
Brown, I so much enjoyed your series on Civilisation.' Four million
viewers are calculated by the BBC. He is inundated with letters, and
spends morning and afternoon answering them. I asked him if he
could not get the BBC to do that, but he says many writers ask sensible questions, or are friends or acquaintances. Then to M. for cup of
tea. The telephone never stopped ringing with requests for interviews
about his new book. I am not entirely pleased that he has given my
name in an *Observer* article as a supporter of his Octavian Society, to
erect some memorial to the Duke of Windsor. I adore M. but not the
D. of W.

Monday, 26th November

We dined last Saturday with the Warrenders† at Widcombe. Large
party given for Robin's father, Victor Bruntisfield and wife‡ who live
in Switzerland. A lovely man. I talked to him after dinner. Has had a
stroke and walks with much difficulty. Otherwise sound in his still
handsome head. Blotchy complexion, but has all his hair. I talked to
him about Polesden Lacey and Mrs Greville, for I saw much of him
in the early 1940s when the N.T. inherited Polesden.§ He said he dis-

* Hon. Peter Coats (1910–90), yr s. of 1st Baron Glentanar; contemporary and cousin of
J.L.-M., who attended the same preparatory school; ADC to Lord Wavell as Viceroy of
India; garden designer and horticultural writer; friend of the politician and diarist Sir
Henry 'Chips' Channon, MP (d. 1958).
† Hon. Robin Warrender (b. 1927), yr s. of 1st Baron Bruntisfield; m. 1951 Gillian
Rossiter; underwriting member of Lloyds.
‡ Victor Warrender (1889–1993); Conservative MP and office-holder, 1923–43; cr. Baron
Bruntisfield, 1942; m. 1st 1920 Dorothy Rawson, 2nd 1948 Tania Kolin.
§ The notoriously malicious Mrs Ronnie Greville bequeathed both her town house in
Charles Street, Mayfair and her country house, Polesden Lacey near Dorking in Surrey,

approved of the bequest. She should have left the place to the Foreign
Secretary, but hated Eden and decided against. She left some money
to Victor and to Robin, her godson. V. said she was not a nice
woman, mischievous and snobbish, as we all knew. He was made a
peer all of forty years ago. Fought in the First World War and has the
Order of St Stanislas. Was with Osbert and Sachie [Sitwell] in the
army. Said Sachie's worst day was when he and Victor were detailed
to play against some other regiment in a cricket match. Sachie did
not know one end of the bat from the other, and dreaded the occasion. He spent days on his knees beforehand praying for rain, the
weather remaining fine. But when the day came, the heavens opened
non-stop. As an MP, Victor was Vice-Chamberlain of the Household
with the duty of writing a weekly account of parliamentary proceed-
ings for George V. The King had been a friend of Victor's father and
liked to hear gossip. V. liked him, but he was devoid of humour. The
reason he wore creases down the sides of his trouser legs was that he
was bandy-legged. Queen Alexandra was adorable. She may have
been stupid but she was the greatest fun, a radiant light in that lugu-
brious royal family.

Tuesday, 27th November

David and Caroline dined alone here. When telling us of the progress
of the works in the big house and mentioning the lift he is putting in,
David went out of his way to stress that he was making no structural
alterations. He seems to think I am critical of what he does or doesn't
do conservation-wise, but I try not to criticise, and don't really care
that much anyway. I did however venture to show him a photograph
in Green's book on Grinling Gibbons of the first Duke's monument,
and pointed out two attendant classical figures which Master removed,
asking him why Master had done this.* He said because it was not safe,
not because Master didn't like them, as he noticed nothing. He agreed
he ought to put them back but was fairly indifferent himself. We
talked of a monument to Master and Mary in the church. Caroline is
anxious to discuss this with Simon Verity, whose name I suggested

---

to the N.T. After her death in September 1942, J.L.-M., as related in his diaries, was
occupied for several years in disposing of the London house and its contents, and preparing Polesden Lacey for eventual opening to the public.
* See *Through Wood and Dale*, 14 August 1976.

months ago to David. David said, 'You can't put up a memorial to someone who is still alive.' But we said that he can get it prepared. All that will be needed is the addition of Mary's name, just as the memorials to Michael Rosse are up in the churches at Birr and Womersley, put there by Anne, who has left liberal space for her own dear name and virtues.*

David told us that his solicitor had come upon files of papers concerning Mary's having set detectives on Master's tracks when he was in love with [Lavinia,] Duchess of Norfolk. On one occasion the detective hid in a cupboard in the very room where they went to bed. All evidence carefully documented. The solicitor said to David, 'Of course I destroyed them all, as you would have wanted me to do.' In fact David would have wanted nothing of the kind. Would have been interested to look through them. But what a devilish thing on the part of the old Duchess [of Beaufort]. She now in her dottiness has turned against Master and tells those she sees that he has left her and run away with the Duchess of Norfolk. That was the affair which touched her most deeply.

Saturday, 1st December

On Thursday for the day to London. Took revised novel to Bruce Hunter, who told me he had already sent previous copy to a reader. This annoyed me, for I have made several important changes and improvements, and incorporated Rupert Loewenstein's corrections of my German phrases. Then to St Martin's-in-the-Fields for Norah Smallwood's memorial service. Enormous attendance. Moving service. Readings of a poem by Stevie Smith, 'Come, Death', and of extract from *Little Gidding* by Jill Balcon.† Anthem of words by George Herbert set to music by Michael Berkeley.‡ Address by Laurens van der Post.§ Theme was the Word, which meant all to Norah who was without religion. But van der P. is clearly a believer in the Trinity, to whom the Word (*Logos*) is Christ, and I wondered

---

* See entry for 15 October 1983.
† Actress; dau. of Sir Michael Balcon, film producer; widow of Cecil Day-Lewis, Poet Laureate 1968–72 and sometime director of Chatto & Windus.
‡ Composer (b. 1948), e. s. of Sir Lennox and Lady Berkeley.
§ South African-born writer (1906–1996) interested in mysticism and the Jungian concept of the collective unconscious; a leading influence on Charles, Prince of Wales.

how many of the congregation would be confused by his meaning.
Norah certainly believed fervently in the purity of English prose. The
first woman chairman of a respected publishing company. I wondered
how long the many people gathered there out of love for her would
remember her.

Had John Phillips* to luncheon at Brooks's. A bore because Nigel
Nicolson whom I met at the service asked me to lunch, which I would
have preferred. Phillips told me that his friend Gordon Brooke-
Shepherd when reading through papers at Windsor for his book on
Edward VII came upon some passionate love letters from Soveral, 'the
Blue Monkey', to Queen Alexandra with whom he had an affair. This
known to King Edward who did not mind, which may account for
the Queen's affability to Mrs Keppel when the King died.

My impotence has altered my character. It has made me judge all
human motives and actions objectively. Is it a virtue, I ask myself? Or
does virtue lie in potency with restraint? Wilde said virtue was the
absence of temptation. Certainly the total absence of lust enables one
to love without ulterior motives. But alas, the revelation of how few
people one does love under such circumstances is rather a shock.

Sunday, 9th December

On Saturday I motored A. to Northamptonshire for a signing of her
book. Complete waste of time. Who benefits? The local shop in
Oundle. We lunched with Mollie Buccleuch at Boughton. Arrived half
an hour late, self-invited too, but Mollie unresentful and sweet. She has
changed and become rather pathetic. Very deaf, teeth giving trouble.
The spark gone, and we didn't feel we were a great success. She has a
new young Scotch couple whom she adores and finds perfect. They
have been with her three months. Nothing too much trouble, love her
dog, love her, would die for her, etc. I have witnessed this so often.
Within a year they will be gone. Disgusting luncheon, unrecognisable
pheasant, watery vegetables. The lovely food we used to get at
Boughton. Does she no longer mind? Mollie was a moth, and now no
candles. The great châtelaine of five houses, with her power and excellent taste, now reduced to a dark corner. No silver, no pearls.

---

* Englishman resident in Florence; executor of Violet Trefusis (d. 1972), with whom J.L.-
M. had corresponded concerning an item of value she had apparently bequeathed to him,
which it had not been possible to locate after her death.

We stay the night at Deene. Marion [Brudenell] is a splendid, efficient, no-nonsense lady. Edmund quite absurd. Won't speak to new
daughter-in-law because she is not out of top drawer. Said Meredyth
Proby* (splendid girl and friend of Nick's) quite nice considering her
father a GP. We spent the morning at Elton [Hall]. About fifty ladies
of the county turned up. A. signed as many books and I signed some
of my paperbacks. Hideous house outside, but magnificent treasures
– some fifteen Reynoldses, old masters in quantity, rare books. A
tiring two days.

Tuesday, 11th December

A's old gardener told her today that he had been given a shilling by
the Prince of Wales when, as a boy, he had opened a gate for him out
hunting. He still cherishes it, for he said, 'He was a great gentleman.'
'Which Prince of Wales do you mean?' A. asked. 'Well, ours of
course.' 'The Duke of Windsor?' 'Yes, that's what they called him. He
was lovely.' A. ventured to remark that some people thought he let
the side down marrying an American divorcée. 'Oh, well, perhaps he
made a mistake. I don't know. But he was a perfect gentleman.'

Thursday, 13th December

Three friends have died this week. George Howard,[†] about whom I
cut out some things in my 1948–49 diaries to avoid offence, was a
Hogarthian Georgian, like Charles James Fox without the geniality.
He was extremely clever, devoid of poetry or romance, extremely
ugly, gross and ungainly, enormously fat, but didn't care a fig what
anyone thought of him. He dressed in a kaftan like a peasant woman,
ate voraciously and messily. Jim Russell says he died from over-eating.
He had been an alcoholic and at times returned to the bottle. He
could be extremely rude and offhand. But he did wonders for Castle
Howard and saved this important house from disappearing. I saw a
good deal of him when we were both Paul Methuen's executors and

---

* Meredyth Brentnall; m. 1974 William Proby of Elton Hall near Peterborough,
Huntingdonshire (President of Historic Houses Association, 1993–8).
† Of Castle Howard, Yorkshire (1920–84); sometime N.T. Historic Buildings
Representative for Yorkshire; Chairman of BBC, 1980–3; Chairman of Museums and
Galleries Commission, 1984; cr. life peer, 1983.

winding up the Corsham estate. His astuteness twisted the rascally solicitors and the Inland Revenue into knots.

Robin McDouall,* a friend from Oxford days, was I suppose a failure. An indiscreet queen, very squalid in his *amours*. I was persuaded against my better judgement to recommend him for the flat which the N.T. decided to let in Carlyle's House to raise money. He allowed *la boue* to visit him at nights, and dear Mrs Strong the caretaker loathed him. He was a good Secretary of the Travellers', but there were scandals there among the black waiters, and Harold Nicolson was wary of him because he was such a gossip. He drank like a fish and disintegrated physically over the last five years, becoming a great trial to saints like Freda Berkeley.

William McKie† was more A's friend than mine, having taught Anthony [Chaplin] music at Radley. An Australian, so decent and pure that he seldom ventured an opinion. A successful choirmaster and organist at the Abbey. He will go straight to Heaven.

A. and I went to London today. Burnet [Pavitt] took us to *Rosenkavalier* at Covent Garden. Beautiful production and costumes. Kiri as the Marschalin drew tears at the end of the first act. I suppose all of us can see ourselves in the Marschalin's shoes at some time of our ageing lives. She behaves with such discretion and generosity that one's heart is wrung. Burnet took us to supper afterwards.

Friday, 14th December

M. breakfasted at Brooks's. Was wearing old tweed jacket and striped shirt with top button undone. Really scruffy. Must tell him if I dare. Odd that the young I like best, him and Nick, are both appalling dressers.

I went to the Stubbs exhibition at the Tate. England on canvas. He is so good with the humbler persons. The grooms wear breeches and long stockings, presumably linen rather than silk, and shoes with buckles. Was this just to be painted in? The jockeys wear little boots. Both the huntsmen and the dukes wear the same caps with broad brims rather than peaks, a little to one side, jauntily. Whistlejacket, a

---

* Squadron-Leader R P. McDouall; Secretary of Travellers' Club, 1945–71; author of *The Pocket Guide to Good Cooking* (1955) and other books on cookery and travel.
† Sir William McKie (1901–84); Organist and Master of the Choristers, Westminster Abbey, 1941–63; kt, 1953; m. 1956 Phyllis Ross.

silky chestnut, very effective prancing in mid-air with no background. Mairi Bury's Hambletonian, enormous. The haymaking scenes, the parson visiting the haymakers on his old cob: we can feel the sizzling heat of mid June. Mrs Pocklington giving a posy of wild flowers to her horse to eat or sniff.

Geoffrey Houghton-Brown and Ralph Dutton lunched. Geoffrey is thin in face but otherwise unchanged. He said, 'I know I look a million, but I just can't believe I am an octogenarian.' Ralph also older, his nose larger than ever. The dearest man. Says now he is a lord people are more deferential, and like working for him. But he gets begging letters daily because Charles Sherborne left an estate valued at £6 million, though not a penny to him. We lunched at the Grosvenor Hotel where G. M. Trevelyan* used to take me between N.T. meetings. He never tipped the waiter more than sixpence. Today's lunch, and the four of us ate moderately, cost me £45.

Saturday, 15th December

I motored to Tredegar Park [Monmouthshire], where I was received and given luncheon by charming young David Freeman.† A touching character, extremely delicate. He told me that, aged twenty-three, he had a growth removed from his stomach. Has recurrent operations and suffers terribly. Is now twenty-eight and looks extremely frail. I can't make out his origins, but he is very sensitive and has excellent taste. Is curator of the house for Newport Borough Council, awful philistines who have already ruined the surroundings with hideous new buildings. He is bringing the house back to life, but says it is a constant battle, as they do not appreciate what he does and treat him vilely. It was totally emptied of Morgan contents save for half a dozen indifferent portraits of the late lords, including my friend, the ineffable John.‡ Tredegar is interesting architecturally. Good mellow brickwork, with those extraordinary heraldic beasts over the pediments of the windows, can't make out whether original or nineteenth-century additions. Dining room, gilt room very splendid; also cedar closet. But dreadful things have happened since John sold. Nuns and a compre-

---

* George Macaulay Trevelyan (1876–1962); historian, Master of Trinity College, Cambridge, 1940–51; Chairman for many years of Estates Committee of N.T.
† Curator of Tredegar Park, 1979–97 (b. 1956).
‡ Frederic Charles John Morgan (1908–62); s. father as 6th and last Baron Tredegar, 1954;

hensive school. Ceilings fell down, dry rot set in, walls disfigured. David is faced with collecting suitable contents and has done extremely well. I was touched by this young person, so lonely, ill and sensitive. Gave him a copy of my *Beckford*.

Sunday, 23rd December

Elaine came to luncheon with Simon and his children yesterday. Was shocked and saddened by her condition. She has become acutely thin and gaunt. Is silent and utterly miserable. After luncheon I asked if she would like to have a talk alone with me in my room. She followed me, sat down without a word, and I sensed she was about to break down. She did, saying between her sobs that she couldn't go on living. Nothing had sense or interest. A. rightly says that her trouble is that she has nothing to do. I think I shall write and suggest that when she returns to Cyprus she take up some voluntary work, in a hospital, or visiting the sick. To talk to other unhappy people might help.

Rowley Winn has died.[*] I hadn't seen him for a long while. He was never my sort. Great friend of Robin Fedden,[†] gallant war, tough, hard-drinking, unsympathetic towards un-normal men. But adored Nostell. Unhappily married, first to daughter of Sir Roderick Jones. I remember staying at Nostell just after my own marriage. When she heard that I spent less than half my time in France and A. could only join me here for three months of the year, her eyes lit up. Eagerly asked how such an arrangement could be arrived at. So I knew she was unhappy. Rowley's second wife was Polish and committed suicide a few years ago. I believe he had a cruel streak.

Thursday, 27th December

We spent three nights at Parkside with the Droghedas. Joan's situation extremely sad. Conversation out of the question, but one makes little remarks of affection. She has become a pretty, touching, sweetly-smiling little doll. All that brightness, fun and quick intelligence, that

---

Eton contemporary of J.L.-M.
[*] Hon. Rowland Winn, MC (1916–84) of Nostell Priory, Wakefield, Yorkshire; s. father (who donated the house to the N.T. on complex terms causing much trouble) as 4th Baron St Oswald, 1957; m. 1st 1952 Laurian Jones, 2nd 1955 Marie Wanda Jaxa-Chamiec.
[†] J.L.-M's successor (1951–68) as Historic Buildings Secretary of N.T. (1909–77).

sharp appreciation of literature, those pertinent comments – gone. Very affectionate, never grumbles and accepts whatever she is told to do. Garrett is too fussy with her, never leaves her alone, presses her to eat when she has no inclination, won't let her walk alone in the garden, ceaselessly asks her whether she is all right. She gave me one of those amused eye-lifts as she used to do when Garrett was being particularly tiresome. Derry and Alexandra came with the baby for the night on Boxing Day. Burnet was to have come but ill with influenza.

Went to St George's Chapel on Christmas morning. A. and I were given seats in the front row of the nave, at the corner of the central aisle. So when the Royals left by the West Door I had to *reculer* so as not to be in their way, and was so busy bowing that I saw little. A. says she can curtsey and look at the same time.

Much excitement on return to Badminton about the body-snatchers having dug up Master's grave to within four inches of the coffin. They were disturbed by Mary Duchess in the middle of the night turning on the lights in her room, declaring to the nurse that she wanted to open her Christmas presents. Vicar thinks this scared them off. They threatened to sever his head and deliver it to Princess Anne. Charming. The village people extremely shocked, old Staines, who never to my knowledge goes to church, saying it was an offence against God.

Caroline said to A. that she thought Master would rather have liked the idea of his body being thrown to hounds at a meet.

Appendices

Appendices

Appendix I

Visit to Vicenza and Asolo with Eardley Knollys
April–May 1982

Saturday, 24th April

12.05 p.m. The Captain informs us we are passing over Paris. I think
of M. somewhere beneath me, resume reading *The Rise and Fall of a
Regency Dandy*, and await snacks. Crisis. Eardley thinks he may have
left spectacles behind. I say I shall then have to read Virginia Woolf's
diaries aloud to him. 'Oh God,' E. exclaims, 'I hate V. Woolf.'
Spectacles discovered in unknown pocket. Rejoicing.

We take water-bus to Venice under a beautiful light never before
seen by me – but I have never before been to Venice in April. The sea
is green and the sky between heliotrope and petunia. We pass by the
cemetery island, so deserted and haunted. I think of Stravinsky buried
there whom I once met in Madrid, an ugly and restless man with
craggy features and round spectacles.

We go straight up Grand Canal to railway station. A fine modern
building, all horizontals. But seen close-to already shoddy, mosaic
ceiling flaking. We dump luggage in second-class compartment. E. sits
with it. Won't look at Venice. Hates it. Why? Sad recollections? I wander
by Grand Canal and enter Carmine Church. Shocked by electric candles
of great ugliness. You put in a coin and press a plastic button. An insult
to the dead. So I don't light a candle for Mama as I always did in Venice.

At Vicenza we take taxi to Albergo Basilica, a humble place. We
have a cell-like room each and share shower and loo. No hot water
however and plugs don't fit basin, which hardly matters as water
declines to run away. We wander to Piazza where we drink far too
much and stagger to pizza restaurant for dinner. Smiling waitresses all
take a swig from enormous jug of red wine as they pass and a puff
from (doped?) cigarette. People of both sexes very plain here.

Sunday, 25th April

E. says, 'This hotel is too simple for me.' Having booked for a week, I balk at leaving tomorrow.

We walk up Holy Stairs to Pilgrimage Church on Monte Bérico. Run into huge crowds. It is Old Bersaglieri Day, old soldiers in khaki and black feathers in hats. We take refuge in large bar. At next table party of nuns and young people stand to attention and sing a hymn unselfconsciously while we sip Cinzano Bianco. We look down on Villa Rotunda, impressive from the hill. We are told the family still live in it and only its garden open to public. In 1950s, when A. and I visited with the Chavchavadzes, we were shown around house by a charming young Count Valmarana, aged nineteen.

E. and I spend afternoon unsuccessfully looking for alternative hotel. I begin to wonder why I have come and whether I will enjoy myself. There is nowhere to sit in the sun. We dine at delicious restaurant called I Due Mori. Must be very old for there are two carved Moors on the façade dating from early eighteenth century.

Monday, 26th April

Sleep well. We are getting used to this squalid little hotel. One gets used to anything, no doubt prisoners-of-war make their camps cosy. One learns where to put one's hairbrush without getting it covered in dust, how to keep plug in plughole without it bouncing out, etc. At least we are in the very centre of old Vicenza. From my bed where I write I look out on a bay of the Basilica, surely the most famous neo-classical building in the world.

My novel, on which my thoughts were focused in England, is now dismissed entirely from my mind. Likewise the war with Argentina. Weather perfect for sightseeing, not too hot or too cold. We spend day happily meandering. All buildings decaying (pollution?). The young men wear snow-white trousers, presumably washed daily.

Palazzo Thiene. Very dilapidated and being restored. Must compare with photographs I bought here in 1930s. Pilaster cartouches by Vittoria over ground-floor windows of classical military scenes.

Palazzo Valmarana. Oblique sunlight at midday on relief panels – Herod on throne, figures pointing at two dogs.

Contrada Riale. Marvellous perspective, curved street of palaces, each better than the last.

Villa Rotunda. Now a main road underneath east side, west still unspoilt. Lovely fresh green cultivated vineyards. Tame hares lollop in the grass. All windows shuttered and barred. View of Monte Bérico: skyline of cypresses and campanile. Odious boys misbehaving, climbing over wall, tearing branches from trees. Guardian throws stones at them. I join in. More estate men arrive. Boys scream abuse but finally retreat in disorder. I commiserate with guardian. He says, 'They are just an example of Italian youth today.'

Villa Valmarana. Palazzina sadly bombed in war and not yet repaired. Enchanting frescos in Forestiera by Gianbattista Tiepolo – boy lying on his front, large behind in air; ladies walking to market, hens in basket; girls in striped silk dresses, hands in muffs; monkey on staircase. Delicious feigned frames, and neo-Gothic room, rare for Italian decoration of 1750s.

Tuesday, 27th April

To Padua for day. Train crammed with students. Walk from Padua station to Mad'dell'Arena, but horde of children crowding this tiny chapel. Walk to Duomo. Little to see but pair of exquisite 'aquasantiere' in marble observed by me, according to pencil marks in guide book, on last visit.

Wander through arcades of old town – very pretty – to Sant' Antonio. The famous equestrian statue by Donatello isn't that marvellous. I prefer the Colleoni in Venice and above all the Marcus Aurelius in Rome. Dazzled by glare and for some time cannot see anything in dark interior of church. Byzantine Gothic. Tiny windows of bad stained glass. Full of splendid Baroque monuments to generals and admirals. Persian slaves staggering under weight of vast temple-like structures. Marble relief scenes of life of St Anthony behind his altar. The faithful praying to the saint with one hand on his tomb slab. Italians must touch and stroke works of art, when they don't write their names on them in indelible ink.

After lunch we return to Madonna dell' Arena. Crowds of children aged eight to ten again line up in groups for admission. What can these little brutes derive from Giotto? Eventually we plunge in. A rich reward. How can they have survived in this superb condition throughout 680 years? What but unwavering faith could have produced them?

Back in Vicenza, we dine at our favourite Due Mori and walk home through Piazza dei Signori. A huge circle of youths and girls

dance in the square, while others clap hands. A couple enter middle
of the circle, dance a mad fandango, and retreat to outer ring, to be
followed by another couple. Much merriment. The English never
behave like this, which is what makes one love the Italians.

Wednesday, 28th April

We decide we shall have had enough of Vicenza by end of week.
Much deliberation about where to go. We visit travel agency where
amiable girl books us two rooms at Albergo Duse, Asolo. We go by
bus on Friday, since none runs on Saturday which is May Day (formerly Our Lady's Day but now universally celebrated as Karl Marx
Day).

We visit National Museum until it shuts at midday. Then to S.
Coronata church which enshrines a thorn from Christ's crown (not
visible). Bellini's *Baptism of Christ* within vast and ornate Renaissance
tabernacle. Stupendous picture only spoilt by God the Father with
wings outspread hovering too heavily over wonderful scenery.
Principal figure of naked Christ to which eye is drawn is nevertheless
below that of Baptist, pouring water from tin-like vessel. Moving
spectacle.

After going to station to ascertain times of trains and buses, E. and
I return to Monte Bérico to see Veronese of St Gregory's *Cena*.
Superb majestic canvas like the Bellini. Odd to see a cinquecento Pope
on throne with Christ a lesser figure on his right hand posing as one
of his poor guests. Sumptuous dishes, damask tablecloth, pages in rich
liveries, dogs, monkey, all the appurtenances of the rich in architectural setting of great splendour.

We walk further up the hill and discover Risorgimento Museum.
We do not enter but sit in the lovely grounds and talk. We talk all day,
every day.

Thursday, 29th April

To Verona for the day in Rapido. Not a square inch of country
between Venice and Verona. All built up. We walk to San Zeno where
I remember being shown round by Kenneth Clark who was eloquent
on thirteenth-century red marble statue of enthroned saint with smile
on lips. This church more swarming with children than any. Like ants,
but din indescribable. Mantegna triptych on high altar too out of

reach to be studied properly. Wonderful bronze door panels of Old and New Testament scenes, twelfth century. Walk miles to Duomo, getting there just as it shuts punctually at twelve.

To Castello Museum after luncheon. Large collection of indifferent pictures. Considering Verona the birthplace of so many great artists, disappointing. Interesting artist called Carotta, almost Impressionist technique. Admire his portrait of young Benedictine, another of dotty little girl holding a childish sketch. We leave Verona at four. Too large a city, and less interesting than Padua.

Friday, 30th April

Pouring with rain. How lucky we have been hitherto. Relieved to be quit of uncomfortable Vicenza hotel and lack of hot water. It is certainly cold. The lower Alps towards which we wend in our bus are covered by new snow. We change at Bassano and walk into this charming little town which I used to visit with Hugh Honour and John Fleming.* We cross covered bridge, built of wood in Renaissance times and exactly rebuilt after destruction in last war. We lunch in excellent restaurant and spend afternoon at Museo Civico. Many pictures by Bassano family which had eight painters. Jacopo so outstanding that his pictures instantly recognisable. A penchant for kneeling figures in foreground, backs bent, behinds presented to spectator, bare dirty peasants' feet. Also several paintings by Magnasco of which refectory of friars eating at long tables with receding perspective most impressive. Alfred Beit once told me that Magnasco was unknown until discovered by the Sitwells, who founded a Magnasco Society. Several busts and figures here by Canova, and a room devoted to Bassano-born opera singer Tito Gobbi, whom I met some years ago dining with the Droghedas.†

We take bus to Asolo, passing the house I twice stayed in with Hugh and John, and Freya Stark's‡ house where I wrote *Earls of Creation* at revolving desk in her work-room. Our hotel is *grande luxe* after Vicenza. Rain has ceased and we think weather may be fine. E. proposes to call on Dame F. Stark. I ask how well he knows her. He says

---

* Hugh Honour (b. 1927) and John Fleming (1919–2001); writers, separately and together, on art and architecture.
† See *Deep Romantic Chasm*, 24 May 1979.
‡ Freya Stark (DBE, 1972), writer and traveller (1893–1992).

hardly at all but it would be a kindness to an old woman of ninety. I question this, and would not dare impose myself on a distinguished lady of letters without an introduction.

At dinner, E. and I discuss the relative merits of general conversation and *tête-à-tête*. I say the only person I knew who insisted on former was Emerald [Cunard]. He says Jean Cocteau did too. I ask if he knew Cocteau. 'Of course,' says E., 'very well indeed in the Twenties.' E. surprises me about persons he has known. He once rented a house here with Vanessa Bell and Duncan Grant. We discuss whether a creative writer should be interested in the arts. E. says of course he should be 'interested', but he need not be an expert and indeed should not be one. Thinks it inconceivable that a civilised being could be indifferent to the arts. I say Harold and Vita were indifferent to music. He ripostes that both were interested in painting and architecture, although their knowledge was superficial. I express doubt that Charlotte Brontë or Trollope were affected by any of the arts. We agree that at least curiosity is more than desirable, that a man cannot be an aesthete who disregards the arts, and must lack sensibility.

Lilac and wisteria tumble over old buildings. Amazed by vast Palladian and post-Palladian villas perched on prominences, some of which, with large wings, colonnades and pavilions, are almost as big as Holkham [Hall, Norfolk]. Are they lived in? Are they empty of fine contents? Do they still belong to the old families? Or do they now house nuns, orphans and delinquents?

Saturday 1st May

Everything stops for two days. We go for longish walk up to La Rocca along path where A. and I used to pick blackberries in 1950s. Path unchanged but view of valley much built-up. Many decent new houses in traditional style for rich Milanese families in summer. Hear many cuckoos. No other birds audible, and horrid sounds of gunfire. Not for years have I heard so many cuckoos as here, where they shoot them. E. says that the painters he has known have never been able to kill anything.

As the day advances, sky turns from a leaden grey first to a gauzy muslin, then forget-me-not, then lapis blue. We enter a bar, order Camparis and soda, and watch coming and going of the Italians, always so busy about nothing. They talk emphatically about their mothers-in-laws' bunions, the carburettors of their new cars, their babies' exploits. They are good-hearted until it comes to money, which is their God. Religion, nature and beauty mean nothing to them, and they hate their historic past.

I stay in my comfortable room all afternoon, perusing my novel so far as it goes, reading Virginia Woolf's diary and snoozing. In evening we go to concert in Eleanore Duse theatre. Bearded cellist in long tail-coat down to heels, and pianist from Vienna who has brought two early nineteenth-century pianos with him. Schubert and Beethoven on old instruments most moving, Debussy rather scratchy.

Sunday, 2nd May

To Mass at eight in large church beneath my window. Liturgy incomprehensible to me, who went to Mass almost daily for twenty-five years. We go for lovely walk up valley, passing through plantation of young chestnuts to a ridge. Lie in the sun looking at a farmhouse such as appears in every settecento Italian landscape. Corrugated tiles, tall cypress, scythed grass, hens cackling, dogs barking. Sun on our faces. What do we talk about? John Hill* and his wife Sheila were both in love with the same Spaniard. Did they go to bed with him, separately or together? Did each know the other loved? In 1920, aged eighteen, E. went to California with his lover Johnnie Campbell, long since dead, whose daughter Chita has always wanted to marry E. and knows nothing of his relationship with her father. What a muddle life is.

Over excellent luncheon, I tell E. I feel horribly inferior to every-one I meet, whether waiter, plumber, dustman or bus driver. E. says nonsense, they could not write a biography of Harold Nicolson. I say they could if they had the education, whereas I could never mend a fuse or drive a lorry if I tried for fifty years. On a desert island I would go under and they would not. That is the ultimate test.

E. and I are both smitten by the most seductive boy. He works in the big bar of the Piazza here. Looks fifteen but might be twenty. Face of such sweetness, especially when he smiles, that our hearts melt. Short, compact, brown hair, low forehead, slightly oriental eyes, slant-ing brows, little nose, but all the expression in the mouth, broad and

---

* Interior designer, brother of the artist Derek Hill, and father of Nicholas (see entry for 19 December 1982).

full, fine teeth, and the smile. He works like a Trojan, dashing from one end of the counter to the other, pouring drinks, scooping ice-creams into cones, fetching orders and bills, carrying trays like lightning. Inspires protective rather than sexual feelings, one wants to watch and hug. His sweetness to the children and the old is so beguiling that one gasps in admiration.

Monday, 3rd May

Another glorious day. We walk aimlessly down main road and descend valley. Wild flowers in abundance, cuckoos shouting their heads off. Have drink at our bar. Alas, the adored one off duty, no doubt worn out by weekend. We shan't see him again. A fleeting spectacle and an eternal memory. The portrait of Innocence, I claim. E. not so sure. Says we are like Aschenbach in *Death in Venice*.

Even after a week together, E. and I still chatter ceaselessly at meals and when walking. A. will enquire what we talked about. What indeed? Painting, sculpture, music; flowers, trees, birds; the war in the Atlantic (we have seen no English papers and spoken to no English person); our loves and adventures; and make-believe. We fashion romances around waiters, shopkeepers, people we see in bars and restaurants. We do not discuss religion, for E. has none and suspects mine to be either insincere or illogical. Nor do we discuss poetry. Sometimes when E. discusses his own painting my mind wanders. 'Yes,' I answer, or 'Oh really?' when I haven't concentrated on a word. This is a bad habit even when what is said is uninteresting. The day will come when I shall be unable to concentrate upon what does interest me.

Tuesday, 4th May

Pack and buy a paper. Our Task Force has sunk an Argentine ship. This does not elate me. Walk to little wine shop which might be a shop in eighteenth century, shelves packed with old-fashioned bottles as used to be in chemist shops, rows of wooden casks with taps. Behind mahogany counter sits an old man in trilby hat, which on our arrival he doffs like a retired ambassador. With old-world courtesy he sells me a bottle of Grappa with picture of Asolo inside. In the church I light a candle to Mama. The Lorenzo Lotto of St Basil shows him leaning on stick yet head turned upwards in adoration of a very plain, governessy Madonna.

Change buses twice. At Treviso we are cheated into buying two tickets, one to Venice, the other to airport. On arrival in Venice we are told airport ticket invalid and obliged to buy another. In aeroplane, E. sits next to what looks like middle aged half-caste lady with peaked green cap pulled down over eyes and dark glasses. Apparition turns and says, 'Hello Eardley,' and kisses him on both cheeks. It is Ram Gopal, Indian dancer with whom he had a roaring affair years ago. Full of charm and Indian whimsy. Tells us to drink tea made from comfrey, to lie always with head lower than feet for blood to flow, to boil water with lemon peel, to be massaged not by another's hands but feet. Then we shall live forever.

Appendix II

Farewell to the National Trust

For James Lees-Milne, the period covered by this volume marked the end of almost half a century of formal involvement in the counsels of the National Trust. From 1936 to 1951 (with a two-year break for war service) he had served as Country Houses (later Historic Buildings) Secretary; he continued to serve as Architectural Consultant until 1966; he was then drafted onto the Properties Committee (successor to the Historic Buildings Committee), from which he retired, according to the rules, on reaching the age of seventy-five in the summer of 1983.*
At the retirement dinner held for him on 13 December 1983 at Fenton House, Hampstead – one of many properties which had come to the Trust largely thanks to his efforts and skill – he was in a mood of happy reminiscence, surrounded as he was by old friends and colleagues.

A few weeks later he defended the National Trust in a letter to *The Times*, written in response to an article by Roger Scruton entitled *Out with the Stately, Enter the State*. The article (published on 21 February 1984) had criticised the social effects of capital taxes, suggesting that there was 'no more vivid example . . . than the fate of our stately houses, and the gradual extension of the dead hand of the National Trust over these once glorious living institutions'. Jim's reply was published on 24 February under the heading 'Helping Hand from the National Trust':

> Roger Scruton's indictment of the National Trust . . . is so misleading that I had to read it twice to make sure it was not meant as a joke.

---

* He continued to serve on the Arts Panel – an advisory body.

His assertion that the Trust is 'an institution which . . . is in truth the smooth apologist for the injustices of the state' is indeed the opposite of the truth. On the contrary, the Trust has always deprecated the penal taxation which compels so many families to leave their country houses.

Mr Scruton 'groans aloud' on the too-frequent occasions when he learns that another 'noble pile' has fallen to the Trust's clutches, 'to be externally fossilized'. But does he groan aloud every month of the year when some noble pile which has not passed into the Trust's safekeeping either falls to the ground from decay or is demolished by the housebreaker ?

He instances Canons Ashby and Kingston Lacy as recent victims of the Trust's 'ghoulish' attentions, i.e., salvation and repair. The first house, which for decades deteriorated in the ownership of an ancient family too poor to maintain it, would undoubtedly have collapsed in ruins; and the second would undoubtedly have been stripped of its incomparable picture collection, even if the fabric survived, had it not been for the National Trust.

Not every house is, or can be, lived in. Hardwick Hall is one such; but that architectural masterpiece is at least preserved intact. There are many country houses belonging to the National Trust in which the original families still reside, if not in the whole, then in part; and within ten miles from where I write beautiful Dyrham Park provides flats for 10 separate families in addition to 14 state rooms enjoyed by the public. There is no sign of 'the dead hand of the National Trust' in this 'mausoleum'.

Jim was pleased (5 March 1984) when this letter prompted the Chairman and Director-General of the National Trust to send him their personal thanks.

It must be said, however, that he did not always express such positive feelings towards the National Trust. For many years, his attitude towards the institution and its policies had been highly ambivalent and often critical – 'that love-hate for the N.T. which in my case is now more hate than love', as he wrote to Eardley Knollys as early as 1958. As it transformed itself into a mass organisation, he bemoaned the fact that its once cosy administration became cumbersome and bureaucratic, that it took less account of the interests of former owners, that the views of 'managers' prevailed over those of 'aesthetes'. Scruton overstated his case and used unfortunate examples; but his two main criticisms – that the Trust transformed 'living' houses into 'dead' museums, and did not do enough to encourage their habitation by the families which had originally owned them – were ones with which Jim generally sympathised (as can be discerned in his later book of National Trust reminiscences, *People and Places*). Jim accepted that many of the changes he deprecated were inevitable; he expressed admiration for many of the staff and their work; he enjoyed visiting 'new' properties (such as Kingston Lacy, Sherborne Castle and Calke Abbey) with old colleagues – but there was nevertheless much head-shaking.

The attitude of the Trust towards Jim was equally ambivalent. After his retirement, many of its figures continued to treat him as the Grand Old Man of the National Trust, seeking his advice, taking him to visit properties, and including him in various events and celebrations. Yet as he noted ruefully on 13 October 1983, the Trust 'definitely refused' to allow his diaries, probably the greatest work of literature to emerge from its history, to be sold in any of its shops – an interdict which appears to continue to this day.

INDEX

Note: Published works of J L-M are given as separate entries; other works are given under authors; current properties of the National Trust are given in small capitals